DIGITAL SAT PREP

SUCCESS 2024-2025

Strategies, Practice Tests, and Insights to maximize your score: 3 full-length Practice Tests + Detailed answer explanation + Effective revision techniques + Bonus Digital Flashcards

a

By Academia Jones

Contents

THIS PAGE IS INTENTIONALLY LEFT BLANK

Introduction Embracing the Digital SAT: Overview

The Advantages of the **Digital SAT** The transition to the Digital SAT represents a significant evolution in standardized testing, aligning with today's technological advancements and learning styles. This digital format offers unique benefits over traditional paper-based tests, providing a **more personalized** testing experience with questions adapting to the test-taker's performance level. Additionally, the digital platform facilitates faster score processing, enabling students to receive their results more quickly.

This introduction to the Digital SAT will explore how this modern approach to testing can enhance preparation strategies, reduce environmental impact, and potentially decrease test anxiety through a familiar digital interface. In this text, we will explore the structure, features, and benefits of the Digital SAT. We will also discuss how students can prepare for and succeed in this updated format, which can open doors to their academic and professional futures.

As the educational landscape transforms, so does the approach to assessing readiness for higher education.

The Digital SAT is a cornerstone of this evolution, streamlining the process and introducing a level of adaptability previously unseen. Its digital interface mirrors contemporary learning tools, potentially easing test anxiety and facilitating a more intuitive testing experience. This change not only indicates a shift towards embracing digital innovation in education but also emphasizes the College Board's commitment to accessibility and efficiency. The following chapters will guide you in mastering this modernized test, ensuring that you are not only prepared but also poised to excel.

To effectively prepare for the SAT using this book, students should first become familiar with the digital SAT format. They should then create a study plan using the strategies outlined, focusing on areas for improvement identified through initial practice tests. Students should regularly practice with the provided questions and utilize the detailed explanations to understand their mistakes.

Finally, they should take full-length practice tests under timed conditions to build confidence and improve time management.

Finally, as the test date approaches, refine your strategy by applying test-taking psychology and revision techniques.

You'll do great!

IMPORTANT REMINDER!

It's crucial for students to remember that in order to take the SAT, they must register for the exam through the official College Board website. Here's a step-by-step guide on how to do so:

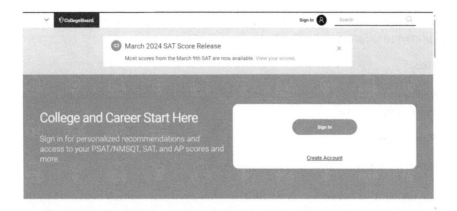

1. **Create a College Board Account:**

   - Navigate to the College Board website.

   - Click on the 'SAT' section.

   - Select 'Register for the SAT'.

   - If you do not already have a College Board account, you will need to create one. This involves providing some personal information, setting up a username, and creating a password.

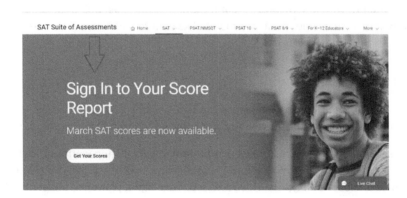

2. **Complete Your Registration:**

   - Once your account is set up, log in and begin the registration process.

   - You will be asked for more detailed personal information. Ensure that the name you use matches the name on your photo ID.

   - Answer the questions about your high school and future college plans. These questions are not mandatory but can help with college and scholarship searches.

3. **Choose Your Test Date and Center:**

   - Select a test date that will give you ample time to prepare and that aligns with your college application deadlines.

- Choose a test center near you. Remember that test centers can fill up quickly, so register early to get your preferred location.

4. **Upload a Photo:**

   - You will need to upload a recent, acceptable photo that adheres to the photo requirements stated on the College Board website.

5. **Review and Make Payment:**

   - Review all the information you have provided.

   - Pay the registration fee with a credit card or other payment method accepted by the College Board.

     The College Board offers test dates throughout the year, which can be found in our SAT test dates guide. The total cost to sit for the exam is $60, but there are also a number of additional fees that must be considered, including:

     A fee of $30 is charged for late registration. A fee of $25 to $35 is charged for cancellation. A fee of $25 is charged for changing test centers. A fee of $12 is charged for each additional score report. A fee of $31 is charged for a rushed score report. A fee of $31 is charged for archived scores. A fee of $55 is charged for hand score verification.

6. **Confirm Your Registration:**

   - After payment, you will receive a confirmation. Print this out and keep it for your records. This confirmation includes important information like your test center location and reporting time.

7. **Prepare for Test Day:**

   - In the days leading up to the test, review the test-day checklist provided by the College Board and make sure you have all necessary items ready, including your photo ID and admission ticket.

As we delve into the strategies for mastering test day, an important logistical step warrants your attention well before you set foot in the test center. A critical component of your SAT preparation involves familiarizing yourself with the digital tools provided by the College Board, most notably, the Bluebook App. This digital platform is essential for those taking the SAT in its digital format, serving as your gateway to the examination interface.

Pre-Test Digital Preparation

A few days before the test, it's imperative to download the **Bluebook App** and meticulously go through the setup steps. Procrastination in this regard can lead to unnecessary stress; therefore, it is advised not to wait until the last moment—specifically, avoid postponing this task until Friday before the test. This proactive approach ensures that, should any technical difficulties arise, you have ample time to seek assistance from your school's IT department or the College Board's support team.

The Bluebook App is designed to simulate the digital SAT testing environment, offering features that will be available on test day. By downloading and **setting up** the app well in advance, you afford yourself the opportunity to become acquainted with its functionality and interface. This familiarity can significantly reduce test-day anxiety, allowing you to focus solely on showcasing your abilities rather than navigating a new digital environment.

Incorporating the Bluebook App into Your Preparation in addition to this book for maximizing your score

Integrate practice sessions using the **Bluebook App** into your study plan. This will not only enhance your comfort with the digital testing format but also refine your time management skills under conditions that closely mimic the actual test. Familiarize yourself with the app's features, such as the timer, the question navigation, and the tools available for different sections of the SAT.

By following these steps, students can ensure their registration for the SAT is completed correctly. It's advisable to register well before the deadline to avoid any last-minute issues. Remember to regularly check the official College Board website for the most up-to-date information regarding the SAT and any changes to testing policies or procedures.

How to Use This Book for Optimal SAT Preparation

This book is designed to be your roadmap through the complex terrain of SAT preparation, providing you with the strategies, tools, and insights necessary to excel on test day. Whether you are just beginning your SAT journey or seeking to refine your skills with advanced techniques, this book will serve as a crucial resource every step of the way.

Structured Approach to Learning

Each chapter of this book is carefully structured to build upon your knowledge and skills systematically. We start with the basics of what the Digital SAT entails, including an overview of its format and the types of questions you can expect. As you progress, each section delves deeper into specific content areas of the SAT—Critical Reading and Writing, Mathematics, and an essential guide on the Psychological Strategies for test-taking.

Interactive and Practical Learning Tools

To ensure that the theoretical knowledge gained is effectively translated into practice, this book includes numerous practice questions and mock tests that mirror the actual Digital SAT format. These are designed to familiarize you with the digital testing environment and to provide a practical application of strategies discussed in each chapter.

Customizable Study Plans

Recognizing that every student has unique needs, this guide offers advice on customizing your study plan to fit your schedule, learning pace, and goals. It includes templates and tips on how to organize your study sessions to maximize efficiency and effectiveness.

Strategies Beyond Preparation

Beyond mere test preparation, this book offers guidance on how to strategically use your SAT scores for college applications and scholarships. It also provides insights into long-term academic and career planning, ensuring that the benefits of your hard work extend far beyond test day.

Using This Book Effectively

1. **Read Sequentially**: Start from the beginning and progress through the chapters in order. This will help you build a solid foundation of knowledge before moving on to more complex topics.

2. **Engage with Practice Materials**: Make extensive use of the practice questions and tests provided throughout the book. This active engagement is crucial for cementing your understanding and improving your test-taking skills.

3. **Review and Reflect**: Regularly review the concepts and strategies discussed. Use the margins for notes and reflections on how you can apply what you've learned to your SAT preparation or broader academic pursuits.

4. **Seek Feedback**: Use the solutions and explanations provided to gauge your performance. If possible, seek additional feedback from instructors or peers to enhance your understanding and approach.

By following these guidelines, this book will not only prepare you for the Digital SAT but also empower you with the skills and confidence to excel in all your academic endeavors. Let's embark on this journey together, with the goal of not just achieving, but exceeding your SAT targets.

Chapter 1: The Digital Interface

Navigating the Test: Features of the Digital Platform

The Scholastic Assessment Test (SAT), a critical instrument in the evaluation of college readiness, has undergone a series of modifications to better align with the instructional and evaluative demands of contemporary education. These alterations manifest as recalibrations to the content, structure, scoring mechanisms, and delivery methods.

Modifications to the SAT Exam: Historically, the SAT transitioned from its origins as an intelligence quotient assessment to a more syllabus-centric evaluative tool. Modifications have included the excision of certain question types, such as analogies, the reconfiguration of the essay component to an optional element, and the transition towards a digital format—these adjustments embody the pedagogical shift towards a test environment that mirrors current educational practices.

Rationale for Changes in the SAT Exam: The impetus for these changes is multifaceted and reflects a commitment to maintaining the exam's relevance:

1. **Curricular Consonance:** The SAT's periodic transformation ensures its coherence with the high school curriculum, thus affirming its validity as a measure of academic preparedness.

2. **Equality and Accessibility:** These changes aim to mitigate socioeconomic and cultural biases, thereby ensuring a more equitable testing environment.

3. **Technological Progression:** In acknowledgment of the digital revolution in educational methodologies, the SAT has adapted to include digital formats, which, among other benefits, allow for adaptive testing techniques.

4. **Institutional Input:** College and university feedback has consistently informed the evolution of the SAT, with the goal of augmenting the exam's predictive value regarding student success in post-secondary education.

Chronology of SAT Revisions: The chronicle of the SAT's evolution is marked by pivotal changes at various junctures. Notably, the reformation in 2005 introduced a writing segment and expanded the quantitative section to cover higher-level mathematical concepts. Furthermore, the most recent adaptations have been towards a digital format, seeking to capitalize on technological advancements and the resultant pedagogical shifts. These changes are enacted with the objective of enhancing the SAT's robustness as a standardized assessment tool, ensuring it remains an equitable and predictive measure of academic aptitude and potential collegiate achievement.

The Digital SAT nowdays is designed to offer a smooth and user-friendly testing experience. It consists of three main sections: **Math, Reading, and Writing.** Each section evaluates a specific set of skills and knowledge that are important for college and career readiness.

The Math section assesses mathematical reasoning and problem-solving abilities, covering a range of topics from algebra to more advanced mathematics. The test may present questions in either multiple-choice format or as student-produced responses, requiring test-takers to calculate and enter their answers.

The Reading Section assesses students' ability to interpret, analyze, and draw conclusions from a variety of texts spanning several genres and periods, reflecting the kind of reading required in college and the workplace. Questions are typically multiple-choice and based on passages provided in the test.

The Writing Section is also included. The section focuses on grammar, usage, and effective language use. Test-takers must read passages and identify errors or ways to improve writing. Questions are multiple-choice and based on written passages, similar to the Reading section.

SAT Digital Parameters	SAT Digital Reading & Writing (RW) Section	SAT Digital Math Section
Format	Two-staged: one tests Reading and the other the Writing section. Both are administered across separately timed modules.	Two-staged: The math section is administered via two separately timed modules.
Test length (total operational and pretest questions)	1st module: • 25 operational questions • 2 pretest questions 2nd module: • 25 operational questions • 2 pretest questions	1st module: • 20 operational questions • 2 pretest questions 2nd module: • 20 operational questions • 2 pretest questions
Time Duration	1st module & 2nd module: 32 minutes each	1st module & 2nd module: 35 minutes each
Total Questions	54	44
Total Time Allocated	64 minutes	70 minutes
Scores Reported	Total score calculation: SAT RW section + SAT Math section scores = 1600	
Question Type(s)	Discrete; MCQs with four options	MCQ (75%) and student-produced response (SPR)(25%)
Topics Tested	Literature, History / Social Studies, Humanities and Science	Science, Social Science and real-world related topics
Informational Graphics	Tested, includes - tables, bar graphs, line graphs	Also tested

In the pursuit of academic excellence and preparation for tertiary education, students approaching the **Digital SAT** will encounter a meticulously structured examination designed to evaluate their scholastic aptitude. This examination comprises two pivotal sections: **Reading & Writing (RW) and Math,** each further bifurcated into two modules with separately timed segments.

The **Reading & Writing** section, which amalgamates assessments of comprehension and linguistic prowess, consists of **54 operational questions**, equally divided between the two modules.

11

Candidates will be afforded **32 minutes** per module to navigate through these queries, cumulating in a total of **64 minutes** of rigorous academic engagement. This portion of the SAT assesses students' ability to interpret and synthesize information from literature, history, social studies, humanities, and sciences, with questions presented in discrete multiple-choice format with four options each.

Simultaneously, the Math section, a bastion of numerical and analytical assessment, presents **44 operational questions** under the same bifurcated module arrangement. In this segment, each module extends to **35 minutes**, leading to a total of **70 minutes** dedicated to exploring scientific, social scientific, and real-world related mathematical problems. The questions are a blend of multiple-choice (75%) and student-produced responses (25%), demanding not only precision but also depth of understanding.

	Questions	Time Limit
Reading and Writing Module 1	27 questions	32 minutes
Reading and Writing Module 2	27 questions	32 minutes
10-minute break		
Math Module 1	22 questions	35 minutes
Math Module 2	22 questions	35 minutes
Total	98 questions	2 hour 14 minutes (excluding break)

The summation of scores from these sections will yield a composite SAT score, with the potential to range up to **1600**, encapsulating a student's readiness for college-level academics. Within these digital pages, students will also engage with various informational graphics such as tables, bar graphs, and line graphs, enhancing their data interpretation skills, which are essential in today's data-driven academic environments.

Through the systematic presentation of the Digital SAT's structure, students are beckoned to a world of academic challenge and discovery, prompting a thorough and strategic approach to mastering the components of this pivotal assessment.

Practice Drills: Getting Comfortable with the Format

Within the initial stages of preparation, students are encouraged to engage with practice drills designed to acclimate them to the **Digital SAT's** format. This acclimatization is twofold, encompassing both the operational fluency of the testing interface and the intellectual mastery of the content.

Practice Drills: Getting Comfortable with the Format

To maximize performance on the **Digital SAT**, students should undertake a series of methodically structured practice drills. These exercises serve to familiarize the examinee with the digital interface's intricacies, ensuring that on the day of the exam, navigating through questions, flagging items for review, and managing the allotted time become almost second nature.

1. **Interface Familiarization:** Prior to delving into content-specific preparation, students should invest time in understanding the operational mechanics of the test. This includes the process of selecting answers, moving between questions, utilizing built-in tools like the calculator and the notes section, and being mindful of the on-screen timer.

The Chilean volcano Calabozos is located in _____ area. Therefore, the risk of loss of human life in the event of an eruption is minimal.

1 ☐ Mark for Review

Which choice completes the text with the most logical and precise word or phrase?

Ⓐ a hazardous

Ⓑ an active

Ⓒ a mountainous

Ⓓ a remote

👤 Carmine Pisano   Question 1 of 27 ∧   Next

2. **Question Navigation Drills:** Simulated exercises that replicate the test environment can be invaluable. Students should practice answering questions within each section, using the same digital tools that will be available during the actual exam. This includes becoming adept at using any on-screen annotation features to highlight or underline key information within passages or problems.

3. **Time Management Exercises:** Time is a critical variable that can influence test outcomes. Hence, drills that focus on time management, encouraging students to allocate specific time slots to different question types based on their difficulty and the individual's strengths and weaknesses, are essential.

4. **Technology Adaptability:** Given that the Digital SAT will likely be taken on a variety of devices with different screen sizes and input methods, students should practice on multiple devices to ensure comfort with various formats, whether they be tablets, laptops, or desktop computers.

5. **Simulated Full-Length Tests:** To synthesize the interface familiarity with content mastery, students should undertake full-length tests that mimic the conditions of the actual exam day. This practice is paramount in building stamina and ensuring that students can maintain concentration over the exam's duration.

By systematically engaging with these practice drills, students can significantly bolster their test-day performance. Through repetitive engagement with the testing interface and the exam content, students transform the once unfamiliar digital landscape into a navigable and comfortable domain, thereby maximizing their potential for superior results.

However, the digital SAT platform will provide a plethora of helpful tools to assist the examinee in navigating the examination

The Desmos Onscreen Calculator

Individuals who own and regularly use a personal handheld calculator are permitted to bring it to the test if it is an approved device. However, the Bluebook testing application includes a Desmos graphing calculator that can be utilized throughout the entire Math section. This calculator enables users to graph lines and curves, plot points, locate x- and y-intercepts, and perform various other calculations.

Those intending to utilize the **Desmos calculator** are encouraged to experiment with the device online and in practice tests to gain familiarity with its diverse capabilities in advance of test day. The embedded onscreen device also incorporates enhanced accessibility features, including conformance with screen readers and other assistive technologies, and it would be prudent to assess these features if they will be utilized.

The Countdown Clock

The digital SAT format will include a countdown timer at the top of the testing screen, indicating the remaining time in any given stage. Those who find the clock anxiety-inducing may choose to hide it. Regardless of whether the clock is visible or concealed, the user will be alerted when five minutes remain on the module.

Section 1, Module 1: Reading and Wr...	31:53		
Directions ∨	Hide	Annotate	More

Approaching the text on the **Digital SAT** requires both a tactical understanding of the material and strategic test-taking skills. Here are some suggestions and tips that can be shared with students to enhance their approach to the text-based sections of the SAT:

1. **Active Reading:**

   - **Advice:** Engage with the text actively by summarizing paragraphs, noting the author's tone, and identifying the main argument as you read. This will improve comprehension and retention of information.

2. **Annotate as You Go:**

   - **Tip:** Use the digital interface to highlight or underline key pieces of information. Annotating can help you locate evidence quickly when answering questions.

3. **Understand Passage Structures:**

   - **Advice:** Recognize that passages may have a particular structure, such as cause-effect, problem-solution, or compare-contrast. Identifying this can guide your understanding and predict the kinds of questions that may be asked.

4. **Predict Before You Peek:**

   - **Tip:** Before looking at the answer choices, try to predict the answer. This can prevent the choices from confusing you and ensure your answer is grounded in the text.

5. **The process of elimination** is a useful tool in identifying incorrect answers on multiple-choice questions. In such instances, it may be more straightforward to eliminate incorrect responses than to determine the correct ones. The strikethrough tool can be employed to eliminate responses that are known to be incorrect. It is possible that the correct answer may be identified through a process of elimination. Furthermore, since points are only awarded for correct responses, but never deducted for incorrect ones, narrowing down the choices to two and then making an educated guess is more likely to result in points being earned than selecting randomly from all four possibilities.

6. **Evidence-based Answers:**

   - **Advice:** Answers must always be supported by evidence from the passage. Even if an answer seems correct based on outside knowledge, it must align with the information presented in the text.

7. **Dissect Difficult Questions:**

   - **Tip:** Break down complex questions by paraphrasing them in simpler terms. Look for keywords that will help you scan the text for the relevant information.

8. **Vocabulary in Context:**

   - **Advice:** When answering vocabulary questions, focus on how the word is used within the context of the passage rather than only its general definition.

9. **Dual Reading:**

   - **Tip:** For paired passages, read one passage thoroughly, answer questions pertaining to it, then move to the second passage. Only tackle comparative questions after understanding both texts.

10. **Time Management:**

    - **Advice:** Allocate your time wisely. Spend more time on passages that align with your strengths and less on those that typically require more effort.

11. **Trust Your First Instinct:**

    - **Tip:** Often your first answer choice is the correct one, especially if you've followed a consistent strategy in approaching the text. Unless you find clear evidence to the contrary, avoid changing your answers on a whim.

12. **Stay Calm and Focused:**

    - **Advice:** Maintain a calm demeanor and focus solely on the passage in front of you. Avoid letting previous questions or sections affect your performance on the current passage.

While the format and content of the new digital SAT will be different from previous years, your approach to the test should be the same. Whether you're taking the SAT, GRE, LSAT, or MCAT, the same skills for maximizing your standardized test scores still apply. So don't be intimidated by the fact that the Digital SAT is "new"-you can still develop these test-taking skills to use in any testing situation.

Read each question thoroughly: Make sure you know exactly what the question is asking, and that the answer you choose answers the question!

Take the test in any order: Take the test in any order you want-you do not have to answer every question in the section in the exact order they are asked. Skip any questions that seem too difficult at the moment, and come back to them after you've answered the easier ones.

What's great about the new digital SAT is that it allows you to skip and bookmark questions, which means you can easily return to difficult questions later. It also means you're less likely to forget to answer a question.

Use the process of elimination: Narrow down your choices when you have to guess a question. Since there's no penalty for getting it wrong on the SAT, you should answer every single question, even if you're guessing. The new test even has a feature that allows you to cross out improbable answers in real time!

By integrating these strategies into their study habits and practice sessions, students can significantly enhance their ability to interpret and analyze texts, thereby improving their performance on the reading and writing sections of the SAT.

On Test Day: A Deep Dive into Effective and Simple Strategies

The day of the SAT is a culmination of your dedication and hard work. Approaching it with a clear mind and a strategic plan can significantly impact your performance. This section provides detailed advice on how to navigate test day from start to finish, ensuring you are at your best when it matters most.

Morning Preparation

- **Wake Up Early:** Allow yourself ample time to wake up fully and engage in your morning routine without rushing. Consider setting multiple alarms if you're not a morning person.

- **Energizing Breakfast:** Choose foods that are high in protein and low in sugar to avoid energy crashes. Think eggs, whole-grain toast, yogurt, or a smoothie.

- **Mindful Moment:** Spend a few minutes in meditation or deep breathing to center yourself. Visualizing success can set a positive tone for the day.

Arrival at the Test Center

- **Document Check:** Double-check that you have all necessary documents and materials before leaving your house. This includes your admission ticket, photo ID, calculator, and any allowed stationery.

- **Arrive Early:** Plan to arrive at the test center at least 30 minutes before the doors open. This extra time can alleviate any stress caused by unexpected delays and allows you to acclimate to the testing environment.

- **Stay Calm:** Keep your composure upon arrival. Engage in light conversation with peers if it helps you relax, but avoid discussions about the test content.

During the Test

- **Strategic Reading:** Skim through the questions quickly before diving into the passages. This approach helps you know what information to look for as you read.

- **Answer Selection:** For multiple-choice questions, eliminate clearly wrong answers first. This tactic can improve your odds if you need to guess.

- **Essay Planning:** If the test includes an essay, spend a few minutes planning your response before you start writing. Outline your main points to make your writing process smoother and more organized.

- **Pace Yourself:** Keep an eye on the clock, but don't let it dictate your pace. Answer easier questions first to secure points, then tackle the more challenging ones.

- **Stress Management:** If you find yourself getting stressed, pause for a moment. Close your eyes, take deep breaths, and then refocus.

Utilizing Breaks

- **Physical Movement:** Use breaks to stand, stretch, or walk around. Physical activity can help reduce tension and rejuvenate your mind.

- **Nutrition and Hydration:** Eat a snack that you brought with you, such as nuts or a granola bar. Drink water to stay hydrated, but be mindful not to drink so much that you're uncomfortable.

- **Mental Reset:** Breaks are an opportunity to clear your mind. Avoid discussing the test with others during breaks to maintain your focus and confidence.

Post-Test

- **Wind Down:** After the test, allow yourself some time to decompress. Engage in activities that help you relax and reflect on the achievement of completing the SAT.

- **Self-Care:** Celebrate your hard work and dedication, regardless of how you feel about your performance. Remember, your worth is not determined by a single test score.

By adopting these strategies, students can approach SAT test day not just with preparedness but with confidence. It's about more than just reviewing material; it's about mental and physical preparation that puts you in the best position to succeed.

Understanding the Digital SAT Scoring Chart

Navigating the intricacies of the SAT scoring system is crucial for students aiming to optimize their performance on this pivotal exam. The Digital SAT scoring chart, a comprehensive framework for evaluating test-takers' proficiency, merits close examination to demystify how scores are calculated and what they signify in the broader context of college admissions. This overview aims to illuminate the scoring process, enabling students to set realistic goals and understand their results more deeply.

The Scoring Scale

The Digital SAT, like its predecessor, employs a scaled scoring system ranging from 400 to 1600. This aggregate score is the sum of two section scores: Evidence-Based Reading and Writing, and Math, each contributing a maximum of 800 points. The scoring model is designed to provide a consistent and equitable measure of academic ability, irrespective of the specific test edition taken.

Calculation Methodology

1. **Raw Scores:** Initially, students earn a raw score for each section, calculated simply by tallying the number of questions answered correctly. The SAT does not penalize for incorrect answers, encouraging students to attempt every question.

2. **Scaled Scores:** Raw scores are then converted into scaled scores through a statistical process known as equating. Equating adjusts for slight differences in difficulty among test versions, ensuring that scores are comparable across different test dates.

3. **Composite Score:** The final step involves adding the scaled scores from the Evidence-Based Reading and Writing section and the Math section to produce the composite score.

Subscores and Cross-test Scores

Beyond the main scores, the SAT also provides subscores and cross-test scores. Subscores offer detailed insights into specific skills and knowledge areas, such as command of evidence, words in context, and algebra. Cross-test scores assess analytical skills across both reading and math contexts, providing a more nuanced perspective on students' abilities to apply their knowledge in varied scenarios.

Interpreting Your Score

Understanding your SAT score involves more than just knowing the numbers. It's about recognizing where you excel and where there is room for improvement. Colleges consider SAT scores in the context of your application as a whole, alongside your academic record, extracurricular activities, essays, and letters of recommendation. Your score is an important component of your college application, but it is not the sole determinant of your academic potential or worth.

Conclusion

The Digital SAT scoring chart offers a clear, objective framework for evaluating academic readiness for college. By comprehensively understanding how scores are calculated and what they represent, students can better navigate their test preparation strategies, set achievable targets, and interpret their performance in a constructive manner. Remember, the goal of the SAT is to showcase your strengths and readiness for college-level work.

Chapter 2: Math Mastery Set

KEY CONCEPTS AND STRATEGIES

As we embark on the exploration of Math Mastery within the SAT, it becomes imperative to not only understand but also strategically apply a core set of mathematical concepts that form the foundation of this section. This pivotal chapter, "**Key Concepts and Strategies**," is designed to equip students with the necessary tools and insights to navigate the complexities of the SAT Math section with confidence and proficiency.

To excel in **the SAT Math section**, students must grasp key concepts that span various branches of mathematics, alongside strategic approaches to apply this knowledge efficiently during the exam. Here's an overview of these critical areas:

Key Concepts

1. **Algebra:**

   - **Linear Equations and Systems**: Ability to solve single variable and systems of equations. This includes interpreting the solution(s) in the context of a problem and understanding systems that have no solution, one solution, or infinitely many solutions.
   - **Quadratic Equations:** Recognize and solve quadratic equations by factoring, completing the square, or using the quadratic formula. Understanding how to manipulate and graph these equations is essential for recognizing their shapes and properties on a graph.
   - **Functions:** Understanding function notation, the concept of domain and range, types of functions (linear, quadratic, polynomial), and how to apply transformations (shifts, stretches, and reflections).

2. **Geometry and Trigonometry:**

   - **Shapes and Properties:** Knowledge of properties related to circles, triangles, rectangles, and other polygons. This includes theorems involving parallel and perpendicular lines, angle sum properties, and properties of circles (tangents, chords, arcs, and sectors).

   - **Trigonometric Ratios:** Familiarity with sine, cosine, and tangent functions for right triangles, as well as their applications.

   - **Area and Volume:** Ability to calculate the area and volume of various shapes, using formulas for rectangles, triangles, circles, trapezoids, cylinders, spheres, and cones.

   - **Unit Circle:** Knowledge of the unit circle and how it relates to the functions and values of sine, cosine, and tangent at key angles

   - **Coordinate Geometry:** Solving geometric problems set within the coordinate plane, such as finding the distance between points, the midpoint of a segment, and the equation of a line.

3. **Problem Solving and Data Analysis:**

   - **Interpretation of Data and Graphs:** Ability to read and analyze tables, graphs, and charts. Analyzing the graphical representations of functions and understanding the graphical implications of algebraic manipulations.

   - **Statistical Principles:** Understanding of mean, median, mode, range, and probability.

   - **Visualization:** Improving the ability to visualize shapes and their transformations on the plane, which is crucial for solving many geometry questions.

4. **Advanced Mathematics:**

   - **Functions:** Comprehension of function notation, transformations, and interactions.

   - **Polynomials and Nonlinear Equations:** Skills in factoring, solving quadratic equations, and understanding the properties of exponential and radical expressions.

Strategies

1. **Understanding the Question:**

   - Take the time to fully comprehend what each question asks. Identify key information and what you need to find.

2. **Time Management:**

   - Prioritize questions based on your strengths. Don't spend too much time on a single problem; remember, each question is worth the same number of points.

3. **Process of Elimination:**

   - Use this approach for multiple-choice questions. Eliminate answers you know are incorrect to increase your chances of choosing the right one.

4. **Estimation and Approximation:**

   - When exact calculations are not necessary, estimate to save time, especially on questions that don't require precise answers.

5. **Strategic Guessing:**

   - Since there is no penalty for wrong answers, make an educated guess if you're unsure. First, eliminate any answers you know are wrong.

6. **Utilizing the Calculator Wisely:**

   - Know when and how to use the calculator efficiently. It's beneficial for complex calculations but shouldn't be a crutch for simpler arithmetic.

7. **Practice with Purpose:**

- Regular, focused practice on each of these key areas. Utilize practice tests to familiarize yourself with the test format and timing.

8. **Review and Reflect:**

   - After practice sessions or mock exams, review your answers, especially the incorrect ones. Understand why you got a question wrong and how to approach similar problems in the future.

The SAT permits the use of approved calculators during one of the Math sections, and understanding how to wield this instrument effectively can enhance accuracy and efficiency.

These practice sets consist of

- a small batch of questions with
- no time limit
- and answers provided after each questiona t the end of the chapter

They are designed to help you learn difficult concepts by practicing in an untimed environment. They differ from our full-length exams.

How to master non linear function

1. Nonlinear functions

Nonlinear functions are characterized by their variable rates of change and typically generate curved, rather than linear, trajectories on a graph. Each category of nonlinear function is distinct, possessing unique properties and practical applications in the real world. A variety of nonlinear functions exist, but for the digital SAT, we will concentrate on four specific types:

1. **Quadratic Functions**: These are described by the equation ax^2+bx+c, where a is not equal to zero. On a graph, they produce parabolas.

2. **Higher-Order Polynomial Functions**: These functions involve variables raised to powers greater than two, exemplified by the formula ax^3+bx^2+cx+d.

3. **Exponential Functions**: Defined by the equation $a \cdot b^x$, where x is an exponent. These functions are known for their swift ascents or descents on a graph.

4. **Absolute Value Functions**: Recognized by the absolute value symbol and typically display a V-shaped graph, represented as $|x|$.

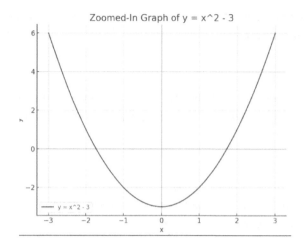

2. Quadratic functions

Quadratic functions are expressed using the equation ax^2+bx+c, with a being a non-zero coefficient. The visual representation of a quadratic function on a graph is a parabola that may arch upward or downward based on the value and sign of a. A thorough comprehension of parabola properties is essential when tackling quadratic equations. This understanding aids in visualizing both the solutions and overall behavior of the function, facilitating more effective problem-solving.

Within the SAT framework, quadratic functions frequently manifest in several variations, such as the standard, factored, and vertex forms. Each variant sheds light on different characteristics of the function, including its roots, vertex, and axis of symmetry. The adaptability of quadratic functions in representing real-world phenomena, like projectile trajectories and calculations of area, makes them a common element in SAT questions.

A deep understanding of the techniques required to resolve these equations, such as factoring, completing the square, and deploying the quadratic formula, is vital for excelling in the SAT's math section.

Let's examine a specific example to demonstrate the procedure for solving a quadratic equation:

Consider the equation $x^2-6x+8=0$. To find the values of x that satisfy this equation, begin by assessing if the equation can be factored conveniently. Here, we search for two numbers whose product is 8 (the constant term) and whose sum is -6 (the coefficient of the linear term). These numbers are -4 and -2, allowing the equation to be expressed as $(x-4)(x-2)=0$.

The subsequent step involves setting each factor to zero and solving for x, resulting in the roots of the equation. Hence, the solutions are $x=4$ and $x=2$, which correspond to the points where the quadratic function's graph crosses the x-axis.

3. Higher-Order Polynomial Functions

Higher-order polynomial functions involve variables elevated to powers exceeding two. These functions may manifest as cubic (third degree), quartic (fourth degree), or even higher-degree polynomials.

A typical expression for a higher-order polynomial function is \($ax^n+ bx^n +..... k$ \), where n represents the degree of the polynomial, and a, b.... k are constants. The dynamics of these functions are more intricate compared to quadratic functions due to their potential for multiple turning points and intercepts on a graph.

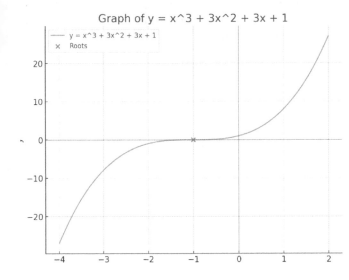

Graph of y = x^3 + 3x^2 + 3x + 1

Addressing higher-order polynomial functions on the SAT involves utilizing a variety of algebraic strategies. Factoring is frequently used, although it becomes increasingly difficult as the degree of the polynomial rises. When direct factoring proves impractical, alternative approaches such as graphical methods might be utilized.

4. Exponential Functions

Exponential functions are characterized by their swift transitions, manifesting either as rapid growth or decline. These functions are typically structured by a formula \(a * b^x$, where a is a constant, b represents the base of the exponential, and x is the exponent.

The distinctive feature of exponential functions is the placement of the variable x in the exponent position, which results in growth or decay rates that surpass those of linear functions. This attribute is frequently observed in real-life phenomena such as population expansion, radioactive decay, and compound interest calculations.

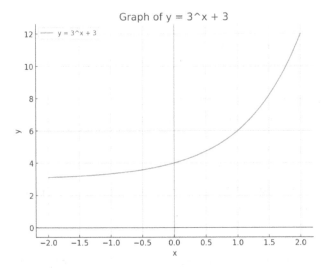

Graph of y = 3^x + 3

When tackling exponential functions on the SAT, it is critical to grasp their characteristics, such as how the rate of change in the function varies as x increases or decreases.

To solve these equations, typically the strategy involves rearranging the formula to isolate x. Recognizing the fundamental patterns of exponential growth and decay—marked by swift increases or decreases—is vital for addressing questions related to graphs.

Consider the following detailed example:

Solve the equation $3^x=81$.

The initial step is to express both sides of the equation using the same base when feasible. Here, 81 is a power of 3 (since $81=3^4$). Thus, the equation can be reformulated as $3^x=3^4$). Once the bases are matched, the exponents must also be the same, allowing us to determine that $x=4$. This method is essential for solving exponential equations, particularly when the numbers are powers of the same base.

5. Absolute Value Functions

Absolute value functions represent a specific category of nonlinear functions, distinguished by their characteristic V-shaped graphs. These functions are described by an equation of the form $y=|ax+b|+c$, where the absolute value of the linear expression $ax+b$ indicates the distance of the value from zero on the number line.

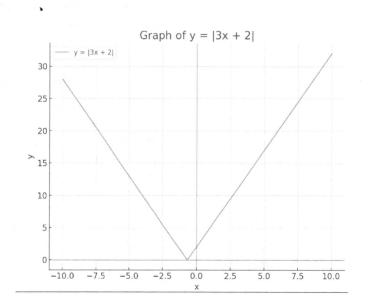

The defining attribute of absolute value functions is their capability to convert all negative inputs into positive outputs, resulting in a graph that reflects symmetrically across the x-axis or a vertical line.

When solving absolute value equations, it is common practice to divide the equation into two scenarios — one where the expression within the absolute value is positive, and another where it is negative. This division facilitates the independent resolution of each corresponding linear equation.

Absolute value functions are commonly included in SAT problems to assess a student's comprehension of piecewise functions and their ability to resolve equations that incorporate absolute values.

Take, for example, the equation $|2x - 3| = 7$. To solve it, we break it down into two cases: $2x - 3 = 7$ and $2x - 3 = -7$. Solving these two linear equations individually, we find $x = 5$ from the first equation and $x = -2$ from the second. These solutions indicate the points where the graph of the absolute value function intersects the x-axis.

6. Tips for Solving Nonlinear Functions Efficiently

Learn Basic Graph Forms: Acquaint yourself with the fundamental graph shapes of prevalent nonlinear functions, including parabolas for quadratic functions, the curves of exponential growth and decay, and the distinctive V-shape associated with absolute value functions. Recognizing these forms is essential for swiftly determining the type of function, a critical skill under the time pressures of the SAT.

Refine Factoring Skills: Proficiency in factoring polynomials is crucial, particularly for quadratic and more complex polynomial functions. Engage in practicing various factoring techniques such as grouping, applying the quadratic formula, and synthetic division. Effective factoring can streamline the solution process for complicated problems, thereby conserving valuable time.

Master Exponents and Logarithms: A thorough understanding of the properties of exponents and logarithms is crucial for managing exponential functions. Knowing how to adeptly manipulate these properties can greatly simplify the process of equation simplification and isolation of variables.

Implement the Substitution Method for Intricate Equations: For dealing with complex equations, the substitution method can be an invaluable strategy. This approach entails replacing a segment of the equation with a simpler variable, solving for that variable, and subsequently back-substituting to resolve the original equation.

Employ Graphing Techniques to Analyze Function Behavior: Drawing quick sketches of graphs can shed light on a function's behavior, proving especially beneficial for pinpointing roots, assessing symmetry, and identifying intervals where the function increases or decreases.

It is highly recommended that students **allocate time to take the practice test,** as it is an **effective method** of preparing for the **SAT.**

DIGITAL SAT MATH

Practice Test 1 Math Module 1 by Topic and sections

DIRECTIONS: This section contains questions pertaining to various fundamental mathematical skills. Calculators may be utilized for all questions. Unless otherwise specified, the following assumptions apply:

• All variables and expressions represent real numbers.

• The provided figures are accurately drawn to scale.

• All figures exist within a two-dimensional plane.

• The domain of a given function f is the set of all real numbers x for which f(x) is also a real number.

---

1. **Category: SAT Problem Solving & Data Analysis**

The expression $x2 - x - 56$ is equivalent to which of the following?

- a. $(x - 14)(x + 4)$
- b. $(x - 7)(x + 8)$
- c. $(x - 8)(x + 7)$
- d. $(x - 4)(x + 14)$

2. **Category: SAT Advanced Math**

The function h is defined as $h(x) = x^3$. The graph of the function is shifted to 4 units to the right. Which of the following expressions represents the new function of the graph?

- a. $g(x)=x3+4$
- b. $g(x)=x3-4$
- c. $g(x)=(x+4)3$
- d. $g(x)=(x-4)3$

3. **Category: SAT Algebra**

Joy purchased a chocolate box for $C. If he purchased a total of 68 boxes, then which of the following expressions represents the total cost of chocolate in dollars?

- a. c + 68

- b. c – 68

- c. 68c

- d. $\frac{68}{c}$

4. Category: SAT Geometry & Trigonometry

The angles formed by the straight line POQ are given in the figure.

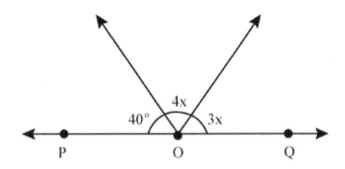

What is the value of x?

- a. 40°

- b. 20°

- c. 30°

- d. 25°

5. Category: SAT Algebra

Which of the following order pair (x, y) is the solution to the equation 2x + y = 6?

- a. (1, 2)

- b. (2, 2)

- c. (2, 1)

- d. (1, 1)

6. Category: SAT Geometry & Trigonometry

The longest side of the right triangle is 15 m, and the other side is 12 m long. What is the measure of remaining side of the right triangle?

- a. 27
- b. 3
- c. 9
- d. 14

7. **Category: SAT Geometry & Trigonometry**

Eight spheres of the same radius form a metallic sphere of 10 cm radius. What is the surface area of each sphere?

8. **Category: SAT Advanced Math**

The function h is defined as $h(x) = x^3$. The graph of the function is shifted to 4 units to the right. Which of the following expressions represents the new function of the graph?

- a. $g(x)=x^3+4$
- b. $g(x)=x^3-4$
- c. $g(x)=(x+4)^3$
- d. $g(x)=(x-4)^3$

9. **Category: SAT Advanced Math**

Which of the following is the equivalent expression, if the expression $3xy + 9y^2$ is subtracted from the expression $15xy + 7x^2 - 3y^2$?

- a. $-12xy-7x^2-12y^2$
- b. $12\ xy +7x^2- 12y^2$
- c. $12\ xy -7x^2- 12y^2$
- d. $12\ xy -7x^2+12y^2$

10. **Category: SAT Algebra**

$x + y - 4 = 0$
$2x + ky - 3 = 0$

Which of the following is the value of k for the system of equation which has no solution?

- a. 0

- b. 2
- c. $\frac{1}{2}$
- d. 6

11. Category: SAT Problem Solving & Data Analysis

When 75% of a number is added to 75, the result is the number again.

What is the number?

- a. 350
- b. 400
- c. 450
- d. 300

12. Category: SAT Problem Solving & Data Analysis

The equation $R = 8000(0.85)^t$ represents the number of road accidents in a city, where t represents the year from 2014. Which of the following sentences is the best interpretation in the context of 8000?

- a. The total number of road accidents
- b. The number of road accidents in 2014
- c. The number of road accidents increases by 8000 per year
- d. The number of road accidents decreases by 8000 per year

13. Category: SAT Algebra

$3(x-1) + 5 = 14$

Which of the following x -value satisfies the above equation?

14. Category: SAT Geometry & Trigonometry

Two right-angled triangles ABC and PQR are similar, right-angled at B and Q, angle A and angle C of triangle ABC correspond to angle P and angle R of triangle PQR respectively. If angle P measures 27°, then what is the measure of angle C?

- a. 63°
- b. 27°
- c. 90°
- d. 153°

15. Category: SAT Problem Solving & Data Analysis

A fair die has six faces, labeled with a number 1 through 6 on each face of a die. If that fair six-sided die is rolled, what is the probability of rolling a number greater than or equal to 4?

- a. $\frac{1}{6}$

- b. $\frac{1}{2}$

- c. $\frac{2}{3}$

- d. $\frac{1}{3}$

16. Category: SAT Advanced Math

If a function h is expressed as h(x) = $(x^2 - 1) + 5$, then for what positive value of the variable x is the function h(x) = 40?

- a. 64

- b. 6

- c. 8

- d. 36

17. Category: SAT Advanced Math

If the function $f(x) = 2x^2 - 7x + 5$ $f(x) = 2x^2 - 7x + 5$ is in the xy -plane, where y=f(x), then what is the value of the x -intercept of the function f(x)?

- a. $(-\frac{5}{2},0)(-\frac{5}{2},0)$

- b. $(-1,0)(-1,0)$

- c. $(0,\frac{5}{2})(0,\frac{5}{2})$

- d. $(1,0)(\frac{5}{2}0)$

18. Category: SAT Algebra

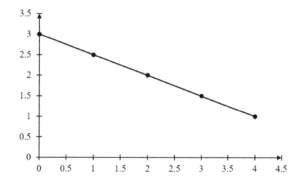

Which of the following linear equations best describes the above linear graph using the highlighted points?

- a. y = 0.5x + 3

- b. y = -0.5x
- c. y = 3x + 0.5
- d. y = -0.5x + 3

19. Category: SAT Geometry & Trigonometry

The base and the height of two right triangles ABC and DEF are given in the ratio 3:2 and 8:5 respectively. Which of the following fractions determines the area of the right triangle ABC by the area of the right triangle DEF?

- a. $\frac{3}{5}$
- b. $\frac{18}{5}$
- c. $\frac{5}{16}$
- d. $\frac{12}{5}$

20. Category: SAT Advanced Math

If a function is represented in the form f(x) = x^2 + 7x + 8, then what is the value of the function f(x) when the value of the variable is x = -1?

21. Category: SAT Geometry & Trigonometry

Which of the following is the equation of the circle in the xy -plane with center at point (0, 5) and a radius with endpoint (-3, 9)?

- a. $(x+3)^2+(y-9)^2=25$
- b. $x^2+(y-5)^2=5$
- c. $x^2+(y-5)^2=25$
- d. $x^2+(y-5)^2=205$

22. Category: SAT Advanced Math

What is the maximum value of the graph of the function f(x) = $-2x^2$ + 25?

- a. 0
- b. 25
- c. 28
- d. 27.5

Detailed Answer Explanations Test 1 Module 1 Math

1.Category: SAT Problem Solving & Data Analysis

C: The question asks for an equivalent form of an expression. If you are given a quadratic in standard form, that is $ax2 + bx + c$, one approach is to factor it. Find two numbers that multiply by 56 and add to -1. These are -8 and 7, so the factored form of the quadratic is $(x - 8)(x + 7)$, which is (C). If a quadratic is more difficult to factor than this one, another approach is to use a graphing calculator. Type in the expression given in the question, then type in the expressions from the answer choices one by one, stopping when one of the answers produces the same graph. By either method, the correct answer is (C).

2.Category: SAT Advanced Math

D: The given function is $h(x) = x^3$

Recall that if the graph of the function $y = f(x)$ is shifted c units to the right, then the new function is represented as follows:

$g(x) = f(x - c)$

The graph of the function h is shifted to 4 units to the right.

The new function can be represented as:

$g(x) = (x - 4)^3$

Thus, if the graph of the function is shifted to 4 units to the right, then the expression represents the new function of the graph is $g(x) = (x - 4)^3$

3.Category: SAT Algebra

C: The product of the number of boxes and the cost per box represents the total cost of the chocolate boxes.

Consider the cost per box $C (as given in the question) and the number of boxes 68.

So, the total cost of chocolate boxes in dollars would be:

Total cost = cost per box * number of boxes
Total cost = c * 68
Total cost = 68c

Therefore, the expression that represents the total cost of chocolate in dollars is 68C.

4.Category: SAT Geometry & Trigonometry

B: Recall that the sum of all angles made on a straight line is 180°.

Add all the angles formed on the straight line and solve for x.

$40° + 4x + 3x = 180°$
$7x = 180° - 40°$
$7x = 140°$
$x = 20°.$

Thus, the value is x = 20°.

5. Category: SAT Algebra

B: The given equation is 2x + y = 6.

The ordered pair (x, y) must satisfy the equation 2x + y = 6.

Put x = 2 and y = 2 in the given equation 2x + y = 6, we get:

$2(2) + 2 = 6$
$4 + 2 = 6$
$6 = 6$

Both sides of the equation are equal, so it satisfies the given equation.

Thus, the solution to the equation is (2, 2).

6. Category: SAT Geometry & Trigonometry

C: In a right triangle, the longest side is the hypotenuse side, and the other two sides are called the legs.

It is given that the longest side (hypotenuse) is 15 m and one of the legs is 12 m long.

Use the Pythagorean Theorem to find the length of the remaining side.

Recall the Pythagorean Theorem that states that in a right triangle, the sum of the squares of the lengths of the legs is equal to the square of the length of the hypotenuse:

$a^2 + b^2 = c^2$

Here, a and b are the lengths of the legs, and c is the length of the hypotenuse.

In this case a = 12, c = 15. Find the value of b as follows:
$b = \sqrt{c^2 - a^2}$
$= \sqrt{15^2 - 12^2}$
$= \sqrt{225 - 144}$
$= \sqrt{81}$
$= 9$

So, the length of the remaining side of the right triangle is 9 m.

314: The radius of the metallic sphere is r = 10cm.

The volume of the sphere is given by the formula:

$V = \frac{4}{3}\pi r^3$

The volume of the metallic sphere is shown below:

$V = \frac{4}{3}\pi(10)^3$

Let the radius of each sphere as R.

Volume of large sphere should be equal to 8 times the volume of sphere with radius R.

$\frac{4}{3}\pi(10)^3 = 8 * \frac{4}{3}\pi R^3$
$1000 = 8R^3$
$R^3 = \frac{1000}{8}$
$= 125$

Take the cube root on both sides.

R = 5cm

The area of the sphere is given by the formula $A = 4\pi R^2$

The area of the sphere is:

$A = 4 * 3.14(5)^2$
$= 314cm^2$

Thus, the area of the sphere is $314cm^2$

8 .Category: SAT Advanced Math

D: The given function is $h(x) = x^3$

Recall that if the graph of the function y = f(x) is shifted c units to the right, then the new function is represented as follows:

g(x) = f(x − c)

The graph of the function h is shifted to 4 units to the right.

The new function can be represented as:

$g(x) = (x − 4)^3$

Thus, if the graph of the function is shifted to 4 units to the right, then the expression represents the new function of the graph is $g(x) = (x − 4)^3$

9.Category: SAT Advanced Math

B: Consider the given expressions $3xy + 9y^2$ and $15xy + 7x^2 - 3y^2$.

Subtract the expression $3xy + 9y^2$ from the expression $15xy + 7x^2 - 3y^2$, we get:

$(15xy + 7x^2 - 3y^2) - (3xy + 9y^2)$

Simplify the expression by distributing -1 inside the parenthesis and then combining the like terms.

$(15xy + 7x^2 - 3y^2) - (3xy + 9y^2) = 15xy + 7x^2 - 3y^2 - 3xy - 9y^2$
$= (15xy - 3xy) + 7x^2 + (-3y^2 - 9y^2)$
$= 12xy + 7x^2 - 12y^2$

Thus, the simplified form is $12xy + 7x^2 - 12y^2$.

10. Category: SAT Algebra

B: Consider the given system of equations:

$x + y - 4 = 0$
$2x + ky - 3 = 0$

If the system of equations has no solution, then the ratio of the coefficients of variables must be equal. $\frac{1}{2} = \frac{1}{k2}$

Solve the equation by cross multiplication.

$k = 2$

Thus, the value is $k = 2$.

11. Category: SAT Problem Solving & Data Analysis

D: Let the number be x.

Given that 75% of a number is added to 75, the result is the number again. So, in the equation form, it can be written as:

75% of x + 75 = x
$\frac{75}{100} * x + 75 = x$
$\frac{3}{4}x + 75 = x$

Simplify the equation for x:

$x - \frac{3}{4}x = 75$
$= \frac{1}{4}x = 75$
$x = 75 * 4$
$= 300$

Thus, the number is 300.

12. Category: SAT Problem Solving & Data Analysis

B: The given equation R = 8000 $(0.85)^t$ represents an exponential function.

Here, t represents the year from 2014.

Put t = 0 in the given equation R = 8000 $(0.85)^t$, we get:

R = 8000(0.85)0(0.85)^0
= 8000(1)
= 8000

Thus, 8000 represents the number of accidents in 2014 (t = 0)

13. Category: SAT Algebra

the only x -value that satisfies the equation 3(x-1) + 5 = 14 is 4.

14. Category: SAT Geometry & Trigonometry

A: Two right-angled triangles ABC and PQR are similar, right-angled at B and Q, angle A and angle C of triangle ABC corresponds to the angle P and angle R of triangle PQR respectively.

Also, angle P measures 27°.

As the triangles ABC and PQR are similar, it is implied that their corresponding angles are equal, so we get $\angle P = \angle A$ and $\angle R = \angle C$.

The measure of $\angle P = 27°$, so we get $\angle A = 27°$.

We know that the sum of three interior angles of a triangle is 180°.

In the triangle PQR, we have $\angle P = 27°$, $\angle Q = 90°$, so the value of $\angle R$ is obtained as follows:

$\angle P + \angle Q + \angle R = 180°$
$27° + 90° + \angle R = 180°$
$117° + \angle R = 180°$
$\angle R = 63°$

Now, $\angle R = 63°$, $\angle R = \angle C$, we get $\angle C = 63°$

Thus, the measure of $\angle C$ is 63°

15. Category: SAT Problem Solving & Data Analysis

B: A fair die has six faces, labeled with a number 1 through 6 on each face of a die; that is, the numbers are 1, 2, 3, 4, 5, 6.

The numbers that are greater than or equal to 4 from the numbers 1, 2, 3, 4, 5, 6 are 4, 5, 6; that is, the count is 3 which means the number of favorable outcomes are 3.

And, the total number count is 6; that is, the total number of outcomes are 6.

The probability, P is represented as follows:

P(E)=Number of Favorable Outcomes/Total Number of Outcomes

So, the probability of rolling a number greater than equal to 4 is obtained as follows:

P (a number greater than or equal to 4) = $\frac{3}{6}$

= $\frac{1}{2}$

Thus, the required probability value is $\frac{1}{2}$

16. Category: SAT Advanced Math

B: The function h is expressed as h(x) = (x^2 – 1) + 5.

Also, it is given that h(x) = 40

Substitute h(x) = 40 into the function h(x) = (x^2 – 1) + 5, and simplify it as follows:

40 = (x^2 – 1) + 5
40 = x^2 – 1 + 5
40 = x^2 + 4

Subtract 4 from both sides of the above term, we get:

x^2 + 4 – 4 = 40 – 4
x^2 = 36

Take a square root on both sides of the above term, and consider only the positive value as follows:

$\sqrt{x^2}=36x2=36$
x = 6

Thus, the function h(x) = 40 when the value of the variable x is 6.

17. Category: SAT Advanced Math

D: The function f(x)=2x^2 −7x+5 is in the xy -plane, where y = f(x).

The x -intercept value of the function is obtained by substituting y = 0 into the given function.

As y = f(x), substitute f(x) = 0 into the function f(x)=2x^2 −7x+5, and simplify the quadratic equation using the factor method as follows:

$2x^2 - 7x + 5 = 0$

$2x^2 - 2x - 5x + 5 = 0$

$2x(x-1) -5(x-1) = 0$

$(x-1)(2x-5) = 0$

From above, we get $x = 1$, $x = \frac{5}{2}$

Thus, the x-intercepts of function f(x) are (1, 0), and $(\frac{5}{2}, 0)$

18.Category: SAT Algebra

D: From the given graph, the highlighted points are obtained as follows:

(0, 3), (1, 2.5), (2, 2), (3, 1.5), (4, 1)

The linear equation using the points (x_1, y_1) and (x_2, y_2) is given as y = mx + b, where m is the slope of the line given as $1m = x_2$ $x_1 y_2 y_1$ and b is the y-intercept value.

Consider the points (x_1, y_1) = (0, 3), and (x_2, y_2) = (1, 2.5) to obtain the slope of the line as follows:

$m = \frac{2.5-3}{1-0}$

$= 2.5 - 3$

$= -0.5$

And the y-intercept value, b is the y-value, when x=0.

From the point (0, 3), we get b = 3.

Substitute m = -0.5, b = 3 into the linear equation form, y = mx + b as follows:

y = -0.5x + 3

Thus, the linear equation describing the given graph is y = -0.5x + 3.

19. Category: SAT Geometry & Trigonometry

D: The base and the height of the two right triangles ABC and DEF are given in the ratio 3:2 and 8:5 respectively.

The formula determining the area of a right triangle with base b, and height h is represented as follows:

$A = \frac{1}{2}bh$

The ratio of the base of the two right triangles ABC and DEF is given as follows:

$\frac{b1}{b2} = \frac{3}{2}$

Similarly, the ratio of the heights of two right triangles ABC and DEF is given as follows:

$\frac{h1}{h2} = \frac{8}{5}$

And, the fraction of the area of the right triangle ABC by the area of the right triangle DEF is given as follows:

$$\frac{a1}{a2} = \frac{\frac{1}{2}(b1)(h1)}{\frac{1}{2}(b2)(h2)}$$

$$= \frac{(b1)(h1)}{(b2)(h2)}$$

$$= \frac{(b1)}{(b2)} \frac{(h1)}{(h2)}$$

Substitute $\frac{(b1)}{(b2)} = \frac{3}{2}$ $\frac{(h1)}{(h2)} = \frac{8}{5}$ in the above fraction, and simplify it as follows:

$$\frac{a1}{a2} = \frac{(b1)}{(b2)} \frac{(h1)}{(h2)}$$

$$= \left(\frac{3}{2}\right) \left(\frac{8}{5}\right)$$

$$= (3) \left(\frac{4}{5}\right)$$

$$= \left(\frac{12}{5}\right)$$

Therefore, the required fraction is $\frac{12}{5}$

20. Category: SAT Advanced Math

2: The correct answer is 2.

The function is $f(x) = x^2 + 7x + 8$, and the variable $x = -1$.

To obtain the value of the function $f(x)$ when the value of the variable is $x = -1$, substitute $x = -1$ into the function $f(x) = x^2 + 7x + 8$ as follows:

$$f(-1) = (-1)^2 + 7(-1) + 8$$
$$= 1 - 7 + 8$$
$$= 1 + 1$$
$$= 2$$

Therefore, the value of the function at $x = -1$ is 2.

21. Category: SAT Geometry & Trigonometry

The radius of the circle, r using the center point (a, b), and an endpoint (c, d) is given as follows:

$$r = \sqrt{(c-a)^2 + (d-b)^2}$$

Substitute the center point (a, b) = (0, 5) and the endpoint (c, d) = (-3, 9) into $r = \sqrt{(c-a)^2 + (d-b)^2}$ to obtain the radius of the circle as follows:

$$r = \sqrt{(-3-0)^2 + (9-5)^2}$$
$$= \sqrt{9+16}$$

$= \sqrt{25}$

$= 5$

The standard equation of the circle with center at point (a, b) and radius, r is represented as $(x-a)^2+(y-b)^2=r^2$

Substitute (a, b) = (0, 5) , r=5 into the standard equation form of the circle, we get the equation of the circle as follows:

$(x-0)^2 + (y-5)^2 = (5)^2$
$x^2 + (y-5)^2 = 25$

Therefore, the equation of the circle is $x^2 + (y-5)^2 = 25$

22. Category: SAT Advanced Math

B: The given equation of parabola is $f(x) = -2x^2 + 25$

Compare the given equation with the equation $f(x) = ax^2 + bx + c$

We get a = -2, b = 0, and c = 25.

Recall the vertex of the parabola as follows:

$(h,k)=(-\frac{b}{2a}, f(\frac{b}{2a}))$

Find the value of h by putting a=-2, and b=0 as follows:

$h=-\frac{0}{2(-2)}$

The value of k represents the y -coordinates (maximum or minimum values) as follows:

Find the value of k as follows:

k = f(h)
= f(0)
$= -2(0)^2 + 25$
= 25

Therefore, the vertex of parabola is (0, 25)

Here, a = -2 < 0, so the parabola opens downwards and the vertex represents the maximum point on the graph.

Thus, the maximum value of the graph is 25.

Practice Test 1 Module 2 Math by Topic and sections

DIRECTIONS: This section contains questions pertaining to various fundamental mathematical skills. Calculators may be utilized for all questions. Unless otherwise specified, the following assumptions apply:

• All variables and expressions represent real numbers.

• The provided figures are accurately drawn to scale.

• All figures exist within a two-dimensional plane.

• The domain of a given function f is the set of all real numbers x for which f(x) is also a real number.

1.Category: SAT Advanced Math

What is the value of $4y - 16$ if $y - 4 = 11$?

2.Category: SAT Advanced Math

$4x + 6 = 18$
Which equation has the same solution as the given equation?

16. a. $4x = 108$
17. b. $4x = 24$
18. c. $4x = 12$
19. d. $4x = 3$

3.Category: SAT Algebra

The charge for parking a car is $50 for an hour. The additional charge for parking is $20. Which of the following expressions represents the total cost of car parking for x hours in dollars?

- a. $50 + 20x$
- b. $20 + 50x$
- c. $20 + 50(x - 1)$
- d. $50 + 20(x - 1)$

4.Category: SAT Algebra

$y = 180 + 20t$

The population of a city is modeled by the above equation, where y is the population and t is the time in years.

What is the population of the city after 4 years?

- • a. 260 million
- • b. 350 million
- • c. 280 million
- • d. 220 million

5. Category: SAT Problem Solving & Data Analysis

The marks obtained by 10 students in monthly exam are given as below:

Students	Marks
1	25
2	34
3	31
4	26
5	22
6	26
7	35
8	28
9	20
10	32

What is the median of the data set?

- • a. 26
- • b. 28
- • c. 27
- • d. 27.5

6. Category: SAT Problem Solving & Data Analysis

In a yoga center, the initial number of students was 300. The number of students increases by 20% every year. What is the total number of students after two years?

7. Category: SAT Advanced Math

$2^x + 2^x + 2^x = 192$

What is the value of x?

- • a. 2

- b. 4
- c. 6
- d. 8

8. Category: SAT Algebra

The sum of x + 1 and x + 3 is 24. What is the value of x?

9. Category: SAT Algebra

$x = -\frac{4}{3}$

$5y + \frac{4}{x} = 7$

What is the value of y?

- a. 2
- b. $\frac{1}{2}$
- c. $\frac{1}{3}$
- d. $\frac{37}{15}$

10. Category: SAT Algebra

What is the x -intercept of the graph of the function f(x) = 3x – 2?

- a. $(\frac{3}{2}, 0)$
- b. $(0, \frac{3}{2})$
- c. $(\frac{2}{3}, 0)$
- d. $(0, \frac{2}{3})$

11. Category: SAT Advanced Math

$4^{x+1} - 4^x = 24$

What is the value of $(2x)^{2x}$?

12. Category: SAT Algebra

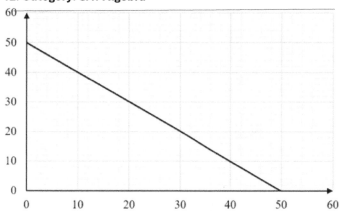

The graph above shows the relationship between the numbers of chocolates bought from Store A represented along the x -axis, and the number of chocolates bought from Store B represented along the y -axis. Which equation could represent this relationship?

- a. 9x + y = 450
- b. x + 9y = 450
- c. x + y = 450
- d. 9x + 9y = 450

13. Category: SAT Problem Solving & Data Analysis

What is two times 16% of 375?

- a. 12
- b. 120
- c. 180
- d. 60

14. Category: SAT Advanced Math

A colony contains 960 mosquitoes, which doubles every 3 hours. Consider the population of mosquitoes as a function of time in hours. What will be the population of the mosquitoes after 18 hours?

15. Category: SAT Algebra

x – 3y = -5
5x = y + 3

Which of the following ordered pairs (x, y) is the solution to the above system of equations?

- a. (11, 2)
- b. (2, 1)

- c. (1, 2)
- d. (-1, 2)

16. Category: SAT Algebra

The present age of Alex is 25 years, and the present age of John is two more than thrice the present age of Alex; what is the present age of John?

- a. 75 years
- b. 36 years
- c. 54 years
- d. 77 years

17. Category: SAT Algebra

An aquarium exhibition costs each of its customers $16 as the entrance fee, and $8 per hour for the time customers spend at the exhibition. A customer spent t hours and spends at most $86 inside the exhibition. Which inequality represents the above situation?

- a. $8t + 4 \leq 43$
- b. $8 + 4t \geq 43$
- c. $8 + 4t \leq 43$
- d. $4t \leq 43$

18. Category: SAT Problem Solving & Data Analysis

12, 9, 5, 16, 12, 8, 10, 17, 5

What is the median value of the above data?

19. Category: SAT Problem Solving & Data Analysis

The velocity with which a train is traveling is at a constant rate of 55 meters per second. What is the velocity of the train, in kilometers per hour?

- a. 186 kilometers per hour
- b. 176 kilometers per hour
- c. 230 kilometers per hour
- d. 198 kilometers per hour

20. Category: SAT Algebra

A teacher is distributing chocolates to 110 students working on an assignment based on the full completion of the assignment and half completion of the assignment. If 30 students fully completed the assignment, and 65 students completed half of the assignment, then which equation represents this situation, where x represents the number of fully completed assignments and y represents the number of half completed assignments?

a. $65x + 30y = 110$

b. $30x - 65y = 110$

c. $30x + 65y = 110$

d. $65y = 30x - 110$

21. Category: SAT Advanced Math

$f(x) = x^2 + 3x - 4$

The above function is defined in the xy -plane. The function g(x) is the result of translating the above function up by 7 units in the xy -plane; what is the expression for the function g(x)?

- a. $g(x) = x^2 + 3x + 3$
- b. $g(x) = x^2 + 3x - 3$
- c. $g(x) = x^2 + 10x - 4$
- d. $g(x) = x^2 + 3x - 11$

22. Category: SAT Algebra

What is the value of x in the equation $7x + 3 = 5x + 9$

Detailed Answer Explanations Test 1 Module 2 Math

1.Category: SAT Advanced Math

The question asks for the value of an expression given an equation. When an SAT question asks for the value of an expression, there is usually a straightforward way to solve for the expression without having to completely isolate the variable. Since 4y is four times y and 16 is four times 4, multiply the entire equation by 4 to get (4)(y – 4) = (4)(11). The equation becomes 4y – 16 = 44. **The correct answer is 44.**

2.Category: SAT Advanced Math

The correct answer is choice C.

Subtracting 6 from both sides of the given equation yields 4x= 12, which is the equation given in choice C. Since this equation is equivalent to the given equation, it has the same solution as the given equation.

3. Category: SAT Algebra

D: Add the initial charge for the first hour and the additional charge for the remaining hours to obtain the total cost.

Let x be the number of hours.

It is given that initial charge for the first hour is $50.

Additional charge for the remaining (x – 1) hours is $20 * (x – 1).

Obtain the equation for the total cost of car parking for x hours in dollars:

Total cost = initial charge + additional charge
Total cost = $50 + $20 * (x – 1)

The expression that represents the total cost of car parking for x hours in dollars is 50 + 20(x – 1).

4.Category: SAT Algebra

A: The population of a city in millions is given by the equation.

y = 180 + 20t

Substitute 4 for t into the equation y = 180 + 20t to find the population after 4 years.

y = 180 + 20(4)
= 180 + 80
= 260

Thus, the population of a city in 4 years is 260 million.

5. Category: SAT Problem Solving & Data Analysis

C: The marks obtained by 10 students in monthly exam are shown below:

25, 34, 31, 26, 22, 26, 35, 28, 20, 32

Arrange the data in the ascending order.

20, 22, 25, 26, 26, 28, 31, 32, 34, 35

The total number of data is 10.

The number of data points is even, so the median will be the average value of the middle two numbers.

$$\text{Median} = \frac{5\text{th}+6\text{th}}{2}$$
$$= \frac{26+28}{2}$$
$$= \frac{54}{2}$$
$$= 27$$

Thus, the median of the data set is 27

6. Category: SAT Problem Solving & Data Analysis

432: The initial number of students is 300.

The increase rate is r = 20%.

The number of time period is t = 2 years

The exponential growth formula is given as:

$f(x) = a(1+r)^t$, where

a = initial amount
r = increase rate
t = time period

Put the given values in the growth formula.

$$f(x) = 300 (1 + 0.20)^2$$
$$= 300(1.20)^2$$
$$= 432$$

Thus, the number of students after two years is 432.

7. Category: SAT Advanced Math

C: Consider the given expression as follows:

$2^x + 2^x + 2^x = 192$

Take common term 2^x out from the expression $2^x+2^x+2^x=192$, we get:

$2^x+2^x+2^x=192$

$= 2^x (1+1+1) = 192$

$= 2^x = \frac{192}{3}$

$= 2^x = 64$

$= 2^x = 2^6$

Use the exponent rule:

$a^m = a^n = \Rightarrow m=n$

Simplify further as:

$2^x = 2^6$

$x = 6$

Thus, the value of x = 6.

8. Category: SAT Algebra

10: The correct answer is 10.

It is given that the sum of x + 1 and x + 3 is 24.

So, add the expressions x + 1 and x + 3, then equate to 24.

$x + 1 + x + 3 = 24$

$2x + 4 = 24$

$2x = 20$

$x = 10$

Thus, the value of x = 10.

9. Category: SAT Algebra

A: The given equations are:

$x = -\frac{4}{3}$

$5y + \frac{4}{x} = 7$

Substitute $-\frac{4}{3}$ for x in the equation $\frac{4}{x} + 5y = 7$ and solve for y as follows:

$\frac{4}{\frac{4}{3}} + 5y = 7$

$= \frac{4*3}{-4} + 5y = 7$

$-3 + 5y = 7$

$5y = 10$

$y = 2$

Thus, the value of $y = 2$

10. **Category: SAT Algebra**

C: The given function is $f(x) = 3x - 2$.

The x-intercept of the graph of the function is the point where $f(x) = 0$

Substitute 0 for $f(x)$ into the function $f(x) = 3x - 2$, we get:

$3x - 2 = 0$

$3x = 2$

$x = \dfrac{2}{3}$

Thus, the x -intercept of the graph of the function is $(\dfrac{2}{3}, 0)$

11. **Category: SAT Advanced Math**

27: The given expression is:

$4^{x+1} - 4^x = 24$

Take out common 4^x from the left-hand side.

$4^{x+1} - 4^x = 24$

$= 4^x(4^1 - 1) = 24$

$= (2^2) \times (3) = 24$

$= 2^2 x = 8$

Rewrite the expression as follows:

$2^2 x = 2^3$

$2x = 3$

$x = \dfrac{3}{2}$

Find the value of the expression $(2)^2 x = $ as follows:

$2)^2 x = (2 * \dfrac{3}{2})^{2 * \frac{3}{2}}$

$= (3)^3$

$= 27$

Thus, the value of the expression is 27.

12. **Category: SAT Algebra**

D: The given graph shows the relationship between the number of chocolates bought from Store A represented along the x-axis and the number of chocolates bought from Store B represented along the y-axis.

The coordinate points obtained from the given graph are as follows:

(0, 50), (10, 40), (20, 30), and so on...

To check which equation represents the relationship shown in the graph, check each equation present in the options one by one using the coordinate points as follows:

Consider option A equation $9x + y = 450$.

Substitute $(x, y) = (0, 50)$ into the equation $9x + y = 450$, we get:

$9(0) + 50 = 450$
$0 + 50 = 450$
$50 = 450$, which is not true

Consider option B equation $x + 9y = 450$.

Substitute $(x, y) = (0, 50)$ into the equation $x + 9y = 450$, we get:

$0 + 9(50) = 450$
$0 + 450 = 450$
$450 = 450$, which is true

But, substituting $=(10,40)(x,y)=(10,40)$ into the equation $x + 9y = 450$ gives:

$10 + 9(40) = 450$
$10 + 360 = 450$
$370 = 450$, which is not true

Consider option C equation $x + y = 450$.

Substitute $(x,y)=(0,50)$ into the equation $x + y = 450$, we get:

$0 + 50 = 450$
$50 = 450$, which is not true

Finally, consider the option D equation $x + y = 450$.

Substitute $(x,y)=(0,50)$ into the equation $9x + 9y = 450$, we get:

$9(0) + 9(50) = 450$
$0 + 450 = 450$
$450 = 450$, which is true

Substitute $(x,y)=(10,40)$ into the equation $9x + 9y = 450$ as follows:

$9(10) + 9(40) = 450$
$90 + 360 = 450$
$450 = 450$, which is also true

Now, substitute (x,y)=(20,30)(x,y)=(20,30) into the equation 9x + 9y = 450 which yields:

9(20) + 9(30) = 450
180 + 270 = 450
450 = 450, which is also true

Thus, the only equation that represents the given relationship in the graph is 9x + 9y = 450.

13. Category: SAT Problem Solving & Data Analysis

B: The expression formed using two times 16% of 375 is as follows:

2(16%) of 375 = 2(16%) * 375
= 32% * 375

Using 1% equivalent to $\frac{1}{100}$ in the above term, we get:

2(16%) of 375 = 32% * 375
$= \frac{32}{100} * 375$
= 8 * 15
= 120

Thus, the value of the given expression is 120.

14. Category: SAT Advanced Math

61440: The correct answer is 61440.

It is given that the country contains 960 mosquitoes, which doubles every 3 hours.

The equation in which the population is increasing at a double rate is represented using the exponential type of equation.

As the initial population is given as P_0 = 960, which doubles every 3 hours, the equation is represented as follows:

$P(t) = P_0 2^{\frac{t}{3}}$
$= 960 \, (2)^{\frac{t}{3}}$

So, the formula that determines the population of mosquitoes as a function of time in hours is

$P(t) = 960 \, (2)^{\frac{t}{3}}$

To obtain the population of mosquitoes after 18 hours, substitute t = 18 into the above equation, we get:

$(18) = 960(2)^{\frac{18}{3}}$
$= 960(2)^6$
= 960 * 64
= 61,440

Thus, the population of the mosquitoes after 18 hours is 61440.

15. Category: SAT Algebra

C: The equations are x – 3y = -5, and 5x = y + 3.

Rewrite the equation 5x = y + 3 as follows:

5x = y + 3
5x – y = 3

Multiply the equation x – 3y = -5 by (-5), and add it with the equation 5x – y = 3 as follows:

(-5)(x – 3y) + 5x – y = (-5)(-5) + 3
-5x + 15y + 5x – y = 25 + 3
-5x + 5x + 15y – y = 28
14y = 28

Now, divide both sides of the above term by 14, we get:

$$\frac{14y}{14} = \frac{28}{14}$$

y = 2

Substitute y = 2 into the equation x – 3y = -5, and simplify it as follows:

x – 3(2) = -5
x – 6 = -5
x = -5 + 6
x = 1

From x = 1, y = 2, the ordered pair of the form (x, y) is (1, 2).

Thus, the ordered pair satisfying the given system of equations is (1, 2).

16. Category: SAT Algebra

D: It is given that the present age of Alex is 25 years, and the present age of John is two more than thrice the present age of Alex.

Let the present age of John be x years.

As the present age of Alex is 25 years, and the present age of John, x, is given using the statement "John is two more than thrice the present age of Alex."

Using the above statement, the expression for the present age of John is formed as follows:

x = 3(25) + 2

Simplify the above expression, we get:

x = 3(25) + 2

= 75 + 2

= 77

From above, we get the present age of John as 77 years.

Thus, the present age of John is 77 years.

17. Category: SAT Algebra

It is given that an aquarium exhibition costs each of its customers $16 as the entering fee, and $8 per hour the time customers spend in the exhibition.

Also, the customer spent t hours and spend at most $86 inside the exhibition.

Let the time spent in the exhibition be t hours, and it costs $8 per hour; that is, $8t.

As the entering fee is $16, and the additional cost is $8t, we get the expression as:

16 + 8t

From the given information, the customer spends at most $86 inside the exhibition.

So, the inequality is as follows:

$16 + 8t \leq 86$

Simplifying the inequality $16 + 8t \leq 86$ as follows:

$16 + 8t \leq 86$

$2(8 + 4t) \leq 2(43)$

Now, divide both sides of the above inequality by 2, we get:

$$\frac{2(8+4t)}{2} \leq \frac{2(43)}{2}$$

$8 + 4t \leq 43$

Thus, the inequality representing the given situation is $8 + 4t \leq 43$

18. Category: SAT Problem Solving & Data Analysis

10: The correct answer is 10.

The data is given as 12, 9, 5, 16, 12, 8, 10, 17, 5.

Rewrite the data 12, 9, 5, 16, 12, 8, 10, 17, 5 in increasing order as follows:

5, 5, 8, 9, 10, 12, 12, 16, 17

If the count of the data values is odd, then the median is the middle term of the data, and if the count is even, then the median is half of the sum of the two middle terms of the data.

As the count of the data values 5, 5, 8, 9, 10, 12, 12, 16, 17 is 9 ,which is odd, so the median of this data is the middle term.

To obtain the median of the data 5, 5, 8, 9, 10, 12, 12, 16, 17, look for the middle term; that is, the 5th term which is 10.

Thus, the median of the given data is 10.

19. Category: SAT Problem Solving & Data Analysis

D: The velocity with which a train is traveling is at a constant rate of 55 meters per second.

The expression 55 meters per second is given as:

$$\frac{55 meters}{1 second}$$

As 1 kilometer = 1000 meters, that is 1 meter = $\frac{1}{1000}$ kilometers.

As 1 hour = 3600 seconds, that is 1 second = $\frac{1}{3600}$ hours.

Using 1 meter = $\frac{1}{1000}$ kilometers, 1 second = $\frac{1}{3600}$ hours in the expression $\frac{55 meters}{1 second}$ as follows:

$$\frac{55 meters}{1 second} = \frac{55 * \frac{1}{1000} kilometers}{\frac{1}{3600}}$$
$$= \frac{55 * 3600 kilometers}{1000 \, hours}$$
$$= \frac{11 * 18 kilometers}{1 \, hour}$$
$$= \frac{198 \, kilometers}{1 \, hour}$$

Thus, the representation in kilometers per hour is 198 kilometers per hour.

20. Category: SAT Algebra

C: There are 110 students working on the assignment.

It is given that 30 students fully completed the assignment, and 65 students completed half of the assignment.

Also, x represents the number of fully completed assignments and y represents the number of half- completed assignments.

So, we get the expression as 30x + 65y.

According to the question "there are 110 students working on the assignment", so the equation becomes:

30x + 65y = 110

Thus, the required equation is 30x + 65y = 110.

21. Category: SAT Advanced Math

A: The function f (x) = x^2 + 3x – 4 is defined in the xy -plane, and the function g(x) is the result of translating the function f(x) up by 7 units in the xy -plane.

The translation of a function up by a units implies that a is added to the function.

As the function f(x) is translated up by 7 units in the xy -plane, we get the representation of the function f(x)=x^2+3x−4 after translation as:

f(x)+7=x^2+3x−4+7

Also, the function g(x) is the result of translating the function f(x) up by 7 units in the xy -plane, we get:

g(x) = f(x) + 7
= x^2 + 3x − 4 + 7
= x^2 + 3x + 3

Therefore, the expression for the function g(x) is g(x) = x^2 +3x + 3.

22. Category: SAT Algebra

3: The given expression is 7x + 3 = 5x + 9 and the value of x can be calculated as follows:

Rearrange the like terms as follows:

7x + 3 = 5x + 9
7x − 5x = 9 − 3
2x = 6
x = 3

Thus, the value of x is 3.

Practice Test 2 Module 1 Math by Topic and sections

DIRECTIONS: This section contains questions pertaining to various fundamental mathematical skills. Calculators may be utilized for all questions. Unless otherwise specified, the following assumptions apply:

• All variables and expressions represent real numbers.

• The provided figures are accurately drawn to scale.

• All figures exist within a two-dimensional plane.

• The domain of a given function f is the set of all real numbers x for which f(x) is also a real number.

1. Question

Category: SAT Problem Solving & Data Analysis

Which of the following is the median of the data set 12, 15, 18, 20, 20, 22, 25, 26?

2. Question

Category: SAT Algebra

What is the value of $(x + y)^2$ according to the solution of the below system of equations?

$2x - y = 3$
$x + 2y = 4$

- a. -9
- b. 9
- c. 5
- d. 4

3. Question

Category: SAT Advanced Math

The expression $x = 2y^2 - k$ shows a relationship between variables x, y, and constant k. Which of the following equations expresses the variable y in terms of variable x and constant k?

- a. $y = \frac{\sqrt{x-k}}{2}$
- b. $y = \frac{\sqrt{x+2}}{2}$
- c. $y = \frac{\sqrt{x+k}}{2}$
- d. $y = \frac{\sqrt{-x+k}}{2}$

4. Question

Category: SAT Advanced Math

The equation $3x^2 - 2x + 1 = 0$ has:

- a. Two real root

- b. One real root

- c. Two distinct real root

- d. No real root

5. Question

Category: SAT Geometry & Trigonometry

Triangle ABC is similar to triangle DEF. If the length of AB is 6 cm and the length of DE is 9 cm, what is the length of BC if the length of EF is 13.5 cm ?

- a. 45 cm

- b. 9 cm

- c. 6 cm

- d. 12 cm

6. Question

Category: SAT Advanced Math

Consider the function $g(d)=500(0.75)^d$, which models the decay of a radioactive substance. The function represents the remaining quantity of the substance after d days, where d is the number of days since the start of an experiment.
Given $0 \le d \le 10$, if z = g(d) is plotted on the dz-plane, which of the following interpretations best fits the z-intercept of the graph in this context?

- a. The maximum estimated quantity of the substance at the beginning of the experiment was 500 units.

- b. The maximum estimated decayed quantity of the substance during the 10 days was 125 units.

- c. The estimated quantity of the substance at the start of the experiment was 125 units.

- d. The estimated quantity of the substance at the start of the experiment was 500 units.

7. Question

Category: SAT Problem Solving & Data Analysis

In a survey, 45% of participants preferred coffee over tea. If the survey included 500 participants, how many preferred coffee?

8. Question

Category: SAT Geometry & Trigonometry

In triangles XYZ and UVW, angles Y and V each have measure 30° and angles Z and W each have measure 45°. Which additional piece of information is sufficient to determine whether triangle XYZ is similar to triangle UVW?

- a. The measure of angle X only

- b. The length of side XY, YZ, and ZX

- c. The ratio of sides XY : UV, and YZ : VW

- d. Measure of any two sides of UVW

9. Question

Category: SAT Advanced Math

In a cafeteria, a sandwich costs 's' dollars and a drink costs 'd' dollars. If Tom buys 3 sandwiches and 2 drinks, and spends $20, which equation represents Tom's purchases?

- a. s + d = 10
- b. 3s – 2d = 20
- c. 2s + 3d = 20
- d. 3s + 2d = 20

10. Question

Category: SAT Algebra

If the slope of a line is 2, then for what value of p another line 3x + py = 7 becomes perpendicular to the first line?

11. Question

Category: SAT Algebra

The graph of y = k(x) + 3 is depicted. Which equation stands for function k?

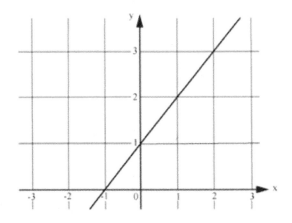

- a. k(x) = x – 1
- b. k(x) = x + 1
- c. k(x) = -x + 1
- d. k(x) = -x – 1

12. Question

Category: SAT Advanced Math

A gardener plans to spend $500 to buy flowering plants. To be eligible for a volume discount, the gardener needs to select at least 15 plants. If the gardener pays $18 per plant for roses and $10 per plant for daisies, what is the maximum number of rose plants the gardener can buy within the budget while meeting the discount requirement?

- a. 16
- b. 17
- c. 18
- d. 19

13. Question

Category: SAT Problem Solving & Data Analysis

In an experiment, a chemical reaction initially contained 1200 grams of a substance. After 15 minutes, the remaining amount was measured to be 300 grams. What is the average rate of substance consumption in grams per minute?

- a. 50 grams/min
- b. 60 grams/min
- c. 20 grams/min
- d. 80 grams/min

14. Question

Category: SAT Problem Solving & Data Analysis

A cyclist rides at a constant speed of 18 km/h. How long, in hours, will it take for the cyclist to travel a distance of 90 km?

- a. 6 hours
- b. 4 hours
- c. 4.5 hours
- d. 5 hours

15. Question

Category: SAT Algebra

In the xy-plane, the function $g(x) = 5x - 20$ has an intercept at the x-axis at $(c, 0)$ and at the y-axis at $(0, d)$. What is the value of $c - d$?

- a. -16
- b. 24
- c. -24
- d. 20

16. Question

Category: SAT Geometry & Trigonometry

The area of a square shaped plate is 36 cm^2. What is the perimeter of the square shaped plate?

17. Question

Category: SAT Advanced Math

The function $A(w) = 5w^2$ represents the area of a square in square units, where w is the length of its side having value of 3 units.

Which of the following statement is correct?

- a. The area of the square is 9 square units
- b. The area of the square is 15 square units
- c. The area of the square is 25 square units
- d. The area of the square is 45 square units.

18. Question

Category: SAT Advanced Math

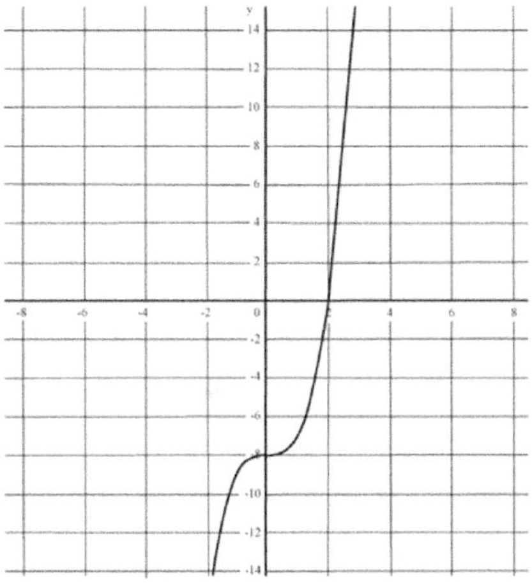

What is the x-intercept of the graph shown?

- a. (2, 0)
- b. (-2, 0)
- c. (0, 2)
- d. (0, -2)

19. Question

Category: SAT Problem Solving & Data Analysis

The line graph depicts the monthly electricity consumption of a residential building over a year, in kilowatt-hours (kWh).

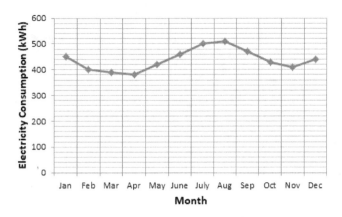

Based on the line graph, in which month did the building consume the least amount of electricity?

- a. February
- b. April
- c. August
- d. November

20. Question

Category: SAT Advanced Math

Consider the equation y = 2.5, and nonlinear equation $y = x^2 - 5x + b$, where b is a positive constant. The equation has a single distinct real solution. What is the value of b that ensures this condition?

21. Question

Category: SAT Algebra

$\sqrt{x}=2$
$y = x^3 - 61$

Consider the above equations of a graph in the x-y plane. What is the value of the y?

- a. -3
- b. 2
- c. 3
- d. 4

22. Question

Category: SAT Problem Solving & Data Analysis

The price, P, of a particular stock t years after its initial public offering is given by $P(t) = 120(1.05)^t$. Which of the following functions best models the price of the stock m months after its initial public offering?

- a. $P(m)=120(1.00416)^m$

- b. $P(m) = 120(1.05)m$
- c. $P(m) = 1440(1.05)m$
- d. $P(m) = 120(1.05)^{\frac{m}{12}}$

Detailed Answer Explanations Test 2 Module 1 Math

1. Question

Category: SAT Problem Solving & Data Analysis

20: correct answer

The data set 12, 15, 18, 20, 20, 22, 25, 26 has a total of n = 8 values.

The total number of values is even, so median of the data set will be same as the mean of its fourth and fifth term.

The fourth and fifth terms are 20 and 20 respectively.

The mean of the fourth and fifth term can be calculated as:

$m = \frac{20+20}{2} \frac{22}{20} + 20$
$m = \frac{40}{2} \frac{22}{40}$
$m = 20$

Thus, the median of the data set is 20.

2. Question

Category: SAT Algebra

B: The system of equations is given as follows:

$2x - y = 3$ ... ... (1)
$x + 2y = 4$ ... ... (2)

Multiply equation (1) by 2 to equate the y coefficient in both equations.

$2(2x - y) = 2(3)$
$4x - 2y = 6$ ... ... (3)

On adding equation (2) and equation (3), we get:

$(x + 2y) + (4x - 2y) = 4 + 6$
$5x = 10$
$x = 2$

On substituting x = 2 in equation (1), we get:

$2(2) - y = 3$
$y = 4 - 3$
$y = 1$

The value of the expression $(x + y)^2$ is given as follows:

$(x + y)^2 = (2 + 1)^2 = 9$

Thus, the value of the expression $(x + y)^2$ is 9.

3. Question

Category: SAT Advanced Math

C: The given expression for variable x in terms of variable y and constant k is $x = 2y^2 - k$

This expression can be converted for variable y in terms of variable x and constant k as follows:

$x = 2y^2 - k$

$x + k = 2y^2$

$y^2 = \frac{\sqrt{x+k}}{2}$

Take positive square root of both sides:

$y = \frac{\sqrt{x+k}}{2}$

Thus, the converted form of expression for y in terms of x and k is $y = \frac{\sqrt{x+k}}{2}$

4. Question

Category: SAT Advanced Math

D: The discriminant of a quadratic equation is given as $D = b^2 - 4ac$.

If D > 0, then equation has two distinct roots.
If D = 0, then equation has two same real roots.
If D < 0, then equation has no real roots.

On comparing the quadratic equation $3x^2 - 2x + 1 = 0$ with general form of quadratic equation $ax^2 + bx + c = 0$, the coefficients are a = 3, b = -2, and c = 1.

The discriminant of the equation $3x^2 - 2x + 1 = 0$ as follows:

$D = (-2)^2 - 4(3)(1)$

$D = 4 - 12$

$D = -8 < 0$

The discriminant of the equation is negative, so no real root of the equation is possible.

5. Question

Category: SAT Geometry & Trigonometry

B: The ratios of corresponding sides of two similar triangles are always equal.

As ΔABC and ΔDEF are similar triangles, so the ratio of their corresponding sides is given as follows:

$\frac{AB}{DE} = \frac{BC}{EF} = \frac{AC}{DF}$

On considering the first two ratios:

$\frac{AB}{DE} = \frac{BC}{EF}$ ....(1)

On substituting AB = 6 cm, DE = 9 cm, and EF = 13.5 cm, we get:

$\frac{6cm}{9cm} = \frac{BC}{13,5\ cm}$

BC = 9 cm

Thus, the length of the side BC is 9 cm.

6. Question

Category: SAT Advanced Math

D: To interpret the d-intercept of the graph in this context, we need to understand that the z -intercept is the point where the graph crosses the z -axis, i.e., where d = 0. This corresponds to the initial quantity of the radioactive substance before any decay has occurred (at the start of the experiment).

The function $g(d)=500(0.75)^d$ represents the remaining quantity of the substance after d days, where d is the number of days since the start of the experiment.

Plugging in d = 0 into the function gives:

$g(0)=500(0.75)^0=500(1)=500$

This means that the initial quantity of the substance (at the start of the experiment) was 500 units. So, the correct answer is "The estimated quantity of the substance at the start of the experiment was 500 units."

7. Question

Category: SAT Problem Solving & Data Analysis

225: The total number of participants in survey is 500 and 45% of participants preferred coffee over tea.

The number of participants who preferred coffee over tea is given as follows:

C = 45% of (500)
$C = (\frac{45}{100})(500)$
C = 225

Thus, the number of participants who preferred coffee over tea is 225.

8. Question

Category: SAT Geometry & Trigonometry

C: For two triangles to be similar, their corresponding angles must be congruent, and their corresponding sides must be in proportion (i.e., their ratios must be equal).

Given that angles Y and V each have a measure of 30°, and angles Z and W each have a measure of 45°, the only piece of additional information that would be sufficient to determine whether triangle XYZ is similar to triangle UVW is:

"The ratio of sides XY : UV, and YZ : VW"

This is because if the ratios of the corresponding sides are equal, then the triangles are similar according to the Angle-Angle (Aa. similarity theorem.)

The given angle information along with the ratios of sides XY : UV and YZ : VW would ensure that all three angles of one triangle correspond to the three angles of the other triangle and that the sides are proportional, satisfying the conditions for similarity.

9. Question

Category: SAT Advanced Math

D: The cost of a sandwich and a drink is $s and $d.

Tom buy's 3 sandwiches, so his spending on sandwiches is S = 3($s).

Tom buy's 2 drinks, so his spending on drinks is D = 2($d).

The total spending of Tom on sandwich and drink costs $20. It can be represented in equation as follows:

S + D = $20
3($s) + 2($d) = $20
3s + 2d = 20

Thus, Tom's purchases can be represented by 3s + 2d = 20.

10. Question

Category: SAT Algebra

A: The slope of the first line is given as:

$m_1 = 2$

The slope of a straight line is given by the ratio of the negative coefficient of x and coefficient of y, so the slope of the line 3x + py = 7 is given as:

$m_2 = \frac{-3}{p} = -\frac{3}{p}$

The two straight lines become perpendicular to each other, if the product of slopes of both lines become equal to -1.

The value of constant p for both lie to be perpendicular is given as:

$m_1 * m_2 = -1$

$(2)\left(\frac{-3}{p}\right) = -1$

$p = \frac{1}{6}$

Thus, the required slope is $\frac{1}{6}$.

11. Question

Category: SAT Algebra

B: The given expression is y = k(x) + 3

This equation shows a straight line passing through the points (0, 1), and (-1, 0).

Find the slope by using these points:

m = slope = 0−1−1−0−1−00−1 = 1

The y-intercept is (1, 0).

So, b = 1.

The function will be k(x) = x + 1.

12. Question

Category: SAT Advanced Math

D: The budget available to purchase flowering plant is P = $500.

The minimum number of plants purchased to avail the discount is n = 15.

The cost of the each rose plant is r = $18 and cost of each daisy plant is d = $10.

The remaining amount after purchasing the 15 daisy plants is given as:

Q = P − n * d
Q = $500 − (15)($10)
Q = $350

The maximum number of rose flower purchased is given as follows:

$N = \frac{q}{r}$

$N = \frac{350}{18}$

$N \approx 19$

Thus, the Gardner can purchase maximum 19 roses.

13. Question

Category: SAT Problem Solving & Data Analysis

B: Consider the initial and final amount of the substance are x = 1200 grams and y = 300 grams.

The time for the chemical reaction is t = 15 min.

The average rate of the substance is the amount of chemical substance burnt in given duration, so it can be given by following formula as:

$R = \frac{(x-y)}{t}$

On substituting all the given values, we get:

$R = \frac{(1200 \, grams - 300 \, grams)}{15 \, min}$

$R = \frac{900 \, grams}{15 \, min}$

R = 60 grams/min

Thus, the average rate of substance consumption in grams per minute is 60 grams/min.

14. Question

Category: SAT Problem Solving & Data Analysis

D: Let t represent the duration to travel the given distance.

The speed of the cyclist is given v = 18 km/h and the distance travelled by the cyclist is 90 km.

The duration to the cover the given distance is given as follows:

$t = \frac{d}{v}$

On substituting v = 18 km/h and d = 90 km in the above equation, we get:

$t = \frac{90 \, km}{18 \, \frac{km}{h}}$

t = 5 hr

Thus, the duration taken by the cyclist to cover the given distance is 5 hours.

15. Question

Category: SAT Algebra

B: Consider the given function g(x).

g(x) = 5x − 20 ... (1)

On substituting x-intercept (c, 0) in the equation (1), we get:

$0 = 5c - 20$

$5c = 20$

$c = 4$

On substituting y-intercept (0, d) in the equation (1), we get:

$d = 5(0) - 20$

$d = 0 - 20$

$d = -20$

The value of difference (c – d) is calculated as follows:

$c - d = 4 - (-20)$

$c - d = 4 + 20$

$c - d = 24$

Thus, the value of difference between x and y intercepts of function $g(x) = 5x - 20$ is 24.

16. Question

Category: SAT Geometry & Trigonometry

24: Let a represents the side of square shaped plate.

The area of square shaped object is equal to the square of the length of its side.

$A = a^2$ ... ... (1)

The value of area of square shaped plate is 36 cm^2.

On substituting A=36 cm^2 in equation (1), we get:

$36\ cm^2 = a^2$

$a = 6\ cm$

The square has four sides of same length and sum of these sides is equal to the perimeter of square.

The perimeter of the square shaped plate is given as follows:

$P = a + a + a + a$

$P = 4a$ ... ... (2)

On substituting a = 6 cm in equation (2), we get:

$P = 4(6\ cm)$

$P = 24\ cm$

Thus, the perimeter of the square shaped plate is 24 cm.

17. Question

Category: SAT Advanced Math

D: The function for the area of the square is given as follows:

$A(w) = 5w^2$ ... ... (1)

On substituting w = 3 in the equation (1), we get:

$A(3) = 5(3)^2$

$A(3) = 5(9)$

$A(3) = 45$

Thus, the area of the square is 45 square units.

18. Question

Category: SAT Advanced Math

A: The graph of the function intersects the x axis at x = 2. The y-coordinates of intersecting point is 0, so the intersecting point of the function at x-axis becomes (2, 0).

Thus, the x- intercept in the graph is (2, 0).

19. Question

Category: SAT Problem Solving & Data Analysis

B: The least value of electricity consumption of residential building is 380 kWh. This least consumption of electricity corresponds to "April".

Thus, the building consumes the least amount of electricity in "April".

20. Question

Category: SAT Advanced Math

8.75: The given non-linear equations are:

$y = 2.5$
$y = x^2 - 5x + b \dots (1)$

Substitute y = 2.5 and simplify equation (1).

$2.5 = x^2 - 5x + b$
$x^2 - 5x + b - 2.5 = 0 \dots (2)$

Above equation (2) is a quadratic equation and it has a single distinct root. Since quadratic equation has a single distinct root, so "discriminant" of this quadratic equation will be greater than or equal to zero.

$D \geq 0$
$(-5)^2 - 4(1)(b - 2.5) \geq 0$
$25 - 4(b - 2.5) \geq 0$

Consider equal sign to find the value of b.

21. Question

Category: SAT Algebra

C: The value of x by using �=2x=2 is calculated as:

$\sqrt{x} = 2$

On squaring of both sides, we get:

$(\sqrt{x}) = (2)^2$
$x = 4$

On substituting x = 4 in the equation $y = x^3 - 61$, we get:

$y = (4)^3 - 61$

$y = 64 - 61$

$y = 3$

Thus, the value of y is 3.

22. Question

Category: SAT Problem Solving & Data Analysis

A: The expression for variation in initial price of stock in years is given as:

$P(t) = 120(1.05)^t$

There are 12 months in a year, so when we convert months in years, we simply divide the time given in years.

The given expression for variation in initial price of stock in years can simply converted into its equivalent expression in months by replacing t by m/12.

The expression for variation in initial price of stock in months is given as:

$P(t) = 120(1.05)^t \equiv P(m) = 120(1.05)^{\frac{m}{12}}$

Take twelfth root of the 1.05.

$P(t) = 120(1.05)^t \equiv P(m) = 120(1.00416)^m$

Thus, the price of the stock m months after its initial public offering is modelled by $P(m) = 120(1.00416)^m$.

Practice Test 2 Module 2 Math by Topic and sections

DIRECTIONS: This section contains questions pertaining to various fundamental mathematical skills. Calculators may be utilized for all questions. Unless otherwise specified, the following assumptions apply:

• All variables and expressions represent real numbers.

• The provided figures are accurately drawn to scale.

• All figures exist within a two-dimensional plane.

• The domain of a given function f is the set of all real numbers x for which f(x) is also a real number.

---

1. Question

Category: SAT Advanced Math

What is the value of $(y^2 - x^2)$ for the given system of equations?

$y = 5x$
$7x + 3y = 22$

- a. -24
- b. 24
- c. 12
- d. -12

2. Question

Category: SAT Geometry & Trigonometry

The area of an equilateral triangle is $4\sqrt{3} \ cm^2$. What is the length of perpendicular drawn from a vertex to its opposite side?

- a. 4 cm
- b. $4\sqrt{3 \ cm}$
- c. $2\sqrt{3 \ cm}$
- d. $\sqrt{3 \ cm}$

3. Question

Category: SAT Algebra

The line represented by 2y + 5x = 15 is translated up 6 units in the xy-plane. What is the y-coordinate of the y-intercept of the resulting graph?

- a. 7.5
- b. 13.5
- c. -7.5
- d. -13.5

72

4. Question

Category: SAT Problem Solving & Data Analysis

The mass of a box is 81.5 kg. Which of the following is equivalent to the mass of the box in grams? (1 kg = 1000 grams).

- a. 81,500 grams
- b. 81,505 grams
- c. 81,050 grams
- d. 815 grams

5. Question

Category: SAT Problem Solving & Data Analysis

Sarah saved up some money this year. She saved 30% of her monthly allowance every month. If her monthly allowance is $200, how much money did Sarah save over the year?

- a. $1200
- b. $2400
- c. $720
- d. $600

6. Question

Category: SAT Advanced Math

Which expressions is equivalent to $17x - (7x - 9)$?

- a. $10x + 9$
- b. $10x - 9$
- c. $-10x - 9$
- d. $-10x + 9$

7. Question

Category: SAT Advanced Math

The expression $((3\sqrt{x} + 4)(8 - 7\sqrt{x})$ is equivalent to:

- a. $32 + 4\sqrt{x} - 21x$
- b. $32 - 4\sqrt{x} - 21x$
- c. $21 - 4\sqrt{x} + 32x$
- d. $4 - 32\sqrt{x} - 21x$

8. Question

Category: SAT Advanced Math

Consider the function $g(x)=4\sqrt[3]{x}$ such that its function value $g(x) = 108$. What is the correct value of x?

- a. 27

- b. 19664

- c. 19683

- d. 19721

9. Question

Category: SAT Algebra

Consider the function $p(x) = -3(x-2)(x+4)$. In the xy-plane, the graph of $y = q(x)$ is obtained by shifting the graph of $y = p(x)$ three units to the right. What is the value of $q(2)$?

10. Question

Category: SAT Advanced Math

Consider the equation $m + 3n = 2p$, where m, n, and p are interconnected numerical values. Which option accurately represents n in terms of m and p?

- a. $\left(\frac{2p+m}{3}\right)$

- b. $\left(\frac{2p-m}{3}\right)$

- c. $\left(\frac{2m+p}{3}\right)$

- d. $\left(\frac{2m-p}{3}\right)$

11. Question

Category: SAT Advanced Math

Consider the expression $\frac{5x^3-15x^2}{10x} + \frac{3x+5}{7}$. Which of the following is equivalent to given expression?

- a. $\frac{(7x^2+15x+10)}{14}$

- b. $\frac{(7x^2-15x-10)}{14}$

- c. $\frac{(7x^2-15x+10)}{14}$

- d. $\frac{(-7x^2-15x+10)}{14}$

12. Question

Category: SAT Geometry & Trigonometry

Circle A has a radius of 7 cm. The circumference of Circle B is 3 times the circumference of Circle A. What is the radius of Circle B?

- a. 7 cm

- b. 21 cm

- c. 14 cm
- d. 42 cm

13. Question

Category: SAT Algebra

The product of two integers is 16. If the first integer is 4 less than two times the second integer, what is the smaller integer?

a. 5

b. -8

c. -5

d. 2

14. Question

Category: SAT Problem Solving & Data Analysis

A smartphone is initially priced at $800. During a clearance sale, the price is reduced by 20%. Later, the price is increased by 15% due to additional features added to the phone. What is the final price of the smartphone?

15. Question

Category: SAT Algebra

Consider the linear equation y = 12x + 30. What is the value of y when x = 3?

16. Question

Category: SAT Geometry & Trigonometry

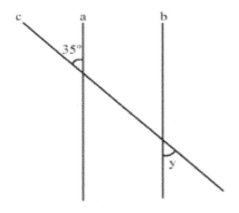

A line c intersects two parallel lines a and b. What is the value of y?

- a. 25°
- b. 15°

- c. 35°

- d. 17.5°

17. Question

Category: SAT Advanced Math

Consider the defined function h(x) = $5x^3 + 2x^2 + 7x - 8$. What is the value of h(-2)?

- a. -62

- b. -54

- c. 54

- d. 62

18. Question

Category: SAT Algebra

For the linear function h(x), if h(0) = -5 and h(5) = 15, which equation defines h?

- a. h(x) = 4x – 5

- b. h(x) = 4x + 5

- c. h(x) = -4x + 5

- d. h(x) = -4x – 5

19. Question

Category: SAT Problem Solving & Data Analysis

A water tank is being filled at a constant rate. The equation V = 10t represents the volume of water V, in gallons, in the tank t minutes after it started filling. What will be the volume of water in the tank 9 minutes after it started filling?

- a. 30 gallons

- b. 50 gallons

- c. 60 gallons

- d. 90 gallons

20. Question

Category: SAT Geometry & Trigonometry

Given a triangle DEF, if angle D exceeds angle E by 10° and angle F measures 70°, how much is angle D?

- a. 50°

- b. 60°

- c. 55°

- d. 65°

21. Question

Category: SAT Advanced Math

The value of constant k for a single solution of quadratic equation $5x^2 - kx + 7 = 0$ is:

- a. 8
- b. 9
- c. 10
- d. 12

22. Question

Category: SAT Problem Solving & Data Analysis

A research study measured the reaction times of two groups, Group P and Group Q, to a certain stimulus. The average reaction time for Group P was 250 milliseconds, and for Group Q, it was 320 milliseconds. If Group P had 90 participants and Group Q had 60 participants, what is the overall average reaction time considering both groups?

- a. 463 ms
- b. 278 ms
- c. 695 ms
- d. 1390 ms

Detailed Answer Test 2 Module 2 Math Explanations

1. Question

Category: SAT Advanced Math

B: Substitute y = 5x in the equation 7x + 3y = 22 to find the value of x.

7x + 3(5x) = 22
7x + 15x = 22
22x = 22
x = 1

The value of y for the given system of equations.

y = 5(1)
y = 5

The value of $(y^2 - x^2)$ is given as follows:

$(y^2 - x^2) = (5)^2 - (1)^2$
$(y^2 - x^2) = 25 - 1$
$(y^2 - x^2) = 24$

Thus, the value of $(y^2 - x^2)$ is 24.

2. Question

Category: SAT Geometry & Trigonometry

C: The formula to calculate the area of an equilateral triangle is given as:

$A = \frac{\sqrt{3}}{4}a^2$

Here, a is the side of equilateral triangle.

On putting $A = 4\sqrt{3}\ cm^2$., we get:

$4\sqrt{3} = \frac{\sqrt{3}}{4}a^2$
$a^2 = 16$
$a = 4$

The length of the perpendicular drawn from a vertex to its opposite side can be given by using the formula $L = \frac{\sqrt{3}}{2}a$

On putting a = 4, we get:

$L = \frac{\sqrt{3}}{4}(4)$
$L = 2\sqrt{3}$

Thus, the length of the perpendicular drawn from a vertex to its opposite side is $2\sqrt{3}$.

3. Question

Category: SAT Algebra

B: The given equation is 2y + 5x = 15 and its y intercept is obtained by putting x = 0.

2y + 5(0) = 15
2y = 15
y = 7.5

This y intercept of line is without any translation.

When the line is translated up by 6 units, the y-intercept shifts along the y-axis by the same amount. Therefore, the new y-coordinate of the y-intercept will be:

Y = y + 6
Y = 7.5 + 6
Y = 13.5

Thus, the y-coordinate of the y-intercept of the resulting graph is 13.5 units after translation of 6 units.

4. Question

Category: SAT Problem Solving & Data Analysis

A: One kilogram mass of box is equal to one thousand grams.

The mass of the box is changed into grams from kilograms as:

m = 81.5 kg
$m = (81.5\ kg)(\frac{1000 gram}{1 kg})$
m = 81500 grams

Thus, mass of the box is equivalent to 81,500 grams.

5. Question

Category: SAT Problem Solving & Data Analysis

C: The monthly allowance of Sarah is $200 and she saves 30% of this monthly allowance, so amount saves from monthly allowance for each month is given as:

$S = (30\%)(\$200)$

$S = (\frac{30}{100})*(200)$

$S = \$60$

There are twelve months in a year.

Sarah saves $60 each month, so the total amount saved by Sarah in a year is given as:

$T = 12S$

$T = 12(\$60)$

$T = \$720$

Thus, the Sarah saves $720 over a year.

6. Question

Category: SAT Advanced Math

A: The given expression is $17x - (7x - 9)$.

Simplify the given expression $17x - (7x - 9)$:

$17x - (7x - 9) = 17x - 7x + 9$

$17x - (7x - 9) = 10x + 9$

Thus, the equivalent expression for expression $17x - (7x - 9)$ is $(10x + 9)$

7. Question

Category: SAT Advanced Math

B: The given expression is $(3\sqrt{x} + 4)(8-7\sqrt{x})$ and it equivalent expression can be calculated as follows:

$(3\sqrt{x} + 4)(8-7\sqrt{x}) = ((3\sqrt{x} (8) - (3(\sqrt{x}) (7(\sqrt{x})+32-(4) (7) \sqrt{x})$

$= (3\sqrt{x} + 4))(8-7\sqrt{x}) = 24\sqrt{x} - 21x + 32 - 28\sqrt{x}$

$= (3\sqrt{x} + 4))(8-7\sqrt{x}) = 21x+32-4\sqrt{x}$

$= (3\sqrt{x} + 4))(8-7\sqrt{x}) = 32-4\sqrt{x} -21x$

Thus, the equivalent expression is $32-4\sqrt{x} -21x$

8. Question

Category: SAT Advanced Math

C: The function is given as:

$g(x)=4\sqrt[3]{x}43x$

The function value is 108, so we can write:

On substituting g(x) = 108 in the given equation, we get:

$108 = 4\sqrt[3]{x}$

$= \sqrt[3]{x} = 27$

On cubing both sides, we get:

$\left(\sqrt[3]{x}\right)^3 = (27)^3$

x = 19683

Thus, the value of x is 19683 for given function.

9. Question

Category: SAT Algebra

27: The given function is p(x) = -3(x – 2)(x + 4).

To obtain y = q(x) the function y = p(x) is shifted to right by three units. It can be represented as:

q(x) = y = p(x – 3) ...(1)

On replacing x by (x – 3) in (x) = -3(x – 2)(x + 4) , we get:

p(x – 3) = -3((x – 3) – 2)((x – 3) + 4)
p(x – 3) = -3(x – 3 – 2)(x – 3 + 4)
p(x – 3) = -3(x – 5)(x + 1)

On substituting p(x – 3) = -3(x – 5)(x + 1) in the equation (1), we get:

q(x) = -3(x – 5)(x + 1) ...(2)

On substituting x = 2 in the equation (2), we get:

q(2) = -3(2 – 5)(2 + 1)
q(2) = -3(-3)(3)
q(2) = 27

Thus, the value of q(2) is 27.

10. Question

Category: SAT Advanced Math

B: The given equation is m + 3n = 2p.

Simplify the given equation m + 3n = 2p to convert it in terms of m and p.

m + 3n = 2p
3n = 2p – m
$n = \frac{2p-m}{3}$

Thus, the equation m + 3n = 2p can be represented in terms of m and p is $n = \frac{2p-m}{3}$.

11. Question

Category: SAT Advanced Math

C: The given expression is $\frac{5x^3 - 15x^2}{10x} + \frac{3x+5}{7}$.

Simplify it to find its equivalent expression.

$$=\frac{5x^3-15x^2}{10x}+\frac{3x+5}{7}=\frac{7(5x^3-15x^2)+(10x)(3x+5)}{7(10x)}$$
$$=\frac{5x^3-15x^2}{10x}+\frac{3x+5}{7}=\frac{35x^3-105x^2+30x^2+50x}{70x}$$
$$=\frac{5x^3-15x^2}{10x}+\frac{3x+5}{7}=\frac{35x^3-75x^2+50x}{70x}$$
$$=\frac{5x^3-15x^2}{10x}+\frac{3x+5}{7}=\frac{(5x)(7x^2-15x+10)}{70x}$$
$$=\frac{5x^3-15x^2}{10x}+\frac{3x+5}{7}=\frac{(7x^2-15x+10)}{14}$$

Thus, the equivalent expression of the given expression is $\frac{(7x^2-15x+10)}{14}$

12. Question

Category: SAT Geometry & Trigonometry

B: The circumference of a circle is given as:

C = 2πr

Here, r is the circle.

The circumference of circle B is equal to the circumference of circle A, so we can write:

$C_B = 3C_A =$
$2\pi r_B = 3(2\pi r_A)$
$r_b = 3r_A ...(1)$

The radius of circle A is 7 cm.

On substituting r_a = 7 cm in the equation (1), we get:

r_b = 3(7 cm)
r_b = 21 cm

Thus, the radius of the circle B is 21 cm.

13. Question

Category: SAT Algebra

B: Let the first and second positive integers be x and y.

First integer is 4 less than two time of second integer, so it can be written as:

x = 2y – 4

The product of integers is 16, so it can be written as:

xy = 16 ... ...(1)

On substituting x = 2y – 4, we get:

(2y – 4)y = 16
$2y^2 - 4y = 16$
$2y^2 - 4y - 16 = 0$
$y^2 - 2y - 8 = 0$
$y^2 - 4y + 2y - 8 = 0$
(y – 5)(y + 2)
y = -2, 5

Find the corresponding x values as follows:

x = 2(-2) – 4
x = -4 – 4
x = -8

And,

x = 2(5) – 4
x = 10 – 4
x = 6

Thus, the smaller integer is -8.

14. Question

Category: SAT Problem Solving & Data Analysis

736: Consider the initial price of the smartphone as P = \$800. The price is reduced by 20% in the clearance sale.

The reduced price of the smartphone in clearance sale is given as:

P_s = P – (20%)P
P_s = \$800 – $(\frac{20}{100})$*(800)
P_s = \$800 – \$160
P_s = \$640

The price of smartphone increases by 15% due to additional features, so final price of the smartphone is given as:

P_f = P_s+ (15%)P_s
P_f = \$640 + $(\frac{15}{100})$ * (640)
P_f = \$640 + \$96
P_f = \$736

Thus, the final price of smartphone is \$736.

15. Question

Category: SAT Algebra

66: The equation given is as follows:

y = 12x + 30

On substituting x = 3 in the above equation, we get:

y = 12x + 30
y = 12(3) + 30
y = 36 + 30
y = 66

Thus, the variation y = 12x + 30 is 66.

16. Question

Category: SAT Geometry & Trigonometry

C: When a transversal line intersects two parallel lines, the corresponding angles, alternate interior, and alternate exterior angles form between transversal line with each parallel lines. The value of corresponding angles, alternate interior and alternate exterior angles for both parallel lines remains the same.

In the given figure the angle transversal line c intersects the parallel lines a and b. The angles shown in figure are alternate exterior angles, so values of these angles must be the same and given as:

y = 35°

Thus, the value of angle y is 35°.

17. Question

Category: SAT Advanced Math

B: The given non-linear function is $h(x) = 5x^3 + 2x^2 + 7x - 8$.

On substituting x = -2 in the given non-linear function, we get:

$h(-2) = 5(-2)3+2(-2)2+7(-2)-85(-2)3+2(-2)2+7(-2)-8$
h(-2) = -40 + 8 – 14 – 8
h(-2) = -54

Thus, the value of the given non-linear function $h(x) = 5x^3 + 2x^2 + 7x - 8$ is -54.

18. Question

Category: SAT Algebra

A: The given function h(x) is a linear function, so it can be written by a linear equation as:

h(x) = mx + c ... (1)

On substituting x = 0 and h(0) = -5 in equation (1), we get:

h(0) = m(0) + c
-5 = c
c = -5

On substituting c = -5 and h(5) = 15 in the equation (1), we get:

h(5) = m(5) + (-5)
15 = m(5) – 5
5m = 20
m = 4

On substituting c = -5 and m = 4 in the equation (1), we get:

h(x) = (4)x + (-5)
h(x) = 4x – 5

Thus, the linear function h is h(x) = 4x – 5.

19. Question

Category: SAT Problem Solving & Data Analysis

A: The volume of the water is related with time as:

$V = 10\sqrt{t}$

On Substituting t = 9 in the above equation, we get:

$V = 10\sqrt{9}$

$V = 10(3)$

$V = 30$

Thus, the volume of water in the tank 9 minutes after it started filling is 30 gallons.

20. Question

Category: SAT Geometry & Trigonometry

B: The angle D of the triangle DEF exceeds by 10° from angle E and it can be written as:

$D = E + 10°...(1)$

The angle F of the triangle DEF measures 70°, so F = 70°.

The sum of interior angles of any triangle is always measures 180°, so angle D is calculated as:

$D + E + F = 180°$
$E + 10° + E + 70° = 180°$
$2E = 180° - 80°$
$2E = 100°$
$E = 50°$

On substituting E = 50° in equation (1), we get:

$D = 50° + 10°$
$D = 60°$

Thus, the value angle D in the triangle DEF is 60°.

21. Question

Category: SAT Advanced Math

D: The discriminant of a quadratic equation is given as $D = b^2 - 4ac$.

If D > 0, then equation has two distinct roots.
If D = 0, then equation has two same real roots.
If D < 0, then equation has no real roots.

On comparing the quadratic equation $5x^2 - kx + 7 = 0$ with general form of quadratic equation $ax^2 + bx + c = 0$, the coefficients are a = 5, b = -k, and c = 7.

The discriminant of the equation $5x^2 - kx + 7 = 0$ as follows:

$D = (-k)^2 - 4(5)(7)$
$D = k^2 - 140$

Equate discriminant D with zero for single solution.

$D = 0$
$k^2 - 140 = 0$
$k = 11.83$
$k \approx 12$

The discriminant of the equation is negative, so no real root of the equation is possible.

22. Question

Category: SAT Problem Solving & Data Analysis

B: To find the overall average reaction time of both groups, we can use the formula:

$$M = \frac{N_{p} \cdot T_{p} + N_{Q} \cdot T_{Q}}{N_{p} + N_{Q}}$$

Here, N_p and N_q are the number of participants in groups P and Q.

T_p and T_q is the average reaction times of participants in group P and Q.

Substitute all the given values in above formula.

$$M = \frac{(90)(250ms) + (60)(320ms)}{90 + 60}$$

$$M = \frac{41700}{150}$$

M = 278 ms

Thus, the overall average reaction time of both groups is 278 ms.

Practice Test 3 Module 1 Math by Topic and sections

DIRECTIONS: This section contains questions pertaining to various fundamental mathematical skills. Calculators may be utilized for all questions. Unless otherwise specified, the following assumptions apply:

• All variables and expressions represent real numbers.

• The provided figures are accurately drawn to scale.

• All figures exist within a two-dimensional plane.

• The domain of a given function f is the set of all real numbers x for which f(x) is also a real number.

1. Question

Category: SAT Geometry & Trigonometry

If a circle has the equation $(x - 4)^2 + (y - 3)^2 = 36$, what is the shortest straight-line distance from the center of the circle to the origin?

2. Question

Category: SAT Problem Solving & Data Analysis

John is taking a rowboat both up and down a 16-kilometer length of a river. A constant current of 1 kilometer per hour makes his trip downstream faster than his trip upstream because he is moving with the current downstream and fighting against the current when traveling upstream. If a round-trip journey took him a total of 4 hours, and if he rowed at a constant pace the whole time, what is the rate in kilometers per hour, to the nearest tenth, at which John is rowing independent of the current?

- a. 7.3
- b. 8.1
- c. 8.9
- d. 9.7

3. Question

Category: SAT Algebra

A function never intersects the y-axis. Which of the following could be an equation of the function?

- a. y = 2x – 5
- b. y = 4

- c. x = 36
- d. y = x

4.Question

Category: SAT Problem Solving & Data Analysis

A particular black hole has a density of 1.0×10^6 kg/m³. A physicist is conducting a thought experiment in which she would like to approximate how much she would weigh if she had the density of a black hole rather than her current weight of 150 pounds, assuming her volume remained the same. Given that her overall body density is approximately 990 kg/m3 and that there are approximately 2.2 pounds in a kilogram, approximately how many pounds would she weigh in her thought experiment?

- a. 2,178
- b.151,500
- c. 990,000,000
- d. 2,178,000,000

5.Question

Catgory: SAT Algebra

Consider the following system of equations with variables A and B and constant integers X and Y:

$A + 2B = 4$

$XA + YB = 4X$

By what number must the sum of X and Y be divisible in order for the two equations to have infinitely many solutions?

6.Question

Category: SAT Problem Solving & Data Analysis

Pam is going to watch a movie on her television at home. She is going to watch the movie as it was shown in movie theaters, in its original aspect ratio of 1.85:1 (length:height). Her television has an aspect ratio of 4:3 and a length of 48 inches. If the movie takes up the entire length of her television screen, how many inches of screen height, to the nearest whole inch, will NOT be used on her TV screen to show the movie?

- a.10
- b.16
- c.22
- d. 44

7.Question

Category: SAT Advanced Math

If $-16 - 6x + x^2 = x^2 - abx - 8b$, where a and b are constants, what is the value of a?

- a. -6
- b. -2
- c. 3
- d. 5

8.Question

Category: SAT Problem Solving & Data Analysis

Bob deposits x dollars into his savings account on January 1, 2015, and the account grows at a constant annual rate of 3%, compounded annually. What will be the amount of dollars in Bob's account on January 1, 2017 assuming that Bob makes no deposits or withdrawals and that there are no account fees or other charges?

- a. $0.06x$
- b. $1.06x$
- c. $1.0609x$
- d. $1.092727x$

9.Question

Category: SAT Algebra

$2(a - 4b)(3 + b^3) = ?$

- a. $2ab^3 - 24b$
- b. $2ab + 6a - 4b^2 - 12b$
- c. $2ab^3 + 4a - 6b^4 - 24b$
- d. $2ab^3 + 6a - 8b^4 - 24b$

10.Question

Category: SAT Problem Solving & Data Analysis

A lamp business uses the following equations to express supply and demand as a function of price and quantity for its lamps:

Supply: Price = 30 - Quantity

Demand: Price = 10 + 3 × Quantity

How many lamps does the business need to sell in order for the supply of lamps to equal the demand for lamps exactly- i.e., for the supply and demand to be at equilibrium?

11. Question

Category: SAT Geometry & Trigonometry

The volume of a particular cylinder is x cubic inches. If the height of the cylinder is tripled while the radius of the cylinder remains the same, what will the new volume of the cylinder be in terms of x?

- a. $2x$
- b. $3x$
- c. $4x$
- d. $5x$

12. Question

Category: SAT Problem Solving & Data Analysis

College football programs are permitted to pay a maximum of 1 head coach, 9 assistant coaches, and 2 graduate assistant coaches. If ABC University wishes to have at least 1 coach for every 4 players, which of the following systems of inequalities expresses the total number of coaches, C, and total number of players, P, possible?

- a. $C = 12$ and $P \leq 4C$
- b. $C \leq 12$ and $P \leq 4C$
- c. $C \leq 10$ and $P \leq 3C$
- d. $C = 1$ and $P \leq 4$

13. Question

Category: SAT Advanced Math

Given that x and n are numbers greater than 1, which of the following expressions would have the greatest overall increase in y values between x values from 2 to 100?

- a. $y = nx + 3$
- b. $y = -nx + 3$
- c. $y = x^n + 3$
- d. $y = x^n + 3$

14. Question

Category: SAT Advanced Math

If $f(x) = 7x + 3$ and $g(x) = 2x^2$, what is the value of $f(g(1))$?

15.Question

Category: SAT Problem Solving & Data Analysis

The approximate relationship between Kelvin (K) and degrees Celsius (C) is given by this equation:

K = 273 + C

The freezing point of water is 0 degrees Celsius, and the boiling point of water is 100 degrees Celsius. What are the approximate freezing and boiling points of water in Kelvin?

- a. Freezing: 0; boiling: 100
- b. Freezing: -273; boiling: -173
- c. Freezing: 273; boiling: 373
- d. Freezing: 473; boiling: 573

16.Question

SAT Geometry & Trigonometry

What is the value of the smallest side in a right triangle with a hypotenuse of 8 and angles of 30 and 60 degrees?

17.Question

Catgory: SAT Algebra

n	Pattern
1	1
2	1 + 3
3	1 + 3 + 5
4	1 + 3 + 5 + 7
5	1 + 3 + 5 + 7 + 9

The table above gives the values of a sum of the first n numbers, starting with 1. Which of the following is a correct statement about n?

- a. The product of n and its corresponding sum decreases as n increases.
- b.The difference between each additional value of n and the previous value of n is increasing exponentially.
- c.The sum of the first n odd numbers equals the square of n.
- d. The sum of the first n numbers is comprised solely of prime numbers.

18.Question

Category: SAT Problem Solving & Data Analysis

A librarian works quickly, putting away 200 books and 20 movies at once. She only puts away books and movies. The total number of items that the librarian shelves during a total of T hours is shown by which expression.

A $220T$

B $20T + 200$

C $220T + 440$

D $200T - 20$

19.Question

SAT Geometry & Trigonometry

The hypotenuse of a right triangle is 20 inches and the side length is 16 inches. What is the length of the third side of the right triangle in inches?

20.Question

Category: SAT Advanced Math

The following equations could all have the constant k equal zero and have a defined solution EXCEPT

- a. $kx = 0$
- b. $3 = k - x$
- c. $4k + x = 7$
- d. $2/k = X$

21.Question

Category: SAT Problem Solving & Data Analysis

A brand-new space tourism firm intends to create a spacecraft capable of safely reentering the Earth's atmosphere without losing their awareness. The doctors consulted by the company told the workers that healthy people can withstand up to 9 grams of force and lose consciousness at 5 grams of force. Which expression gives the range of g-force values, g, that the company's engineers should ensure the spacecraft can provide during reentry?

- a. $g < 5$
- b. $g > 5$
- c. $5 < g < 9$
- d. $g > 9$

22.Question

Category: SAT Problem Solving & Data Analysis

A company operates four different stores at four different locations throughout a large city. The company gathered data pertaining to the initial prices, sale prices, and the corresponding quantities sold for a specific item.

Store	Price Before Sale	Quantity Sold Before Sale	Sale Price	Quantity Sold During Sale
Store A	$12.50	350	$11.00	400
Store B	$13.25	260	$10.00	520
Store C	$11.75	550	$9.50	625
Store D	$14.00	220	$10.25	460

Look at how many of the particular item Stores A and B sold at the presale price. What is the arithmetic mean of this set of values to the nearest tenth?

- a. 8.1
- b. 9.7
- c. 10.5
- d. 12.8

Detailed Answer Test 3 Module 1 Math Explanations

1.Question

Category: SAT Geometry & Trigonometry

Correct Answer: 5

5 Based on the general equation of a circle, $(x - h)^2 + (y - k)^2 = r^2$, the center point is (h, k). For this circle, the center point is (4, 3). This point is a distance of 5 from the origin, which has the coordinates (0, 0). The graph of the circle is as follows:

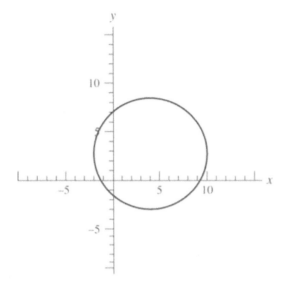

You can calculate the shortest straight-line distance by using the distance formula or, even easier, recognizing that these numbers form a Pythagorean triple: 3-4-5. Recognizing that this is a Pythagorean triple will save you the time and trouble of calculating the distance using the distance formula.

2.Question

Category: SAT Problem Solving & Data Analysis

Correct Answer: B

(B) Use the formula Distance = Rate x Time to make your calculations. The distance is 16 km/hour for the journey in either direction. The rates, however, are different. The rate going upstream is 1 km/hr less than the rate at which John is actually rowing because he is going against the current. The rate going downstream is 1 km/hr more than the rate at which he is actually rowing because he is going with the current. If x is the rate at which John is rowing, the time, u, to go upstream is:

$$d = ru \rightarrow 16 = (x - 1) \rightarrow u = \frac{16}{x - 1}$$

The time going downstream, t, can be calculated in a similar way:

$$d = rt \rightarrow 16 = (x + 1)t \rightarrow t = \frac{16}{x + 1}$$

Since the total time of the journey is 4 hours, combine these two expressions together into one equation:

$$\frac{16}{x - 1} + \frac{16}{x + 1} = 4$$

Then solve for x:

$$\frac{16}{x-1} + \frac{16}{x+1} = 4 \rightarrow \frac{16(x+1)}{(x-1)(x+1)} + \frac{16(x-1)}{(x+1)(x-1)} = 4 \rightarrow$$
$$\frac{16(x+1) + 16(x-1)}{x^2 - 1} = 4 \rightarrow \frac{16x + 16 + 16x - 16}{x^2 - 1} = 4 \rightarrow$$

$$\frac{32x}{x^2 - 1} = 4 \rightarrow 32x = 4x^2 - 4 \rightarrow 4x^2 - 32x - 4 = 0 \rightarrow x^2 - 8x - 1 = 0$$

Use the quadratic formula to solve:

$$\frac{-b \pm \sqrt{b^2 - 4ac}}{2a} \rightarrow \frac{8 \pm \sqrt{(-8)^2 - 4 \cdot 1 \cdot (-1)}}{2 \cdot 1} = \frac{8 \pm \sqrt{68}}{2} =$$

$$\frac{8 \pm 2\sqrt{17}}{2} = 4 \pm \sqrt{17}$$

You get two solutions. However, you can use only $4 + \sqrt{17}$, because velocity cannot be negative. The value of $4 + \sqrt{17}$ is approximately 8.1.

3.Question

Category: SAT Algebra

Correct Answer: C

(C) $x = 36$ does not have a y-intercept, because it runs parallel to the y-axis. Therefore, this equation never intersects the y-axis. Here is a graph of $x = 36$:

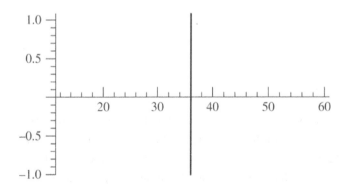

All of the other choices intersect the y-axis one time, because they have a y- value when $x = 0$.

4.Question

Category: SAT Problem Solving & Data Analysis

Correct Answer: B

(B) Divide 1.0×10^6 kg/m^3 by 990 kg/m^3 to determine by what multiple her weight will increase. Her weight will be 1,010 times greater. Then multiply 1,010 by 150 pounds to get 151,500 pounds.

5.Question

Category: SAT Problem Solving & Data Analysis

Correct Answer: 3

3 There will be infinitely many solutions if the two equations are multiples of the same equation. The coefficients of the A and B terms in $A + 2B = 4$ add up to 3 because they are 1 and 2. Since $XA + YB = 4X$ is divisible by 4 on the right-hand side, as is the other equation, the sum of X and Y must also be divisible by 3 in order for the two equations to be multiples of one another. To replicate the structure of the first equation, Y must equal $2X$ so that the two equations will be multiples of one another. To see this with greater clarity, consider this example:

$A + 2B = 4$

$XA + YB = 4X$

If the second equation had $X = 2$ and $Y = 4$, the equation would be twice the first equation: $2A + 4B = 8$. This equation is simply a multiple of the first one, making them essentially identical. As a result, there are infinitely many solutions since the equations overlap each other when graphed.

6.Question

Category: SAT Problem Solving & Data Analysis

Correct Answer: A

(A) The height of Pam's television is 36 inches, as 48:36 reduces to her screen ratio of 4:3. To determine the height of the movie image on Pam's TV, a ratio can be set up: 1/1.85 = x/48. This yields an approximate value of 26 for the height of the image. The remaining screen height, which is not occupied by the movie, can be determined by subtracting the height of the movie from the height of the TV screen. This yields the result 36 - 26 = 10.

7.Question

Category: SAT Advanced Math

Correct Answer: C

(C) The different terms on the two sides of the equation equal each other. So $-16 = -8b$, $-6x = -abx$, and $x^2 = x^2$. Why? This occurs because the constants must equal each other, the terms with an x must equal each other, and the terms with an x^2 must equal one another. Since $-16 = -8b$, $b = 2$.

Plug in 2 for b in the second equation and cancel out the -x to solve for a:

$-6x = -abx \rightarrow 6 = a \cdot 2 \rightarrow a = 3$

8.Question

Category: SAT Problem Solving & Data Analysis

Correct Answer: C

(C) To determine a 3% increase on an original amount of x, add 3% to the original amount:

$x + 0.03x = 1.03x$

To save time, you can simply multiply x by 1.03 to get the sum of x plus 3% interest. The amount in the account is compounded twice. So multiply x by 1.03 twice:

$x \cdot 1.03 \cdot 1.03 = 1.0609x$

9.Question

Category: SAT Algebra

Correct Answer: D

(D) Use FOIL to calculate the product of the terms in parentheses:

$2(a - 4b)(3 + b^3) = 2(3a + ab^3 - 12b - 4b^4) = 6a + 2ab^3 - 24b - 8b^4$

To put the values in the order shown in the choices, rearrange them.

$2ab^3 + 6a - 8b^4 - 24b$

10.Question

Category: SAT Problem Solving & Data Analysis

Correct Answer: 5

5 Since the supply and demand are at equilibrium, set the two expressions equal to one another and solve for the number of lamps:

30 - Quantity = 10 + 3 × Quantity

20 = 4 × Quantity

5 = Quantity

11.Question

Category: SAT Geometry & Trigonometry

Correct Answer: B

(B) The volume for a cylinder is one of the given formulas: $V = \pi r^2 h$. If the height is tripled while the radius remains the same, the volume of the new cylinder will be

$$\pi r^2 (3h) \rightarrow 3\left(\pi r^2 h\right).$$

So, it is triple the original value, making the correct answer $3x$.

12. Question

Category: SAT Problem Solving & Data Analysis

Correct Answer: B

(B) The programs are permitted a maximum of 12 coaches. So C must be equal to or less than 12. Choice (B) is the only option with this statement. All of the other options do not allow for the full range of possible values for the number of coaches. Moreover, the number of players will be limited by the number of coaches if the university is to maintain a ratio of a maximum of 4 players per coach. By making the number of players less than or equal to 4 times the number of coaches, $P \le 4C$, the university will ensure that it has at least 1 coach for every 4 players.

13. Question

Category: SAT Advanced Math

Correct Answer: C

Choice (C) clearly has the greatest overall increase, going from 11 to 1,000,003. Try plugging in some sample values for x, like 2 and 100, and assume n is a constant, like 3. Alternatively, you can simply realize that a number greater than 1 to a power more than 1 will be greater than the other possibilities.

Equation	Substitute $x = 2$ and $n = 3$	Value when $x = 2$ and $n = 3$	Substitute $x = 100$ and $n = 3$	Value when $x = 100$ and $n = 3$
A. $y = nx + 3$	$y = 3 \times 2 + 3$	9	$y = 3 \times 100 + 3$	303
B. $y = -nx + 3$	$y = -3 \times 2 + 3$	-3	$y = -3 \times 100 + 3$	-297
C. $y = x^n + 3$	$y = 2^3 + 3$	11	$y = 100^3 + 3$	1,000,003
D. $y = x^{-n} + 3$	$y = 2^{-3} + 3$	$3\frac{1}{8}$	$y = 100^{-3} + 3$	3.000001

14. Question

Category: SAT Advanced Math

Correct Answer: 17

17 Work inside out by first solving for $g(1)$:

$g(x) = 2x^2 \to g(1) = 2(1)^2 = 2$

Then put 2 in for x in the $f(x)$:

$f(x) = 7x + 3 \to f(2) = 7(2) + 3 = 17$

15.Question

Category: SAT Problem Solving & Data Analysis

Correct Answer: C

(C) The freezing point of water in degrees C should be plugged into the equation.

$K = 273 + C$

$K = 273 + 0 = 273$

Choice (C) is the only option that has 273 for the freezing point. You can also plug in 100 for the boiling point in degrees C. You will get 373 as the result.

16.Question

Correct Answer: 4

SAT Geometry & Trigonometry

Below is a drawing showing the side lengths of this particular triangle.

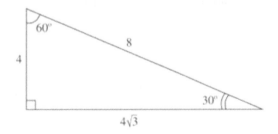

This triangle is 30-60-90, so you can easily calculate the side lengths. So the side lengths can be expressed as x, $\sqrt{3}x$, and $2x$. (This formula is provided at the beginning of the Math section.) The hypotenuse of 8 equals $2x$, and the shortest side equals x. Do the calculations to find the length of the shortest side:

$8 = 2x$

$x = 4$

You could also recognize that the ratio of the smallest side to the hypotenuse in a 30-60-90 triangle is 1:2. The value of the smallest side of a right triangle with a hypotenuse of 8 in a right triangle is 4.

17. Question

Catgory: SAT Algebra

Correct Answer: C

(C) Rewrite the table by calculating the actual sums:

n	Pattern	Sum
1	1	1
2	1 + 3	4
3	1 + 3 + 5	9
4	1 + 3 + 5 + 7	16
5	1 + 3 + 5 + 7 + 9	25

Each value in the "Sum" column is the corresponding value of n squared: $1 = 1^2$; $4 = 2^2$; $9 = 3^2$; $16 = 4^2$; $25 = 5^2$

18. Question

Category: SAT Problem Solving & Data Analysis

Correct Answer: A

(A) For each hour the librarian works, he or she shelves a total of 220 items. So, the number of things the librarian has stored for T hours is 220 times T. The other answers have constants added or taken away from the term multiplied by T. This doesn't make sense because it would mean that the librarian could store or remove items without spending any time doing it.

19. Question

Category: SAT Geometry & Trigonometry

Correct Answer: 12

12. Use the Pythagorean Theorem, $a^2 + b^2 = c^2$, to solve for the unknown side. Use 20 for the c, because it is the hypotenuse. Use 16 for a, because it is one of the legs of the triangle (you could also use 16 for b). Solve for the unknown side as follows:

20.Question

Category: SAT Advanced Math

Correct Answer: D

(D) $2/k = x$ is undefined if $k = 0$. Divide by 0 to get an undefined solution. All the other equations have solutions for x when $k = 0$.

21.Question

Category: SAT Problem Solving & Data Analysis

Correct Answer: A

(A) Since the company does not want the passengers to lose consciousness, the passengers must not experience g forces equal to or greater than 5. The passengers must not experience g forces equal to or greater than 5. The only possible range of g-values is $g < 5$, in which all the g-values are less than 5.

$$a^2 + b^2 = c^2 \rightarrow 16^2 + b^2 = 20^2 \rightarrow$$
$$256 + b^2 = 400 \rightarrow b^2 = 400 - 256 \rightarrow b^2 = 144 \rightarrow$$
$$b = \sqrt{144} = 12$$

22.Question

Category: SAT Problem Solving & Data Analysis

Correct Answer: D

(D) The arithmetic mean is the average. Solve this problem using a weighted average. In other words, calculate the average by factoring in the relative amounts of the item sold by each store.

Store	Price Before Sale	Quantity Sold Before Sale	Sale Price	Quantity Sold After Sale
Store A	$12.50	350	$11.00	400
Store B	$13.25	260	$10.00	520
Store C	$11.75	550	$9.50	625
Store D	$14.00	220	$10.25	460

Store A sold 350 items for $12.50 each, and Store B sold 260 items for

$13.25 each. The total number of items sold is 350 + 260. You can compute the average as follows:

Total Income/Total Number of Items Sold = [(12.50 × 350) + (13.25 × 260)]/(350 + 260) ≈ 12.8

Practice Test 3 Module 2 Math by Topic and sections

DIRECTIONS: This section contains questions pertaining to various fundamental mathematical skills. Calculators may be utilized for all questions. Unless otherwise specified, the following assumptions apply:

• All variables and expressions represent real numbers.

• The provided figures are accurately drawn to scale.

• All figures exist within a two-dimensional plane.

• The domain of a given function f is the set of all real numbers x for which f(x) is also a real number.

1.Question

Category: SAT Problem Solving & Data Analysis

Isabel grows potatoes in her garden. She harvested 760 potatoes this year and saved 10% to plant next year. How many of the harvested potatoes did Isabel reserve for planting next year?

- a.66
- b.76
- c.84
- d.86

2.Question

Category: SAT Advanced Math

What length, in centimeters, is equivalent to a length of 51 meters? (1 meter = 100 centimeters)

- a.0.051
- b.0.51
- c.5,100
- d.51,000

3.Question

Category: SAT Problem Solving & Data Analysis

A bus is traveling at a constant speed along a straight portion of road. The equation d = 30t gives the distance d, in feet from a road marker, that the bus will be t seconds after passing the marker. What's the distance between the bus and the marker in two seconds?

- a. 30
- b. 32

- c. 60
- d. 90

4.Question

Catgory: SAT Algebra

Which expression is equivalent to 20w − (4w + 3w)?

- a.10w
- b.13w
- c.19w
- d.21w

5.Question

Catgory: SAT Algebra

If 6+ x = 9, what is the value of 18 + 3x?

6.Question

Catgory: SAT Algebra

Which expression is equivalent to 9x2 + 5x?

- a. x (9 x + 5)
- b.5x(9 x + 1)
- c.9x(x + 5)
- d. x2 (9x + 5)

7.Question

Catgory: SAT Algebra

y = 3x

2x + y = 12

The solution to the given system of equations is (x ,y). What is the value of 5?

- a. 24
- b.15
- c.12
- d. 5

8.Question

Category: SAT Geometry & Trigonometry

A cube has an edge length of 41 inches. What is the volume, in cubic inches, of the cube?

- a.164
- b.1,681
- c.10,086
- d. 68,921

9.Question

Category: SAT Advanced Math

6x + 7y = 28 2x + 2y = 10 The solution to the given system of equations is (x, y). What is the value of y ?

- a.−2
- b.7
- c.14
- d.18

10.Question

Category: SAT Advanced Math

The minimum value of x is 12 less than 6 times another number, which is n. Which inequality illustrates the possible values of x?

- a. x ≤ 6n − 12
- b. x ≥ 6n − 12
- c. x ≤ 12 − 6n
- d. x ≥ 12 − 6n

11.Question

Category: SAT Problem Solving & Data Analysis

The data set A comprises the heights of 75 buildings, with a mean of 32 meters. The data set B comprises the heights of 50 buildings, with a mean of 62 meters. The data set C comprises the heights of the 125 buildings from data sets A and B. What is the mean, in meters, of data set C?

12.Question

Catgory: SAT Algebra

−9x 2 + 30x + c = 0 In the given equation, c is a constant.

The equation has exactly one solution. What is the value of c ?

- a.3
- b.0
- c. −25
- d. −53

13.Question

Category: SAT Advanced Math

Which expression is equivalent to 12x³-5x³?

- a.$7x^6$
- b.$17x^3$
- c. $7x^3$
- d.$17x^6$

14.Question

Catgory: SAT Algebra

x+ y = 18

5= y x

What is the solution (x, y) to the given system of equations?

- a. (15, 3)
- b. (16, 2)
- c. (17, 1)
- d. (18, 0)

15.Question
Category: SAT Problem Solving & Data Analysis

A truck with a towing capacity of 4,600 pounds can tow a trailer with a maximum combined weight of 4,600 pounds, including the weight of the trailer and the boxes it contains. What is the maximum number of boxes that can be towed in a trailer with a weight of 500 pounds, with each box weighing 120 pounds?

- a.34
- b.35
- c.38
- d.39

16.Question

Category: SAT Problem Solving & Data Analysis

The table summarizes the distribution of color and shape for 100 tiles of equal area.

	Red	Blue	Yellow	Total
Square	10	20	25	55
Pentagon	20	10	15	45
Total	30	30	40	100

If one of the tiles is selected at random, what is the probability of selecting a red tile? Please express your answer as a decimal or fraction, not as a percent.

17.Question

Category: SAT Problem Solving & Data Analysis

A proposition to establish a new library was included on a ballot in an election. A radio show indicated that the number of people who voted in favor of the proposal exceeded the number of those who opposed it by threefold. A social media post indicated that the number of people who voted in favor of the proposal exceeded that of those who voted against it by 15,000. Based on these data, what was the number of people who voted against the proposal?

- a.7500
- b.15,000
- c.22,500
- d.45,000

18.Question

Category : SAT Geometry & Trigonometry

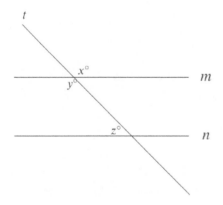

In the provided figure, lines m and n are parallel. If

x = 6k + 13 and y = 8k – 29, what is the value of z?

- a.
- b.
- c.
- d.

19.Question
Category: SAT Problem Solving & Data Analysis

A candle is composed of 17 ounces of wax. During the candle's combustion, the quantity of wax within the candle is diminished by 1 ounce every 4 hours. If 6 ounces of wax remain in this candle, for how many hours has it been burning?

- a. 3
- b. 6
- c. 24
- d. 44

20.Question

Category: SAT Advanced Math

The rational function f is defined by an equation in the form $f(x) = \frac{a}{x+b}$, where a and b are constants. The partial graph of y = f(x) is shown. If g(x)= f (x + 4), which equation could define function g?

- a. $g(x)=\frac{6}{x}$
- b. $g(x)=\frac{6}{x+4}$
- c. $g(x)=\frac{6}{x+8}$
- d. $g(x)=\frac{6(x+4)}{x+4}$

21.Question

Category: SAT Problem Solving & Data Analysis

Poll results

Angel Cruz 483
Terry Smith 320

The table presents the results of a poll. A total of 803 randomly selected voters were asked which candidate they would vote for in the upcoming election. According to the poll, if 6,424 people vote in the election, by how many votes would Angel Cruz be expected to win?

- a.163
- b.1,304
- c. 3,864
- d.5,621

22.Question

Category : SAT Geometry & Trigonometry

A sample of oak has a density of 807 kilograms per cubic meter. The sample is in the shape of a cube, with each edge measuring 0.90 meters in length. To the nearest whole number, what is the mass, in kilograms, of this sample?

- a. 588
- b. 726
- c. 897
- d. 1,107

Detailed Answer Test 3 Module 2 Math Explanations

1.Question

Category: SAT Problem Solving & Data Analysis

Choice B is correct.

To figure out how many potatoes Isabel saved to plant next year, multiply the total number of potatoes she harvested (760) by the amount of potatoes she saved. Since she saved 10% of the potatoes she harvested, the proportion of potatoes she saved is $\frac{10}{100}$, or 0.1. Multiplying 760 by this proportion gives 760 0.1 ( ), or 76, potatoes that she saved to plant next year

2.Question

Category: SAT Advanced Math

Choice C is correct.

Since 1 meter is equal to 100 centimeters, 51 meters is equal to 51 meters $(\frac{100\ centimeters}{1\ meter})$, or 5,100 centimeters.

3.Question

Category: SAT Problem Solving & Data Analysis

Choice C is correct.

It's given that t represents the number of seconds after the bus passes the marker. Substituting 2 for t in the given equation d t =30 yields d =30(2), or d =60. Therefore, the bus will be 60 feet from the marker 2 seconds after passing it

4.Question

Catgory: SAT Algebra

Choice B is correct.

Combining like terms inside the parentheses of the given expression, 20w- (4w+ 3w) yields 20w -(7w). Combining like terms in this resulting expression yields 13w .

5.Question

Catgory: SAT Algebra

The correct answer is 27.

Multiplying both sides of the given equation by 3 yields 36 39 ( ) ( ) + = x , or 18 3 27 + =x . Therefore, the value of 18 3 + x is 27

6.Question

Catgory: SAT Algebra

Choice A is correct.

Since x is a factor of each term in the given expression, the expression is equivalent to x (9x)+x (5) , or x(9x+5).

7.Question

Catgory: SAT Algebra

Choice C is correct.

It's given by the first equation in the system that y =3x .

Substituting 3x for y in the equation 2x + y + = 12 yields 2x+ 3x= 12 , or 5x= 12 .

8.Question

Category : SAT Geometry & Trigonometry

Choice D is correct.

The volume of a cube can be found using the formula $V=s^3$, where s is the edge length of the cube. It's given that a cube has an edge length of 41 inches. Substituting 41 inches for s in this equation yields $V = 41^3$ cubic inches, or V =68,921 cubic inches. Therefore, the volume of the cube is 68,921 cubic inches

9.Question

Category: SAT Advanced Math

Choice A is correct.

The given system of linear equations can be solved by the elimination method. Multiplying each side of the second equation in the given system by 3 yields (2x+2y)(3)=(10)(3) or 6x+ 6y =30 . Subtracting this equation from the first equation in the given system yields (6x+ 7y)- (6x+ 6y)= (28)- (30) which is equivalent to (6x – 6x) + (7y- 6y)= 28 -30 or y =-2.

10.Question

Category: SAT Advanced Math

Choice B is correct.

It is known that the minimum value of x is 12 less than 6 times another number n. Therefore, all possible values of x are greater than or equal to 12 less than 6 times n. The value of 6 times n is given by the expression 6n. The value of 12 less than 6n is given by the expression 6n- 12 . Therefore, the possible values of x are all greater than or equal to 6n - 12. This can be shown by the inequality x ≥ 6n – 12.

11.Question

Category: SAT Problem Solving & Data Analysis

The correct answer is 44.

The mean of a data set is computed by dividing the sum of the values in the data set by the number of values in the data set. It is assumed that data set A consists of the heights of 75 buildings and has a mean of 32 meters.

This can be represented by the equation $\frac{x}{75}$ = , where x represents the sum of the heights of the buildings in data set A, in meters. Multiplying both sides of this equation by 75 yields x =75(32), or x =2,400 meters.

It can be demonstrated that the sum of the heights of the buildings in data set A is 2,400 meters. Furthermore, data set B consists of the heights of 50 buildings and has a mean of 62 meters.

This can be represented by the equation $\frac{y}{50}$=62 , where y represents the sum of the heights of the buildings in data set B. Multiplying both sides of this equation by 50 yields y = 50 (62), or y = 3,100 meters.

Therefore, the sum of the heights of the buildings in data set B is 3,100 meters. Given that data set C comprises the heights of the 125 buildings from data sets A and B, it follows that the mean of data set C is the sum of the heights of the buildings in meters from data sets A and B, divided by the number of buildings represented in data sets A and B. This yields 44 meters, which is equivalent to $\frac{2400+3,100}{125}$ Consequently, the mean, in meters, of data set C is 44.

12.Question

Catgory: SAT Algebra

The correct answer is Choice C.

It can be demonstrated that the equation $-9x^2+30x+c=0$ has precisely one solution. This is the case for a quadratic equation of the form ax^2 bx +c =0, which has precisely one solution if and only if its discriminant, $-4ac+b^2$, is equal to zero. Consequently, for the given equation, a = -9 and b = 30. Upon substituting -9 for a and 30 for b into b^2- 4ac, the result is 30^2-4(-9)(c) or 900 36c. Since the discriminant must equal zero, 900 =36c. Subtracting 36c from both sides of the equation yields 900= 36c. Dividing each side of the equation by -36 yields – 25=c. Therefore, the value of c is -25.

13.Question

Category: SAT Advanced Math

Choice C is correct.

The given expression shows subtraction of two like terms. The two terms can be subtracted as follows: $12x^3$-$5x^3$=(12-5)x^3,or $7x^3$.

14.Question

Catgory: SAT Algebra

Choice A is correct.

The second equation in the given system defines the value of x as 5y. Substituting 5y for x into the first equation yields 5 y +y =18 or 6y=18 . Dividing each side of this equation by 6 yields y =3. Substituting 3 for y in the second equation yields 5(3)= x or x =15. Therefore, the solution (x,y) to the given system of equations is (15,3).

15.Question

Category: SAT Problem Solving & Data Analysis

The correct answer is Choice A.

It is a given that the truck can tow a trailer if the combined weight of the trailer and the boxes it contains is no more than 4,600 pounds. If the trailer has a weight of 500 pounds and each box weighs 120 pounds, the expression 500 +120b, where b is the number of boxes, provides the combined weight of the trailer and the boxes. Given that the combined weight must be no greater than 4,600 pounds, the possible numbers of boxes the truck can tow are determined by the inequality $500+120b \leq 4,600$. Subtracting 500 from both sides of the inequality yields $120b \leq 4,100$. Dividing both sides of the inequality by 120 yields $b \leq \frac{205}{6}$ or b is less than or equal to approximately 34.17. Given that the number of boxes, b, must be a whole number, the maximum number of boxes that the truck can tow is the greatest whole number less than 34.17, which is 34.

16. Question

SAT SAT Problem Solving & Data Analysis

The correct answer is $\frac{3}{10}$. It is assumed that there are a total of 100 tiles of equal area, which represents the total number of possible outcomes. According to the table, there are a total of 30 red tiles. The probability of an event occurring is defined as the ratio of the number of favorable outcomes to the total number of possible outcomes. By definition, the probability of selecting a red tile is given by $\frac{30}{100}$, or $\frac{3}{10}$. It should be noted that 3/10 and .3 are examples of ways to enter a correct answer.

17. Question

Catgory: SAT Problem Solving & Data Analysis

Choice A is correct.

It can be reasonably deduced that the aforementioned radio show indicated that there were three times as many individuals who voted in favor of the proposal as those who voted against it. Therefore, let x represent the number of individuals who voted against the proposal. Consequently, it can be inferred that 3x represents the number of individuals who voted in favor of the proposal, and 3x- x represents the number of individuals who voted in favor of the proposal and who also voted against it. Additionally, a social media post indicated that 15,000 more individuals voted in favor of the proposal than voted against it. Consequently, 2x= 15,000. Given that 2x= 15,000, it can be deduced that the value of x must be half of 15,000, or 7,500. Therefore, 7,500 individuals voted against the proposal.

18. Question

Category: SAT Geometry & Trigonometry

The correct answer is Choice C.

Vertical angles, which are angles that are opposite each other when two lines intersect, are congruent. The figure shows that lines t and m intersect. Therefore, the angle with measure x^0 and the angle with measure y^0 are vertical angles, so x=y. It is given that x = 6k+ 13 and y = 8k-29. Substitution of 6k +13 for x and 8k- 29 - for y in the equation x =y yields 6k+ 13= 8k. Subtraction of 6k from both sides of this equation yields 13= 2k- 29. Upon adding 29 to both sides of the equation, we obtain 42= 2k , or 2k= 42. Dividing both sides of the equation by 2 yields k = 21. It is assumed that lines *m* and *n* are parallel, and the figure illustrates that lines m and n are intersected by a transversal, line t. If two parallel lines are intersected by a transversal, then the same-side interior angles are supplementary.

It can be demonstrated that the same-side interior angles with measures y^0 and z^0 are supplementary, thus $y + z = 180$. Substitution of 8k- 29 for y in this equation yields 8k- 29+z= 180. Substitution of 21 for k in this equation yields 8(21)- 29+z= 180. Subtraction of 139 from both sides of this equation yields z = 41. Consequently, the value of z is 41.

19.Question

Category: SAT Problem Solving & Data Analysis

The correct answer is Choice D.

It is assumed that the candle initially contains 17 ounces of wax and that 6 ounces of wax remain after a specified period of time. The amount of wax lost by the candle during this period can be determined by subtracting the remaining amount of wax from the amount of wax present at the beginning, which yields 17 - 6 = 11 ounces. This indicates that the candle has lost 11 ounces of wax over the specified period. It is assumed that the amount of wax decreases by 1 ounce every 4 hours. If h represents the number of hours the candle has been burning, it follows that $\frac{1}{4} = \frac{11}{h}$. Multiplying both sides of this equation by 4h yields h = 44. Therefore, the candle has been burning for 44 hours.

20.Question

Category: SAT Advanced Math

Choice C is correct.

It's given that $f(x) = \frac{a}{x+b}$ and that the graph shown is a partial graph of y= f(x). Substituting y for f(x) in the equation f(x)= $\frac{a}{x+b}$ yields y=$\frac{a}{x+b}$. The graph passes through the point (- 7,- 2) . Substituting -7 for x and -2 for y in the equation y=$\frac{a}{x+b}$ yields - 2=$\frac{a}{-7+b}$ = . Multiplying each side of this equation by - 7 + b yields – 2(-7+b) =a, or 14-2b=a. The graph also passes through the point (-5;-6). Substituting -5 for x and -6 for y in the equation y=$\frac{a}{x+b}$ yields - 6=$\frac{a}{-5+b}$. Multiplying each side of this equation by -5+ b yields -6 (-5+b)=a or 30- 6b=a. Substituting 14 -2b for a in this equation yields 30- 6b= 14-2b. Adding 6b to each side of this equation yields 30= 14+ 4b. Subtracting 14 from each side of this equation yields 16= 4b. Dividing each side of this equation by 4 yields 4= b. Substituting 4 for b in the equation 14- 2b= a yields 14- 2 (4) =a, or 6= a. Substituting 6 for a and 4 for b in the equation f(x) = $\frac{6}{x+b}$yields f(x) =$\frac{6}{x+4}$. It's given that g (x)=f(x+4). Substituting x +4 for x in the equation f (x) $\frac{6}{x+4}$ yields f(x+4)=$\frac{6}{x+4+4}$ which is equivalent to f (x+4)= $\frac{6}{x+8}$= . It follows that g(x) $\frac{6}{x+8}$.

21.Question

Category: SAT Problem Solving & Data Analysis

The correct response to this question is Choice B.

It is known that 483 out of 803 respondents indicated their intention to vote for Angel Cruz. Therefore, the proportion of respondents who indicated their intention to vote for Angel Cruz is $\frac{483}{803}$. It is also known that there are a total of 6,424 voters in the election. Consequently, the total number of individuals who would be anticipated to cast their ballots in favor of Angel Cruz is 6,424, or 3,864. Given that 3,864 of the 6,424 total voters are expected to vote for Angel Cruz, it follows that 6,424 - 3,864 = 2,560 voters are expected to vote against Angel Cruz. The difference in the number of votes for and against Angel Cruz is 3,864 - 2,560 = 1,304 votes. Consequently, if 6,424 individuals cast their ballots in the election, it is anticipated that Angel Cruz will emerge as the victor by a margin of 1,304 votes.

22.Question

Category: SAT Geometry & Trigonometry

Choice A is correct

It can be reasonably deduced that the sample in question is a cube with edge lengths of 0.9 meters. Consequently, the volume of the sample can be calculated as 0.90^3, or 0.729, cubic meters. Furthermore, it is assumed that the sample has a density of 807 kilograms per 1 cubic meter. Consequently, the mass of the sample can be calculated as follows:

0.729 cubic meters $\frac{807 \; kilograms}{1 \; cubic \; meter}$, 588,303 kilograms. s. Rounding this mass to the nearest whole number gives 588 kilograms. Therefore, to the nearest whole number, the mass, in kilograms, of this sample is 588

THIS PAGE IS INTENTIONALLY LEFT BLANK

READING & WRITING SAT

Chapter 3: Critical Reading and Writing

Strategies for Reading Comprehension

In the pursuit of academic excellence, particularly in the context of the SAT, the ability to navigate the complexities of reading comprehension is paramount. This section of our guide is dedicated to elucidating strategies that will empower students to dissect, understand, and analyze the diverse array of passages presented in the Critical Reading and Writing component of the exam. Mastery in this area is not only a testament to one's literacy and critical thinking skills but also a crucial determinant of overall SAT success.

Understanding the Structure of Texts

Each passage encountered in the SAT is a window into a distinct narrative, argument, or exposition. Students must become adept at identifying the underlying structure of these texts, whether they are linear narratives, argumentative pieces with supporting evidence, or expository texts with complex concepts. Recognizing the structure aids in anticipating the types of questions that may follow.

The most crucial aspects of grammar to master for the digital **SAT Reading and Writing** sections are those pertaining to punctuation. It bears emphasizing that those who utilize the aforementioned grammar tips to master the SAT punctuation rules will see their Reading and Writing scores increase significantly.

What, then, are the essentials of punctuation on the digital SAT? The answer lies in clauses. The number of grammatical rules that determine the type of punctuation that can be used is finite. These rules depend on the separation of the punctuation.

- **The first rule of punctuation in the SAT is that a semicolon is used to separate two complete sentences.**

This is a relatively straightforward question. In almost every instance, the semicolon is identical to a period. In the event that a complete sentence precedes and a complete sentence follows the semicolon, the latter is always the appropriate punctuation.

Conversely, if the semicolon is situated between a complete sentence and an incomplete one, it is incorrect. To ascertain the correct answer, it is sufficient to examine the content of the sentences on either side of the semicolon.

- **It is a fundamental rule of punctuation that a comma cannot be used to separate two complete sentences.**

Mastery of this SAT grammar rule will enable the elimination of a significant number of incorrect answer options. This is a relatively straightforward rule, with no exceptions: a comma is never used to separate two complete sentences.

The explanation is straightforward. The technical term for this is a "comma splice," but the crucial point is the ability to identify it when it occurs. In the event that one is aware that a question pertaining to the use of punctuation on the SAT is being considered, and one encounters a comma within an answer option, the initial step is to ascertain whether the comma is separating two complete sentences. In such a case, the answer is incorrect.

- **The third rule of punctuation in the SAT is that a colon should follow a complete sentence.**

It is not uncommon for students to find colons confusing. However, they are not as difficult to understand as one might think. The most crucial rule regarding the use of colons in the context of the digital SAT is that they can only be employed after the completion of a sentence.

What, then, of what follows the colon? The colon may be used to introduce either a complete sentence or an incomplete sentence. However, it must also explain something that the preceding text does not address. One might consider the colon to be akin to a piece of a larger puzzle. It signals that whatever follows it will serve to elucidate the preceding text.

- **The forth rule of punctuation in the SAT is that dashes indicate an interruption in a complete sentence.**

The purpose of dashes is a topic that has been the subject of much debate. Dashes are another punctuation mark that can be challenging to use correctly. However, we will provide an overview of the two main ways that dashes are used on the digital SAT, which should help you to become more familiar with them in a relatively short period of time.

The most straightforward interpretation of the dash is as a signal indicating a change in direction within a sentence. There are two ways in which this can occur. Should one wish to introduce additional information at the conclusion of a complete sentence, a single dash is sufficient.

In this instance, it is sufficient to ascertain that the dash follows a complete sentence in order to ascertain its correctness.

In the more common format employed by the SAT, dashes are used to introduce an interruption into the middle of a complete sentence. In this instance, they function in a manner analogous to that of parentheses. If two dashes are employed, it should be possible to remove everything between them and be left with a complete sentence that still makes sense.

Mastery in this section requires a nuanced understanding of grammatical rules and the ability to apply these rules in varied contexts to improve clarity and precision in writing

Verb Tenses

- **Consistency is Crucial:** Ensure that verb tenses remain consistent throughout a sentence or passage unless a shift in the timeline necessitates a change. This rule helps maintain clarity and coherence in writing.

Punctuation

- **Commas and Dashes:** Use commas or dashes to set off non-essential information within a sentence. This punctuation not only clarifies the sentence structure but also adds nuance to the written expression.

Sentence Structure

- **Parallel Structure:** Employ parallelism to ensure symmetry and balance in lists or sequences of ideas within a sentence. This enhances readability and stylistic sophistication.

- **Subordination and Coordination:** Utilize subordination to emphasize primary ideas and coordination to link ideas of equal importance, thus enriching the text's complexity and depth.

Agreement

- **Subject-Verb Agreement:** Always match the verb in a sentence with its subject in both number and tense, a fundamental rule for ensuring grammatical accuracy.

- **Pronoun-Antecedent Agreement:** Pronouns should agree in number and gender with the nouns they refer to, preventing ambiguity.

Modifiers

- **Correct Placement:** Place modifiers near the words they describe to avoid confusion and misinterpretation, such as in cases of misplaced or dangling modifiers.

Concision and Clarity

- **Eliminate Redundancy:** Remove unnecessary words or redundant phrases to streamline writing and enhance its effectiveness.

- **Choose Precise Words:** Select specific and appropriate vocabulary to express ideas clearly and accurately.

Advanced Punctuation

- **Using Colons and Semicolons:** Apply colons to introduce lists or explanations, and use semicolons to connect closely related independent clauses, thereby improving the flow and coherence of paragraphs.

Active Reading

Active reading is the cornerstone of comprehension. It involves:

- **Annotation:** Marking key points, noting unfamiliar words, and summarizing paragraphs in the margins.

- **Questioning:** Asking questions about the passage's purpose, the author's perspective, and the implications of certain statements.

- **Predicting:** Anticipating where the text is headed or what argument the author is building towards.

Inference and Analysis

Many questions in the reading section require making inferences—that is, drawing conclusions based on evidence within the text rather than direct statements. This necessitates a critical analysis of the passage, understanding nuances, and evaluating the effectiveness of the author's arguments or the impact of specific word choices.

Evidence-Based Answers

The SAT emphasizes evidence-based answers. Students must not only identify the correct answer but also select the piece of evidence that best supports that answer. This dual-step process reinforces a deeper engagement with the text and cultivates a meticulous approach to evidence selection.

Vocabulary in Context

Understanding vocabulary in the context of the passage is crucial. Students should focus on how words are used within the text to grasp their meanings, rather than relying solely on prior knowledge. This context-based approach allows for a more nuanced understanding of the text.

Strategies for Time Management

Given the time constraints of the SAT, efficient reading is essential. This does not mean rushing through passages but rather developing a reading strategy that allows for thorough comprehension within the allotted time. Techniques include skimming for main ideas, prioritizing passages based on personal strengths, and allocating time proportionately to the number and difficulty of questions.

Practice and Reflection

Consistent practice with a variety of texts and question types is vital. After each practice session, reflecting on the strategies that were effective and those that need improvement can help refine reading comprehension skills.

By cultivating these strategies, students will enhance their ability to interpret complex texts, analyze arguments critically, and select evidence judiciously. This chapter not only aims to improve SAT scores but also to enrich students' academic and intellectual journey, laying a strong foundation for future scholarly endeavors.

These grammar rules are not only foundational for scoring well on the SAT but are also crucial for effective writing and communication in academic and professional settings. To excel on the SAT Writing and Language section, students should practice these rules extensively through targeted exercises and by revising their own written work to identify and correct errors.

Before to start

As students embark on the journey to master the Critical Reading and Writing section of the SAT, engaging with practice tests emerges as a pivotal step in their preparatory regimen. This introduction serves as a primer to the comprehensive suite of practice exercises specifically designed to mirror the intricacies and demands of the actual SAT. It is within these practice environments that students can hone their analytical skills, deepen their comprehension, and refine their writing, all within the framework of the SAT's rigorous standards.

Objective of the Practice Test

The practice **Reading & Writing** test is meticulously crafted to simulate the real SAT experience. It aims to familiarize students with the types of passages they will encounter, the breadth of questions they will need to answer, and the critical thinking required to discern the subtleties of text interpretation and analysis. Beyond mere preparation, these practice tests are a litmus test for the students' readiness, offering valuable insights into their strengths and areas for improvement.

Components of the Practice Test

The digital SAT Reading and Writing section comprises four main categories of question types. Collectively, these questions test a range of skills, including knowledge of proper punctuation and syntax, as well as the ability to analyse data in passages.

The four categories of questions are as follows:

- Standard English Conventions
- Expression of Ideas
- Craft and Structure
- Information and Ideas

Let us now examine the question types in each category in greater detail.

- **Standard English Conventions:**
  Approximately 11-15 of the Reading and Writing questions on the digital SAT fall into the Standard English Conventions category.

  The question types in this category include grammar questions dealing with the following:

  -subject-verb agreement
  -pronoun-antecedent agreement
  -plural and possessive nouns
  -verb forms
  -modifier placement

  This category encompasses two distinct types of questions: those pertaining to extra information that is not necessary for the sentence to be complete, and items in a list.
  The category also encompasses questions pertaining to the proper use of punctuation in general, including the use of commas, semicolons, colons, and dashes (and periods).

- **Expression of Ideas:**
  Approximately 8-12 of the Reading and Writing questions on the digital SAT fall into the category of Expression of Ideas. The question types in this category include:

  Transition: questions that require the selection of an appropriate transition word or phrase from a list of options to fill a blank in the passage. These blanks may appear within a sentence or between two sentences. Examples of transition words include "though," "therefore," and so forth.

  Rhetorical Synthesis: questions that require the selection of an answer choice that most effectively synthesizes bulleted notes from the passage to accomplish a specific goal. For instance, the goal may be to demonstrate a similarity or contrast.

- **Craft and Structure:**
  Approximately 13-15 of the Reading and Writing questions on the digital SAT fall into the Craft and Structure category. The question types in this category include:

  Structure: questions that require the identification of the answer choice that best describes the organizational structure of the passage, including the manner in which the author presents the information, the sequence of events, and the overall structure of the passage.
  Main Purpose: questions that require the identification of the author's primary objective in writing the passage. In other words, what the author does overall in the passage (e.g., argues against something, provides an explanation for something, etc.).

  Specific Purpose: questions that ask us what the function of a particular underlined portion of the passage is, for example, a particular sentence.
  In this section, we will examine words in context. This type of question requires us to either fill in a blank within a passage with the most fitting word among the answer choices or select the word among the answer choices that best conveys the meaning of an underlined word in the passage. It would be beneficial to engage in some vocabulary practice with these words.

Cross-Text Connections: Questions that ask us to relate two paired passages to each other in some way. For example, we might be asked to consider how someone discussed in Passage 1 would feel about the views of someone discussed in Passage 2

- **Information and Ideas:**

  Approximately 12-14 questions on the Reading and Writing section of the digital SAT are classified under the category of Information and Ideas. These question types include:
  Main Idea: Questions that prompt identification of the central idea of a given passage

  Detail: Questions requiring identification of a particular idea within a passage, typically expressed in a specific sentence

  Inference: Questions that require identification of the answer choice that logically completes the passage. Each answer choice presents a significant portion of what would be the final sentence of the passage.

  Command of Evidence (Textual): Questions that ask us which answer choice most effectively "illustrates" a claim from the passage or most strongly "supports" a claim or hypothesis from the passage. These questions may accompany either literature-based or science-based passages.

  Command of Evidence (Quantitative): Questions that request the completion of the passage with the statement among the answer choices that most accurately employs data from a table or graph.

To divide and summarize these 4 macro areas we can split into:

- **Reading Comprehension**: This component includes passages from a broad range of disciplines—literature, historical documents, social sciences, and natural sciences—each followed by questions that test the students' ability to understand, analyze, and interpret texts.

- **Writing and Language**: Here, students will encounter passages that require revision and editing. The questions assess grammar, usage, consistency in style and tone, and the logical flow of ideas, challenging students to apply their knowledge of the English language in a context that mimics real-world writing scenarios.

Strategies for Maximizing Practice Test Efficacy

1. **Simulate Testing Conditions**: To reap the full benefits of the practice test, students are encouraged to simulate actual testing conditions—adhering to the time limits, using only approved calculators, and minimizing interruptions.

2. **Analyze Performance**: Post-test analysis is as critical as the test-taking itself. Students should carefully review their answers, especially those they got wrong, to understand their mistakes and learn from them.

3. **Focus on Weak Areas**: Identifying and focusing on weaker areas allows for targeted improvement, turning potential vulnerabilities into strengths.

4. **Practice Regularly**: Consistency is key. Regular practice not only solidifies the students' skills but also builds confidence and reduces test-day anxiety.

5. **Seek Feedback:** Where possible, students should seek feedback on their performance, whether from teachers, tutors, or through self-assessment tools. Constructive feedback is invaluable for growth and improvement.

Conclusion

The Practice Reading & Writing Test is not just a preparatory tool; it is a **critical component** of the learning process. It offers students a practical and insightful means to gauge their readiness, refine their skills, and approach the actual SAT with confidence and a clear understanding of what to expect. Engaging with these practice tests is a step towards not only SAT success but also towards the cultivation of lifelong skills in critical reading and effective writing.

Practice Test 1 Module 1: Reading & Writing Practice Sets

The questions in this section cover a range of important reading and writing skills. Each

question consists of one or more passages, which may include a table or graphic. Read each passage and question carefully, and then choose the best answer to the question based on the passage(s).

All questions in this section are multiple-choice with four possible answers. Each question has a single best answer.

1.Question

Category: SAT Standard English Conventions

In a small, quaint town, the summer festival brought joy and laughter to the streets. Families and friends gathered together for fun-filled activities, like face-painting and balloon-animal making. The locals – ever-friendly and welcoming – organized a community potluck, where everyone shared their delicious, home-cooked dishes. The festival-goers couldn't help but feel a sense of togetherness and camaraderie as they danced and sang under the star-lit sky. It was a truly unforgettable night, and the memories created _____ would linger for years to come.

Which choice completes the text so that it conforms to the conventions of Standard English?

- a. heartwarming and cherished

- b. heartwarming and cherished –

- c. – heartwarming and cherished –

- d. , heartwarming and cherished –

2. Question

Category: SAT Information & Ideas

The melting of the Arctic Sea ice is a serious problem having a number of negative impacts on the Arctic region. The impacts of climate change are already being felt in the Arctic and they are only going to get worse in the future. It is important to take action to address climate change in order to protect the Arctic region and the people who live there. The chart shows the average temperature of the Arctic Sea ice from 1980 to 2023. The line graph shows that the average temperature has been decreasing over time, _____.

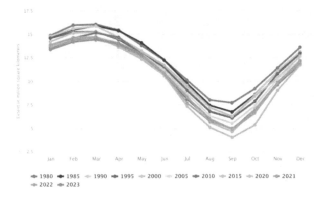

Average monthly sea ice extent in the Northern Hemisphere from January 1980 to May 2023

Which choice most effectively uses data from the table to complete the statement?

- a. from -17.4 degrees Celsius in 1980 to -13.5 degrees Celsius in 2023.

- b. from -17.4 degrees Fahrenheit in 1980 to -13.5 degrees Fahrenheit in 2023.

- c. from 0 degrees Celsius in 1980 to 3.5 degrees Celsius in 2023.

- d. from 15 million square kilometers in 1980 to 10 million square kilometers in 2023.

3. Question

Category: SAT Standard English Conventions

Throughout history, the captivating art of origami has mesmerized people around the world. The ancient Japanese tradition of folding paper into intricate shapes and figures _____ time, with its origins dating back centuries. Surprisingly, there is no definitive evidence that origami is indigenous to Japan, leading scholars to speculate about its mysterious origins.

Which choice completes the text so that it conforms to the conventions of Standard English?

- a. to transcended

- b. having transcended

- c. has transcended

- d. transcending

4. Question

Category: SAT Expression of Ideas

While researching a topic, a student has taken the following notes:

- The Great Fire of London was a major conflagration that swept through the central parts of the English city of London in September 1666.

- The fire burned for three days, destroying over 13,000 homes and 87 churches.

- It is estimated that only 6 people died in the fire, leaving over 70,000 people homeless.

- The fire was caused by a baker's oven that was left unattended.

- The rebuilding of London after the fire led to the creation of the modern city we know today, with wide streets and brick buildings replacing the narrow, wooden structures of the past.

The student wants to emphasize the uniqueness of the modern city creation. Which choice most effectively uses relevant information from the notes to accomplish this goal?

- a. The rebuilding of London after the Great Fire of London in 1666 led to the creation of the modern city we know today, with wide streets and brick buildings replacing the narrow, wooden structures of the past.

- b. The Great Fire of London in 1666 was a major conflagration that swept through the central parts of the city, destroying over 13,000 homes and 87 churches. The rebuilding of London after the fire led to the creation of a modern city with wide streets and brick buildings.

- c. The Great Fire of London in 1666 burned for three days, leaving over 70,000 people homeless. The rebuilding of London after the fire led to the creation of the modern city we know today, with wide streets and brick buildings replacing the narrow, wooden structures of the past.

- d. The Great Fire of London in 1666 was caused by a baker's oven that was left unattended. The rebuilding of London after the fire led to the creation of the modern city we know today, with wide streets and brick buildings replacing the narrow, wooden structures of the past.

5. Question

Category: SAT Craft & Structure

Text 1:

Astronomers have long puzzled over the coexistence of multiple galaxies in the universe, each containing billions of stars and vast cosmic structures. According to traditional theories, gravitational forces should eventually lead to the merging of galaxies, resulting in the dominance of a single, larger galaxy. However, observations have shown that numerous galaxies coexist in close proximity, raising questions about the mechanisms that maintain their separate identities and prevent complete assimilation.

Text 2:

Astronomer Sarah Turner and her team propose a novel explanation for the persistence of multiple galaxies in close proximity. They suggest that the vast distances between galaxies create a sparse and gravitationally diluted environment. The immense cosmic voids between galaxies hinder their ability to interact directly, reducing the frequency of galaxy mergers. In this vast cosmic expanse, direct gravitational competition occurs less frequently than previously assumed, allowing multiple galaxies to persist over time.

Which choice best describes a difference in how the author of Text 1 view Astronomer Sarah Turner's proposal in Text 2?

- a. The author of Text 1 views Astronomer Sarah Turner's proposal in Text 2 as a radical departure from traditional theories.

- b. The author of Text 1 views Astronomer Sarah Turner's proposal in Text 2 as a more nuanced explanation for the persistence of multiple galaxies in close proximity than traditional theories.

- c. The author of Text 1 views Astronomer Sarah Turner's proposal in Text 2 as a more likely explanation for the persistence of multiple galaxies in close proximity than traditional theories.

- d. The author of Text 1 views Astronomer Sarah Turner's proposal in Text 2 as a complementary explanation to traditional theories.

6. Question

Category: SAT Information & Ideas

In the field of wildlife conservation, biologist Dr. Sarah Walker embarked on a mission to protect endangered species and their habitats. During her research, she noticed that certain animal calls and behaviors were challenging for automated recording systems to detect accurately, but trained field biologists had no trouble identifying them. Inspired by this observation, Dr. Walker developed a novel method to safeguard wildlife reserves from illegal poaching and human intrusion. She created a specialized security test that required users to distinguish between authentic animal calls and background noises in audio recordings. This innovative test not only helped keep poachers and intruders at bay but also contributed valuable data to her ongoing research on wildlife populations and behavior.

According to the text, why did Dr. Sarah Walker develop a specialized security test for wildlife reserves?

- a. She wanted to make it more difficult for poachers and intruders to enter the reserves.

- b. She wanted to create a more challenging challenge for field biologists.

- c. She wanted to make it more difficult for poachers and intruders to disguise their activities.

- d. She wanted to develop a more effective way to protect endangered species and their habitats from illegal poaching and human intrusion.

7. Question

Category: SAT Craft & Structure

Research conducted by psychologist Dr. Emily Martinez explores the intriguing link between weather patterns and decision-making in the workplace. In her study, she analyzed data from various industries over a five-year period, investigating how different weather conditions influenced managers' financial decisions. Dr. Martinez discovered a fascinating correlation between rainy weather and risk aversion. When managers were exposed to prolonged periods of rain during the weeks leading up to important financial decisions, they tended to adopt a more cautious approach. This was evident in their conservative earnings forecasts and business strategies, reflecting a tendency to play it safe during uncertain times.

Which choice best describes the function of the underlined portion in the text as a whole?

- a. It introduces a new research topic unrelated to weather patterns and decision-making.

- b. It provides a summary of the main findings of the study.

- c. It presents a counterargument to the main thesis of the passage.

- d. It supports the claim that rainy weather is linked to risk aversion in managers' financial decisions.

8. Question

Category: SAT Information & Ideas

In the heart of a dense and ancient forest, a symphony of life unfolds with each passing day. Towering trees stretch their limbs toward the heavens, their leaves whispering tales of forgotten ages. Among the emerald foliage, an array of vibrant creatures dance through the undergrowth, each playing a role in the intricate web of life that thrives in this natural sanctuary. The forest floor teems with life, bustling with insects of all sizes scurrying about their daily tasks. From the tiniest ants to the majestic beetles, they toil tirelessly, their endeavors essential to the forest's delicate balance. These miniature architects shape the soil, aerating it and recycling organic matter, while also _____.

Which choice most logically completes the text?

- a. serving as a vital source of nourishment for the creatures higher up the food chain.

- b. providing a safe haven for small mammals and reptiles to live and breed.

- c. helping to disperse seeds and pollen, which helps to propagate new plants.

- d. competing with larger animals for food and resources.

9. Question

Category: SAT Craft & Structure

The migratory behavior of certain bird species enhances its survival during harsh weather conditions. Ornithologist Dr. Sarah Johnson and her team found in their 2021 study that these birds accomplish this ____ by sensing changes in the Earth's magnetic field. This enables them to navigate long distances and find suitable habitats with abundant food sources.

Which choice completes the text with the most logical and precise word or phrase?

- a. magically

- b. unconsciously

- c. biologically

- d. miraculously

10. Question

Category: SAT Standard English Conventions

When exploring the literary works of renowned author Maria Santiago, it is common for critics to highlight her incorporation of Western influences into her storytelling. However, what often goes unnoticed is Santiago's profound connection to her native Latin American heritage and her deep engagement with its rich artistic traditions, such as magical realism. Throughout her literary career, _____, blending the fantastical with the realistic in her narratives. While some critics praise her use of Western literary techniques, they may overlook the subtle nods to Latin American folklore, where myths and legends seamlessly intertwine with everyday life.

Which choice completes the text so that it conforms to the conventions of Standard English?

- a. Santiago has demonstrated a masterful fusion of diverse cultural elements

- b. Demonstrating a masterful fusion of diverse cultural elements, Santiago was blending the fantastical with the realistic in her narratives

- c. Demonstrated a masterful fusion of diverse cultural elements, Santiago has blended the fantastical with the realistic in her narratives

- d. Santiago's masterful fusion of diverse cultural elements was demonstrated

11. Question

Category: SAT Expression of Ideas

Engrossed in the captivating world of marine biodiversity, a dedicated student embarks on a research journey, meticulously documenting the following fascinating notes:

- The Great Barrier Reef is the world's largest coral reef system, stretching over 2,300 kilometers along the northeastern coast of Australia.

- This natural wonder is a biodiverse haven, home to an astounding variety of marine life, including over 1,500 species of fish and around 400 species of coral.

- The Great Barrier Reef's significance transcends its immense beauty, as it provides habitat and shelter to a myriad of marine species, some of which are endangered or threatened.

- Apart from its ecological importance, the reef system plays a crucial role in supporting Australia's tourism industry, attracting visitors from across the globe who wish to witness its breathtaking splendor.

Which choice most effectively uses information from the given sentences to emphasize the relative size of the Reef's diversity?

- a. The Great Barrier Reef is home to over 1,500 species of fish and around 400 species of coral, making it one of the most diverse marine ecosystems in the world.

- b. The Great Barrier Reef is so large that it can be seen from outer space. It is also home to an incredible variety of marine life, including over 1,500 species of fish and around 400 species of coral.

- c. The Great Barrier Reef is home to over 1,500 species of fish, which is more than any other marine ecosystem in the world. It also has a greater diversity of coral species than any other reef system, with around 400 species.

- d. The Great Barrier Reef is home to more species of fish than any other marine ecosystem in the world. It also has a greater diversity of coral species than any other reef system.

12. Question

Category: SAT Craft & Structure

In the realm of culinary artistry, the renowned chef Julia Simmons wields her knife with skill, conjuring delights of joy and satisfaction with every dish she crafts. With a keen understanding of the human palate, she delves into the hearts and minds of those who taste her creations, evoking memories and emotions reminiscent of cherished moments. Just as a seasoned botanist deciphers the language of flowers, Julia reads the flavors and aromas of ingredients, blending them harmoniously into culinary symphonies. Even the most delicate of broths and sauces respond to her culinary command, as she summons forth the essence of flavors with a mere touch of her spatula.

Which choice best states the main purpose of the text?

- a. To describe the culinary skills of Julia Simmons

- b. To explain how Julia Simmons creates culinary symphonies

- c. To compare Julia Simmons to a botanist

- d. To present Julia Simmons as a culinary artist who creates dishes that evoke memories and emotions

13. Question

Category: SAT Craft & Structure

Starting in the late 19th century, botanist and environmental activist Rachel Carson tirelessly dedicated herself to promoting environmental conservation and public awareness. This all-encompassing _____ involved conducting extensive research on pesticides' detrimental effects, authoring groundbreaking books like "Silent Spring," and advocating for stronger regulations to protect the environment and human health.

Which choice completes the text with the most logical and precise word or phrase?

- a. pursuit
- b. adventure
- c. quest
- d. endeavor

14. Question

Categoria: SAT Standard English Conventions

Inside African turquoise killifish eggs, survival hinges on a remarkable adaptation known as diapause. These tiny eggs, laid in temporary water bodies, face the harsh reality of unpredictable and often drying environments. To cope with these challenging conditions, the embryos enter a state of suspended animation, essentially putting their development on hold. This dormant state, known as diapause, allows the eggs _____ for much longer than the life span of an adult killifish.

Which choice completes the text so that it conforms to the conventions of Standard English?

- a. remain viable
- b. remaining viable
- c. having remain viable
- d. to remain viable

15. Question

Category: SAT Expression of Ideas

Amidst the vast realm of scientific exploration, a curious student embarks on a research journey, carefully documenting the following intriguing facts

- Olivia Anderson, a visionary scientist, was honored with the prestigious 2021 Nobel Prize in Physics, a testament to her groundbreaking contributions to the field.

- Anderson's academic roots lie in a quaint town in Switzerland, where she was born and nurtured a passion for the mysteries of the cosmos. Presently, she spearheads research initiatives at a renowned research institution in the United States.

- Among the diverse array of scientific publications authored by Dr. Anderson, her seminal work titled "Stellar Symphony" has captured the hearts of numerous scientists and stargazers alike. This revolutionary research has been applauded for its remarkable insights into the formation of stars and galaxies.

- "Stellar Symphony" transcends the boundaries of traditional astrophysical studies; it is an ambitious cosmological journey that explores the birth and evolution of celestial objects throughout the universe's history.

The student wants to introduce "Stellar Symphony" to an audience unfamiliar with the novel and its author. Which choice most effectively uses relevant information from the notes to accomplish this goal?

- a. Dr. Olivia Anderson, a visionary scientist who was awarded the prestigious 2021 Nobel Prize in Physics, wrote the groundbreaking book "Stellar Symphony." This book explores the formation of stars and galaxies throughout the universe's history.

- b. Dr. Olivia Anderson, a scientist who was born in Switzerland and currently works in the United States, wrote the book "Stellar Symphony." This book is about the formation of stars and galaxies throughout the universe's history.

- c. Dr. Olivia Anderson's book "Stellar Symphony" is a groundbreaking work that explores the formation of stars and galaxies throughout the universe's history. This book has been applauded for its remarkable insights and its ability to transcend the boundaries of traditional astrophysical studies.

- d. Dr. Olivia Anderson, a visionary scientist who was awarded the prestigious 2021 Nobel Prize in Physics, wrote the groundbreaking book "Stellar Symphony." This book transcends the boundaries of traditional astrophysical studies by exploring the birth and evolution of celestial objects throughout the universe's history. "Stellar Symphony" has been applauded for its remarkable insights into the formation of stars and galaxies, and it is sure to appeal to anyone who is interested in the mysteries of the cosmos.

16. Question

Category: SAT Craft & Structure

In the early 1990s, linguist Dr. Emily Hughes encountered a curious phenomenon during her research on speech recognition technology. She noticed that certain regional accents and dialects were particularly challenging for the technology to understand accurately. Inspired by this observation, Dr. Hughes devised an ingenious application that would not only improve speech recognition but also serve as an educational tool. The result was the creation of an innovative language proficiency test known as "Accento Test." This test required users to repeat a standard set of phrases and words, as well as some phrases from diverse regional dialects. The correct pronunciation of the regional phrases by users contributed valuable data for refining the speech recognition algorithms, while also aiding in the preservation and documentation of various linguistic variations across different cultures.

Which choice best states the main purpose of the text?

- a. To describe the development of the Accento Test language proficiency test.

- b. To discuss the challenges of speech recognition technology in understanding regional accents and dialects.

- c. To highlight the importance of linguistic variations across different cultures.

- d. To explain how the Accento Test language proficiency test was created to improve speech recognition technology and preserve linguistic variations.

17. Question

Category: SAT Standard English Conventions

In the remote deserts of Namibia, a peculiar phenomenon baffles researchers and visitors alike. In the arid expanse of the Namib Desert, there lies a place known as Fairy Circles _____. These mysterious formations, ranging from a few feet to several meters in diameter, have captivated scientists for decades due to their peculiar origin and behavior.

Which choice completes the text so that it conforms to the conventions of Standard English?

- a. ; where barren circular patches dot the landscape

- b. , where barren circular patches dot the landscape

- c. where barren circular patches dot the landscape

- d. : where barren circular patches dot the landscape

18. Question

Category: SAT Craft & Structure

Text 1

In the world of astronomy, researchers have been fascinated by the discovery of mysterious fast radio bursts (FRBs). Unlike regular radio waves, these bursts are intense but short-lived, lasting only a fraction of a second. Astronomers have been investigating the origins of these enigmatic bursts to unravel the secrets of the universe. While FRBs have been detected from various sources, their exact nature and mechanisms remain a subject of intense study.

Text 2

When Dr. Michael Thompson and his team found that fast radio bursts (FRBs) share certain characteristics with known celestial phenomena, it sparked excitement among astronomers. However, the researchers have highlighted that the nature of FRBs might be very different from the sources they resemble. Dr. Thompson likens FRBs to cosmic light switches that activate other processes in space, but the specifics of how these bursts operate and what they represent in the cosmic landscape are still shrouded in mystery.

Which choice best describes a difference in how the author of Text 1 and the author of Text 2 view fast radio bursts (FRBs)?

- a. The author of Text 1 views FRBs as more mysterious than the author of Text 2.
- b. The author of Text 1 views FRBs as more powerful than the author of Text 2.
- c. The author of Text 1 views FRBs as more common than the author of Text 2.
- d. The author of Text 1 views FRBs as more puzzling than the author of Text 2.

19. Question

Category: SAT Standard English Conventions

The art of music and its emotional resonance take center stage in Daniel's symphonic compositions. In his magnum opus, "Harmony of the Heart," Daniel's character, a talented composer named Alexander, finds solace and connection through the melodies he creates. Each note becomes a poignant link to his past, evoking memories of his childhood home and the enchanting sounds that filled the air during his formative years. In "Harmony of the Heart," Alexander's music _____ as a gateway to his native city, a place he left behind years ago in pursuit of his dreams.

Which choice completes the text so that it conforms to the conventions of Standard English?

- a. had served
- b. serves
- c. served
- d. was serving

20. Question

Category: SAT Craft & Structure

Text 1

Genetic engineering has revolutionized modern agriculture, offering numerous advantages for both farmers and consumers. Through genetic modification, scientists have developed crops that are more resistant to pests, diseases, and adverse weather conditions. This increased resilience reduces the need for harmful chemical pesticides and promotes sustainable farming practices. Additionally, genetically engineered crops can have enhanced nutritional content, benefiting human health. For example, biofortified crops with increased levels of essential vitamins and minerals can address malnutrition in vulnerable populations. Embracing genetic engineering in agriculture can lead to higher crop yields, lower production costs, and ultimately, greater food security for a growing global population.

Text 2

While genetic engineering in agriculture offers certain advantages, it also raises significant ethical concerns that must be addressed. Critics argue that the long-term effects of genetically modified crops on human health and the environment remain uncertain. The widespread adoption of genetically engineered crops may lead to unintended consequences, such as the development of resistant pests and the loss of biodiversity. Additionally, there are concerns about the ownership and control of genetically modified seeds by a few large corporations, potentially limiting farmers' autonomy and increasing dependency on specific biotechnology companies. The introduction of genetically modified organisms (GMOs) into natural ecosystems may also disrupt ecological balance. It is essential to approach genetic engineering in agriculture with caution, taking into account its potential risks and ethical implications.

Based on the texts, how would the author of Text 2 most likely respond to the discussion in Text 1?

- a. The author of Text 2 would agree with the author of Text 1 that genetic engineering is a promising new technology with the potential to revolutionize agriculture.

- b. The author of Text 2 would argue that the potential risks of genetic engineering outweigh the potential benefits.

- c. The author of Text 2 would argue that the discussion in Text 1 is incomplete because it does not address the potential risks and ethical concerns of genetic engineering.

- d. The author of Text 2 would suggest that more research is needed to determine the long-term effects of genetically modified crops on human health and the environment.

21. Question

Category: SAT Standard English Conventions

In the realm of architecture, a visionary designer named Emily Carter revolutionized the way buildings adapt to changing environmental conditions. Seeking a sustainable and flexible solution, she developed a prototype of the first adaptive facade system, which could seamlessly respond to varying weather patterns and enhance energy efficiency. _____ stemmed from her fascination with biomimicry, drawing inspiration from the natural world to solve engineering challenges

Which choice completes the text so that it conforms to the conventions of Standard English?

- a. Emily's innovation

- b. Emily innovation

- c. Emilys innovation

- d. Emilys' innovation

22. Question

Category: SAT Information & Ideas

Father was not the kind of man who confined himself to the solemn routine of work and business. He made sure to set aside quality time for his family, always ready to engage in playful activities with the children and lend a hand with their school assignments. When he wasn't working, he enjoyed reading stories to them and crafting tales of his own, filling their evenings with enchanting adventures. Birthdays and special occasions were never dull, as Father had a knack for composing humorous poetry that brought smiles and laughter to everyone's faces.

What does the text most strongly suggest about Father's approach to family time and special occasions?

- a. Father was a workaholic who didn't have time for his family.

- b. Father was a boring man who didn't know how to have fun.

- c. Father was a loving and devoted father who made sure to create special memories with his family.

- d. Father was a creative man who loved to entertain his family.

23. Question

Category: SAT Information & Ideas

Josephine Baker's life and legacy serve as a powerful reminder of the transformative impact one individual can have on society. Her journey from a young girl in New Orleans to a trailblazing entertainer and activist stands as a beacon of courage and determination. Baker's commitment to breaking down racial and gender barriers through her art and advocacy has left an indelible mark on American history. Her influence continues to resonate with generations, inspiring others to stand up for justice and equality. Josephine Baker's remarkable contributions to both the entertainment world and the civil rights movement have solidified her position as an iconic figure and a symbol of empowerment and resistance. Her enduring legacy serves as a testament to the potential for positive change when individuals dare to challenge the status quo and fight for a more inclusive and just society. In conclusion, Josephine Baker's life and work stand as a shining example of the enduring power of perseverance and the pursuit of equality.

Which finding, if true, would most directly support author's conclusion?

- a. Josephine Baker was a successful entertainer and activist.

- b. Josephine Baker's work inspired others to stand up for justice and equality.

- c. Josephine Baker's work helped to break down racial and gender barriers in the entertainment industry and the civil rights movement.

- d. Josephine Baker's work had a lasting impact on American society.

24. Question

Category: SAT Information & Ideas

The towering baobab trees of the African savanna have long fascinated researchers and nature enthusiasts alike. These majestic trees can reach heights of over 80 feet and boast massive trunks with diameters exceeding 30 feet, making them some of the largest trees in the world. Scientists have delved into the mysteries behind their extraordinary growth, and while some have attributed their immense size to specific factors such as rich soil and favorable climate, there is evidence to suggest that_____.

Which choice most logically completes the text?

- a. other elements have played crucial roles in their evolution

- b. Baobab trees are actually not trees at all, but giant cacti.

- c. Baobab trees are actually not native to Africa, but were introduced from South America.

- d. are able to grow so large because they have a symbiotic relationship with a type of bacteria that helps them to store water.

25. Question

Category: SAT Craft & Structure

Considering the extreme temperatures and hostile conditions of deep-sea hydrothermal vents, scientists have long puzzled over the discovery of diverse and thriving ecosystems around these vent sites. The enigmatic nature of these ecosystems has left researchers without a definitive _____ explanation. However, marine biologists Dr. Maria Rodriguez and Dr. James Anderson made significant progress in understanding these ecosystems by using advanced imaging technology and deep-sea exploration to uncover the complex interactions between microbes and specialized organisms that sustain life in this seemingly inhospitable environment.

Which choice completes the text with the most logical and precise word or phrase?

- a. complete
- b. final
- c. ultimate
- d. comprehensive

26. Question

Category: SAT Craft & Structure

In the field of wildlife conservation, biologist Dr. Patel embarked on a mission to protect endangered species and their habitats. During her research, she noticed that some animal calls and behaviors were challenging for automated recording systems to detect accurately, but trained field biologists had no trouble identifying them. Inspired by this observation, Dr. Patel developed a novel method to safeguard wildlife reserves from illegal poaching and human intrusion. She created a specialized security test that required users to distinguish between authentic animal calls and background noises in audio recordings. This innovative test not only helped keep poachers and intruders at bay but also contributed valuable data to her ongoing research on wildlife populations and behavior.

Which choice best describes the overall structure of the text?

- a. A comparison of wildlife conservation methods used by biologists.
- b. A description of Dr. Patel's background and education.
- c. An analysis of the challenges faced by automated recording systems.
- d. A presentation of Dr. Patel's innovative method for safeguarding wildlife reserves.

27. Question

Category: SAT Standard English Conventions

In the early 2000s, an innovative engineer named Alan Chambers faced a daunting challenge when his tech startup was on the verge of collapse. Seeking a way to revitalize the company, he turned to his childhood friend and creative strategist, Emily Collins, for advice. Drawing inspiration from their shared passion for interactive storytelling, Emily _____ an ingenious transformation for the company's struggling virtual reality platform.

Which choice completes the text so that it conforms to the conventions of Standard English?

- a. Proposed
- b. Proposes
- c. Had proposed
- d. Was proposing

Solutions Reading & Writing Test 1 Module 1: Detailed Answer Explanations

1. Question

Category: SAT Standard English Conventions

C: Option C is the correct choice because the phrase "heartwarming and cherished" is an extra information given in the sentence.

Thus, it is correctly placed between two "-"

2. Question

Category: SAT Information & Ideas

A: Option A is correct it is the only option that uses data from the table to complete the statement. The table shows that the average temperature of the Arctic Sea ice has decreased from -17.4 degrees Celsius in 1980 to -13.5 degrees Celsius in 2023.

3. Question

Category: SAT Standard English Conventions

C: Option C is the correct choice because it uses the present perfect tense, which is used to describe actions that have been completed but have some connection to the present.

The sentence is about the fact that origami has transcended time, and the present perfect tense accurately describes this action. The present perfect tense is also the most concise option, and it does not use any unnecessary words or phrases.

4. Question

Category: SAT Expression of Ideas

A: Option A is the correct choice because it directly states that the rebuilding of London after the Great Fire led to the creation of the modern city, which was characterized by wide streets and brick buildings replacing the narrow, wooden structures of the past.

This information is relevant to the student's goal of emphasizing the uniqueness of the modern city creation and is supported by the notes provided.

5. Question

Category: SAT Craft & Structure

B: Option B is correct because the author of Text 1 does acknowledge that Astronomer Sarah Turner's proposal is a new explanation that needs to be considered.

The author of Text 1 also states that traditional theories suggest that gravitational forces should eventually lead to the merging of galaxies, but observations have shown that numerous galaxies coexist in close proximity.

This suggests that the persistence of multiple galaxies in close proximity is a more complex phenomenon than traditional theories suggest.

6. Question

Category: SAT Information & Ideas

D: Option D is correct because it takes into account all of the evidence in the text. The text states that Dr. Walker noticed that certain animal calls and behaviors were challenging for automated recording systems to detect accurately, but trained field biologists had no trouble identifying them.

This observation inspired Dr. Walker to develop a novel method to safeguard wildlife reserves from illegal poaching and human intrusion.

The test that she developed is more effective at detecting poachers and intruders than automated recording systems, and it also contributes valuable data to Dr. Walker's ongoing research on wildlife populations and behavior.

7. Question

Category: SAT Craft & Structure

D: In the passage, Dr. Emily Martinez's research explores the relationship between weather patterns and decision-making in the workplace.

The specific sentence "When managers were exposed to prolonged periods of rain during the weeks leading up to important financial decisions, they tended to adopt a more cautious approach" provides evidence for a fascinating correlation between rainy weather and risk aversion in managers' financial decisions.

This supports the main function of the passage, which is to present the findings of Dr. Martinez's research and establish the link between weather conditions and managers' behaviors in financial decision-making.

Thus, Option D is the correct choice.

8. Question

Category: SAT Information & Ideas

A: Option A is the correct choice because the passage describes the forest as a "symphony of life" and an "intricate web of life." This suggests that the forest is a complex ecosystem where different creatures interact with each other in a variety of ways.

The passage also mentions that insects are "essential to the forest's delicate balance." This suggests that insects play an important role in the ecosystem.

It is the only option that mentions the role of insects as a food source. The passage mentions that insects are a vital source of nourishment, so this option logically follows.

9. Question

Category: SAT Craft & Structure

C: Option C is correct because it suggests that the birds' ability to sense changes in the Earth's magnetic field is a biological phenomenon.

This is consistent with the passage, which states that Dr. Johnson and her team have found a scientific explanation for this ability. The word **biologically** means "relating to the body or to living organisms."

This suggests that the birds' ability to sense changes in the Earth's magnetic field is a natural phenomenon that is caused by their biological makeup.

The word **biologically** is consistent with the tone and style of the passage. The passage is written in a serious and matter-of-fact tone, and the word **biologically** reflects this tone.

In addition, the word **biologically** is more precise than the other options. The other options, such as **magically, miraculously,** and **unconsciously,** do not provide any specific information about how the birds are able to sense changes in the Earth's magnetic field.

The word **biologically,** on the other hand, suggests that the birds' ability is caused by a specific biological mechanism.

10. Question

Category: SAT Standard English Conventions

A: Option A is the correct choice because it is concise and accurately summarizes the main point of the sentence. The sentence is about Santiago's use of Western and Latin American influences in her storytelling, and this option accurately describes how she does this.

The option also uses the correct verb tense, "has demonstrated," which indicates that Santiago's use of diverse cultural elements is a past event that has continuing effects.

11. Question

Category: SAT Expression of Ideas

C: Option C is the correct choice because the sentence states that the Great Barrier Reef is home to over 1,500 species of fish, which is more than any other marine ecosystem in the world.

Additionally, it mentions that the reef system has a greater diversity of coral species than any other reef system, with around 400 species.

By explicitly comparing the number of fish species and coral species in the Great Barrier Reef to other marine ecosystems and reef systems, Option C highlights the exceptional level of biodiversity present in the reef.

This emphasis on being the leader in both fish and coral species underlines the Reef's unparalleled ecological significance, making it an extraordinary haven for marine life.

12. Question

Category: SAT Craft & Structure

D: Option D is correct because the text does present Julia Simmons as a culinary artist who creates dishes that evoke memories and emotions.

The text does this by describing her skills, her understanding of the human palate, and her ability to create culinary symphonies. The text supports this main purpose by providing evidence, such as descriptions of Julia's skills and her ability to evoke memories and emotions.

13. Question

Category: SAT Craft & Structure

D: The passage is about Rachel Carson, a botanist and environmental activist who dedicated herself to promoting environmental conservation and public awareness. The passage begins by stating that Carson began her work in the late 19th century, and that she continued to work tirelessly until her death in 1964. The word **endeavor** is consistent with the tone and style of the passage.

The passage is written in a serious and matter-of-fact tone, and the word **endeavor** reflects this tone. The word **endeavor** accurately describes the nature of Rachel Carson's work. Carson's work was a serious and sustained effort to promote environmental conservation and public awareness.

14. Question

Category: SAT Standard English Conventions

D: Option D is the correct choice because the word "to" indicates that the ability to remain viable is something that the eggs have the potential to do. This is the most accurate way to describe the eggs' ability to develop and remain alive for a long period of time.

15. Question

Category: SAT Expression of Ideas

D: Option D is the correct choice because it uses relevant information from the notes to accomplish the goal of introducing "Stellar Symphony" to an audience unfamiliar with the novel and its author. The option mentions Dr. Anderson's Nobel Prize, her research, and the book's unique approach to astrophysical studies.

These details are likely to be of interest to many people, and they will help to introduce "Stellar Symphony" in a way that is both informative and engaging.

16. Question

Category: SAT Craft & Structure

D: The passage states that Dr. Emily Hughes, a linguist, was working on speech recognition technology in the early 1990s. She noticed that certain regional accents and dialects were particularly challenging for the technology to understand accurately. This inspired her to create a new language proficiency test called AccentoTest. The AccentoTest test requires users to repeat a standard set of phrases and words, as well as some phrases from diverse regional dialects.

The correct pronunciation of the regional phrases by users contributes valuable data for refining the speech recognition algorithms. The test also helps to preserve and document various linguistic variations across different cultures. In short, the passage describes the creation of the AccentoTest test and its potential benefits for speech recognition technology and linguistic preservation. Option D is correct because it accurately states the main purpose of the text, which is to explain how the AccentoTest test was created to improve speech recognition technology and preserve linguistic variations.

The correct option accurately states the main purpose of the text, which is to explain how the AccentoTest test was created to improve speech recognition technology and preserve linguistic variations. The correct option is consistent with the tone and style of the passage.

17. Question

Category: SAT Standard English Conventions

B: Option B is the correct choice because it uses a comma to separate the independent clause from the phrase "where barren circular patches dot the landscape." The comma is used to indicate that the phrase is an adverbial clause, which modifies the independent clause by providing additional information about where the Fairy Circles are located.

18. Question

Category: SAT Craft & Structure

D: The author of Text 1 uses the word "enigmatic" to describe FRBs, which suggests that they are puzzling or difficult to understand. The author of Text 2 uses the word "shrouded in mystery" to describe FRBs, which suggests that they are hidden or concealed.

The word "enigmatic" is more specific than the word "mystery," so it suggests that the author of Text 1 views FRBs as more puzzling than the author of Text 2. Thus, the Option D is the correct choice.

19. Question

Category: SAT Standard English Conventions

B: Option B is the correct choice because it conveys the idea that Alexander's music currently acts as a means of connecting him to his native city. The present tense "serves" indicates an ongoing and current action, which is appropriate in this context.

20. Question

Category: SAT Craft & Structure

C: Option C is correct because the author of Text 2 does acknowledge the potential benefits of genetic engineering; the discussion in Text 1 is incomplete because it does not address the potential risks and ethical concerns. The author of Text 2 would likely argue that these concerns need to be addressed before genetic engineering can be widely adopted.

21. Question

Category: SAT Standard English Conventions

A: Option A is the correct choice because it uses the possessive form of the noun "Emily," which is necessary to show that the innovation belongs to Emily. The possessive form is created by adding an apostrophe and an "s" to the end of the noun.

22. Question

Category: SAT Information & Ideas

C: Option C is correct because the text provides several examples of how Father made time for his family and ensured that they had fun together. For example, the text mentions that he was always ready to engage in playful activities with the children, lend a hand with their school assignments, read stories to them, and compose humorous poetry.

23. Question

Category: SAT Information & Ideas

C: Option C is correct because it directly supports the author's conclusion. The author argues that Josephine Baker's work stands as a shining example of the enduring power of perseverance and the pursuit of equality.

This finding directly supports the author's conclusion because it shows how Josephine Baker's work helped to break down racial and gender barriers, which are two major obstacles to equality.

24. Question

Category: SAT Information & Ideas

A: Option A is correct because it suggests that there are other factors, in addition to the ones listed in the passage, that have helped baobab trees to evolve and grow so large. For example, it is possible that baobab trees have a genetic predisposition to grow large, or that they have benefited from the presence of other plants or animals in the African savanna.

25. Question

Category: SAT Craft & Structure

D: The word **comprehensive** means "covering all or nearly all aspects of something." This suggests that a comprehensive explanation of the deep-sea hydrothermal vent ecosystems would need to take into account all of the complex interactions between microbes and specialized organisms that sustain life in this seemingly inhospitable environment.

The word **comprehensive** is consistent with the tone and style of the passage. The passage is written in a serious and matter-of-fact tone, and the correct option reflects this tone.

26. Question

Category: SAT Craft & Structure

D: Option D is the correct choice because the passage predominantly describes Dr. Patel's innovative method for safeguarding wildlife reserves from illegal poaching and human intrusion using a specialized security test.

It emphasizes the importance of this method in protecting endangered species and contributing valuable data to ongoing research on wildlife populations and behavior.

27. Question

Category: SAT Standard English Conventions

A: Option A is the correct choice because it uses the simple past tense, which is used to describe actions that happened in the past. The sentence is about Emily Collins proposing an ingenious transformation for the company's struggling virtual reality platform, and the simple past tense accurately describes this action.

Practice Reading & Writing Test 1 Module 2: Reading & Writing Practice Sets

The questions in this section cover a range of important reading and writing skills. Each

question consists of one or more passages, which may include a table or graphic. Read each passage and question carefully, and then choose the best answer to the question based on the passage(s).

All questions in this section are multiple-choice with four possible answers. Each question has a single best answer.

1. Question

Category: SAT Expression of Ideas

As the student immerses himself in the captivating world of art and creativity, he embarks on a research journey, carefully documenting the following intriguing notes:

- Renowned artists Leonardo da Vinci and Michelangelo are credited with creating numerous masterpieces during the Italian Renaissance.

- Despite being credited as the creators of many artworks, it is believed that some works attributed to Leonardo or Michelangelo might have been the collaborative efforts of both artists.

- The exact authorship of certain parts of these masterpieces has been a subject of historical debate, with art historians and experts scrutinizing brushstrokes and stylistic elements to unravel the mysteries behind their creation.

- In the pursuit of shedding light on these artistic enigmas, scholars such as Dr. Elena Martinez and Dr. Alessio Bianchi have utilized advanced art analysis techniques to analyze the content and style of Leonardo and Michelangelo's works.

- Through rigorous analysis and comparison, they have uncovered intriguing patterns and similarities in brushwork and artistic expression, providing valuable insights into the collaborative nature of some masterpieces.

The student wants to make a generalization about the kind of work created by Leonardo da Vinci and Michelangelo. Which choice most effectively uses relevant information from the notes to accomplish this goal?

- a. Leonardo da Vinci and Michelangelo were both renowned artists who created many masterpieces during the Italian Renaissance. Some of their works were collaborative efforts, and art historians have studied these works to try to determine the exact authorship of certain parts.

- b. Leonardo da Vinci and Michelangelo were both masters of their craft, and their works are characterized by their intricate detail, realism, and use of light and shadow. Some of their most famous works include the Mona Lisa, the Last Supper, and the David.

- c. Leonardo da Vinci and Michelangelo were both versatile artists who worked in a variety of media, including painting, sculpture, and architecture. Their works are characterized by their innovation and creativity, and they continue to inspire artists and art lovers today.

- d. Leonardo da Vinci and Michelangelo were both masters of Renaissance art, and their works are characterized by their realism, attention to detail, and use of light and shadow. They often collaborated on their works, and their combined talents resulted in some of the most iconic masterpieces in history.

2. Question

Category: SAT Standard English Conventions

In the realm of contemporary art, renowned painter and illustrator Mia Hernandez finds inspiration in the works of iconic surrealist Salvador Dali. With a masterful brush and vivid imagination, she weaves elements of Dali's dreamlike landscapes and melting clocks into her own original creations _____ that pay homage to the surrealist master.

Which choice completes the text so that it conforms to the conventions of Standard English?

- a. giving rise to a series of mesmerizing artworks,
- b. , giving rise to a series of mesmerizing artworks
- c. giving rise to a series of mesmerizing artworks
- d. – giving rise to a series of mesmerizing artworks

3. Question

Category: SAT Standard English Conventions

As the sun dipped below the horizon, casting a warm, golden glow over the picturesque landscape, the couple strolled hand in hand along the sandy beach. The gentle waves whispered sweet nothings to the shore, while seagulls soared gracefully in the evening sky. This serene moment captured the essence of their love: a timeless bond of laughter, shared dreams, and unconditional support. With each passing second, their hearts beat in harmony, knowing that this fleeting moment would forever be etched in their memories_____.

Which choice completes the text so that it conforms to the conventions of Standard English?

- a. : a beautiful chapter in the story of their love.
- b. a beautiful chapter in the story of their love.
- c. ; a beautiful chapter in the story of their love.
- d. a beautiful chapter, in the story of their love.

4. Question

Category: SAT Craft & Structure

Text 1:

Early childhood education plays a crucial role in a child's development and lays the foundation for future learning. Research shows that children who receive quality early education are more likely to perform better academically and have improved social and emotional skills. It helps promote language development, cognitive abilities, and problem-solving skills at a critical stage of brain development. Furthermore, early education provides a supportive environment for children to explore and discover their interests, fostering a lifelong love for learning. Investing in early childhood education is not only beneficial for individual children but also for society as a whole, as it leads to better educational outcomes and reduces disparities in academic achievement.

Text 2:

While early childhood education is widely recognized for its potential benefits, it is essential to acknowledge its limitations and potential challenges. Critics argue that an excessive focus on formal education at a young age may lead to stress and pressure on young children. Some children may not be developmentally ready for structured learning, and early academic pressures could hinder their natural curiosity and creativity. Moreover, the quality of early childhood education programs varies significantly, and not all children have access to high-quality learning environments. Socioeconomic disparities can further exacerbate unequal educational opportunities, perpetuating existing inequalities. To fully harness the benefits of early childhood education, it is crucial to address these challenges and ensure that all children have equal access to quality learning experiences.

Which choice best describes how Text 1 and Text 2 relate to each other?

- a. Text 1 presents a one-sided view promoting early childhood education, while Text 2 presents a balanced perspective by discussing both its benefits and limitations.

- b. Text 1 and Text 2 present contrasting viewpoints on early childhood education, with Text 1 emphasizing its positive impact, and Text 2 highlighting its potential challenges.

- c. Text 1 and Text 2 complement each other, with Text 1 providing evidence to support the claims made in Text 2 about the benefits and challenges of early childhood education.

- d. Text 1 and Text 2 present unrelated perspectives on different aspects of education, without any clear connection between the two passages.

5. Question

Category: SAT Information & Ideas

Among the diverse wonders that adorn our planet, coral reefs stand as mesmerizing underwater ecosystems that captivate both scientists and nature enthusiasts. These intricate and vibrant communities, composed of corals, fish, and a plethora of marine species, create an otherworldly spectacle beneath the waves. However, coral reefs face an unprecedented threat—coral bleaching. This phenomenon, linked to rising ocean temperatures, poses a grave danger to the delicate balance of these marine sanctuaries, _____.

Which choice most logically completes the text?

- a. causing the death of coral reefs and the loss of biodiversity.

- b. leading to the collapse of the marine food chain.

- c. raising concerns about the future of these biodiverse habitats

- d. prompting calls for action to protect coral reefs.

6. Question

Category: SAT Expression of Ideas

Climate change is a pressing global issue that requires immediate attention. Human activities, such as burning fossil fuels and deforestation, are major contributors to the increase in greenhouse gas emissions. _____, natural factors, like volcanic eruptions and solar radiation, also play a role in influencing the Earth's climate.

Which choice completes the text with the most logical transition?

- a. Nevertheless

- b. Moreover

- c. Although

- d. Furthermore

7. Question

Category: SAT Information & Ideas

In a groundbreaking research study, psychologist Dr. Lisa Thompson investigated the effects of ambient noise levels on decision-making in the workplace. Utilizing data collected from various companies over a span of five years, Dr. Thompson's team analyzed the correlation between noise exposure and the accuracy of financial forecasts made by managers. The findings were intriguing: managers who were exposed to higher levels of ambient noise in their work environment tended to make more conservative forecasts, while those in quieter settings exhibited a greater inclination towards optimistic predictions. This research sheds light on how external environmental factors, such as noise levels, can influence decision-makers' behavior and perceptions of future outcomes.

Based on the passage, how did managers in quieter settings tend to make financial forecasts?

- a. They tended to make more conservative forecasts.

- b. They tended to make more risky forecasts.

- c. They tended to make inaccurate forecasts.

- d. They tended to make no forecasts at all.

8. Question

Category: SAT Information & Ideas

The researchers' claim that retail sales of clothing, footwear, and leather goods in the United States have been growing steadily in recent years. This growth is likely to continue in the future, driven by a number of factors. One factor is the increasing disposable income of consumers. As consumers have more money to spend, they are more likely to purchase clothing, footwear, and leather goods. Another factor is the growing popularity of online shopping. Consumers can now easily and conveniently shop for clothing, footwear, and leather goods from the comfort of their own homes. Finally, the increasing demand for fashionable and stylish clothing and footwear is also driving the growth of the retail market for these products. Consumers are looking for clothing and footwear that makes them look good and feel confident.

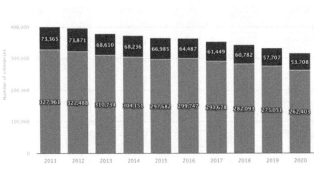

Number of specialized stores for the retail sale of clothing, footwear and leather goods in the European Union (27 countries) from 2011 to 2020

Which choice best describes data from the table that support the researchers' claim?

- a. The number of specialized stores for the retail sale of clothing, footwear, and leather goods in the European Union increased from 2011 to 2020.

- b. The average sales per store for the retail sale of clothing, footwear, and leather goods in the European Union increased from 2011 to 2020.

- c. The total retail sales of clothing, footwear, and leather goods in the European Union increased from 2011 to 2020.

- d. The retail sales of clothing, footwear, and leather goods per capita in the European Union increased from 2011 to 2020.

9. Question

Category: SAT Information & Ideas

"Reflections of the Soul" is a contemporary poem by Maya Johnson. In this poetic work, Johnson addresses the readers directly, implying that they have yet to fully comprehend the complexity and depth of their own emotions and experiences. Through vivid imagery and evocative language, the poet encourages introspection, urging the readers to delve into the recesses of their minds and hearts. She emphasizes the importance of self-awareness and self-acceptance, portraying it as a transformative journey towards self-discovery.

Which quotation from "Reflections of the Soul" most effectively illustrates the Maya's emphasis on "the importance of self-awareness and self-acceptance, portraying it as a transformative journey towards self-discovery"?

- a. "Look within yourself, and you will find the answers you seek."

- b. "Do not be afraid to explore the darkness of your soul, for it is there that you will find your true self."

- c. "To truly know oneself is to accept oneself, flaws and all. It is to embrace the darkness as well as the light, the pain as well as the joy."

- d. "The journey of self-discovery is a long and winding one, but it is a journey that is worth taking."

10. Question

Category: SAT Information & Ideas

Humans have been harvesting the small, dry seeds known as grain for thousands of years. The two main categories of grains are cereals, such as wheat, rye, and corn, and legumes, such as beans, lentils, peanuts and soybeans. Many grains are capable of being stored for long periods of time, easily transported over long distances, processed into flour, oil, and gas, and consumed by animals and humans. The use of grains in producing ethanol has increased significantly in recent years. Researchers' claim that corn is the most important grain produced globally.

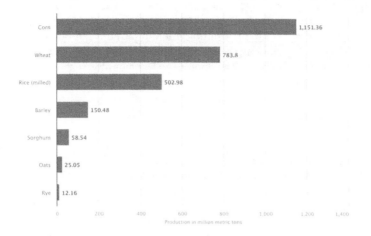

Worldwide production of grain in 2022/23, by type (in million metric tons)*

Which choice best describes data from the table that support the researchers' claim?

- a. Corn is the most produced grain in the United States, with a total production of 1,151.36 million metric tons.

- b. Corn has a total production of 783.8 million metric tons

- c. Corn has the has the lowest total production and per capita production of any grain.

- d. Wheat is a versatile grain that can be used to produce a variety of products, such as food, animal feed, and biofuels.

11. Question

Category: SAT Craft & Structure

Embracing the ethos of sustainable agriculture, local farmers and agricultural research institutions form mutually beneficial partnerships in crop experimentation and development. In one such collaborative initiative between a farming cooperative and a renowned agricultural university, they adopted the same model: farmers actively collaborated with scientists to co-create _____ farming techniques, and they continue to work together in gathering and analyzing agricultural data.

Which choice completes the text with the most logical and precise word or phrase?

- a. conventional

- b. effective

- c. innovative

- d. traditional

12. Question

Category: SAT Craft & Structure

Text 1

145

In recent years, solar energy has emerged as a promising and sustainable alternative to traditional fossil fuels. Advocates of solar power argue that harnessing energy from the sun offers numerous benefits, both for the environment and the economy. Solar panels generate electricity without emitting greenhouse gases, reducing our carbon footprint and combating climate change. Moreover, solar energy is abundant and inexhaustible, unlike finite fossil fuel reserves. As technology has improved, the cost of solar panels has decreased significantly, making solar energy more accessible to a wider range of consumers. Embracing solar power can lead to energy independence, create jobs in the renewable energy sector, and contribute to a cleaner, greener future.

Text 2

While solar energy presents certain advantages, it is essential to consider its limitations and challenges. Critics of solar power point out that solar panels are dependent on sunlight, making them less reliable in regions with inconsistent or limited sunlight. Additionally, the manufacturing and disposal of solar panels can produce environmental waste and toxins, raising concerns about the overall sustainability of solar energy. The initial investment in solar panels can also be prohibitive for many individuals and businesses, even with decreasing costs. Furthermore, the efficiency of solar panels decreases over time, requiring periodic maintenance and replacements. To fully transition to solar energy, significant infrastructural changes and technological advancements are necessary. While solar energy is a step in the right direction, it is not without its drawbacks and demands careful consideration.

Based on the texts, both authors would most likely agree with which statement?

- a. Solar energy is a perfect solution for all our energy needs.

- b. Solar energy is not a viable option for most people.

- c. Solar energy is a promising alternative to traditional fossil fuels, but it has some limitations that need to be addressed.

- d. Solar energy has the potential to be a major source of clean energy, but it is important to be aware of its limitations and challenges.

13. Question

Category: SAT Craft & Structure

George, an urban artist and architect, spent most of his life amidst the bustling cityscape, surrounded by towering skyscrapers and concrete jungles. Despite this, he had a deep appreciation for the harmony of architectural symmetry and design. Whenever he encountered a striking building or a well-designed public space, he felt a sense of connection, as if the urban landscape resonated with his artistic sensibilities. The city, with its constant movement and vibrant energy, became a reflection of his own dynamic personality.

Which choice best describes the function of the underlined sentence?

- a. To provide an example of George's appreciation for architectural symmetry and design.

- b. To explain why George felt a sense of connection to the urban landscape.

- c. To provide a contrast between the cityscape and George's artistic sensibilities.

- d. To provide a conclusion of the passage.

14. Question

Category: SAT Standard English Conventions

Established in the early 2000s with a mission to conserve the world's most precious natural areas and the rich biodiversity they harbor; the Global Wildlife Conservation (GWC) organization has been at the forefront of global conservation efforts. Initially focusing on protecting endangered species and their habitats, the GWC's scope and impact _____ exponentially over the years, propelling it to the forefront of the conservation movement.

Which choice completes the text so that it conforms to the conventions of Standard English?

- a. have grown
- b. had grown
- c. grows
- d. has grown

15. Question

Category: SAT Information & Ideas

John was not the type of person to sit idle and let life pass him by. He actively engaged in his children's lives, always there to play with them and read them bedtime stories. John took an active role in their education, assisting them with their homework and encouraging their curiosity. He even claimed that he took the time to write personalized stories for them, which he would read aloud during family gatherings. On special occasions like birthdays, he would compose humorous and heartwarming poetry, making every celebration memorable and joyful for his loved ones.

Which finding, if true, would most directly support the John's claim?

- a. John's children all say that he was a very active and involved father.
- b. John's children all have fond memories of him reading them bedtime stories and writing personalized stories for them.
- c. John's children all have good grades in school.
- d. John's children all say that they had a happy childhood.

16. Question

Category: SAT Information & Ideas

The following text is adapted from Emily Dickinson's poem "Hope is the Thing with Feathers," written in the mid-19th century. The poem reflects on the concept of hope as an intangible and uplifting force in the face of adversity.

Hope is the thing with feathers

That perches in the soul,

And sings the tune without the words,

And never stops at all,

And sweetest in the gale is heard;

And sore must be the storm

That could abash the little bird

That kept so many warm.

I've heard it in the chilliest land,

And on the strangest sea;

Yet, never, in extremity,

It asked a crumb of me.

Which choice best states the main idea of the text?

- a. Hope is a bird that sings in the soul.

- b. Hope is a powerful force that can overcome any obstacle.

- c. Hope is an intangible and uplifting force that can help us to cope with adversity.

- d. Hope is a gift that we should cherish.

17. Question

Category: SAT Craft & Structure

Former marine biologist Dr. Alex Johnson asserts that while he cannot predict the exact timeline, he firmly believes that humanity will _____ face the necessity of inhabiting environments beyond Earth's boundaries. This conviction drives his passion for advocating further exploration and research missions to the depths of the ocean.

Which choice completes the text with the most logical and precise word or phrase?

- a. inevitably

- b. eventually

- c. certainly

- d. maybe

18. Question

Category: SAT Standard English Conventions

In the depths of the lush rainforest, a peculiar creature_____ exhibits a stunning display of colors that perplexes researchers. Unlike other insects that rely on camouflage to avoid predators, this brightly adorned leafhopper appears to flaunt its vibrant hues for all to see. As researchers delve into the enigmatic world of this little creature, they begin to unravel the mystery behind its striking coloration.

Which choice completes the text so that it conforms to the conventions of Standard English?

- a. , known as the flamboyant leafhopper

- b. known as the flamboyant leafhopper,

- c. , known as the flamboyant leafhopper,

- d. ; known as the flamboyant leafhopper,

19. Question

Category: SAT Information & Ideas

In the vast and enigmatic realms of the cosmos, astronomers have been tirelessly peering into the depths of space, striving to unlock the mysteries of the universe. Among the countless celestial wonders they have discovered, black holes stand out as some of the most captivating and puzzling entities. These cosmic enigmas, with their unfathomable gravitational pull, possess an intense allure that has captured the imagination of scientists and the public alike. As researchers delve deeper into the intricacies of black holes, they have uncovered tantalizing evidence that suggests these cosmic giants _____.

Which choice most logically completes the text?

- a. are actually not holes at all, but giant stars.

- b. may hold the keys to unveiling profound truths about the nature of space, time, and the fabric of reality

- c. are actually not real, but a figment of our imagination.

- d. are simply empty spaces in space.

20. Question

Category: SAT Expression of Ideas

While researching a topic, a student has taken the following notes:

- A significant period in history marked by the widespread transition from agrarian and handcraft-based economies to industrial and machine-based production methods.

- The Industrial Revolution originated in Britain during the late 18th century and gradually spread to other parts of Europe and North America.

- Key technological advancements that fueled the Industrial Revolution included the steam engine, which revolutionized transportation and powered factories, and the mechanization of textile production, which led to the rise of factories and mass production.

- The Industrial Revolution brought about profound social changes, such as urbanization, as people migrated from rural areas to cities in search of employment opportunities. It also led to the formation of the working class and the rise of labor movements.

- The shift to industrialization resulted in significant economic growth and increased productivity, but it also led to income inequality and exploitation of labor in many industries.

Given this information, which question effectively utilizes relevant details from the notes to accomplish the student's objective?

- a. "How did the Industrial Revolution impact the working class and labor movements?"

- b. "What were the key technological advancements during the Industrial Revolution that drove its growth?"

- c. "Can you explain the origin and spread of the Industrial Revolution?"

- d. "What were the consequences of the Industrial Revolution on income distribution and labor exploitation?"

21. Question

Category: SAT Standard English Conventions

In the vast expanse of the desert, extreme temperatures and arid conditions pose formidable challenges to survival. The relentless heat and dryness exert a profound impact on the physiological processes of desert-dwelling creatures _____ the intricate structures of their cellular proteins. However, these resilient organisms have evolved a remarkable adaptation to counter the harsh environmental stress: the chemical compound trehalose.

Which choice completes the text so that it conforms to the conventions of Standard English?

- a. particularly
- b. ; particularly
- c. , particularly
- d. : particularly

22. Question

Category: SAT Information & Ideas

Throughout the dynamic landscape of Post-War and Contemporary art, the year 2022 illuminated the United States as a towering presence. With a commanding presence on the global stage, the United States carved out the highest share of auction revenue, researchers' claim. This accomplishment speaks to the nation's unwavering influence and prominence within the art market. The United States' remarkable achievement in securing the top spot in Post-War and Contemporary art auction revenue is a testament to its thriving art ecosystem. The country's galleries, collectors, artists, and institutions have collectively contributed to this monumental success. Their dedication to fostering creativity, innovation, and artistic expression has propelled the nation to the forefront of the global art scene.

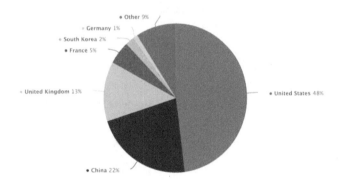

Geographical distribution of Post-War and Contemporary art auction revenue worldwide in 2022

Which choice best describes data from the table that supports the researchers' claim?

- a. The U.S. alone generated 48 percent of the global auction sales value in this art segment.
- b. China was the third leading market in 2022
- c. UK represented 22 percent of auction sales in the year 2022.
- d. The U.K. generated enough global auction sales value in this art segment.

23. Question

Category: SAT Information & Ideas

Several ancient manuscripts discovered within the archives of medieval monasteries reveal depictions of monks diligently transcribing texts illuminated by candlelight. Certain researchers have contended that the presence of illuminated manuscripts indicates the deep spiritual significance of this practice, as the manuscripts often contained religious texts. However, art historian Maria Rodriguez posits that illuminated manuscripts may also signify the reverence for knowledge and the pursuit of wisdom that monks held dear. The fact that such meticulous attention was given to the illumination of texts, therefore, _____.

Which choice most logically completes the text?

- a. demonstrates the monks' artistic inclinations and aesthetic preferences.

- b. underscores the practical necessity of proper lighting for transcription.

- c. highlights the monks' dedication to preserving historical records.

- d. reflects the harmonious fusion of artistic craftsmanship and spiritual devotion

24. Question

Category: SAT Standard English Conventions

In the realm of investment banking, derivatives are complex financial contracts _____, like stocks or bonds, but derive their value from other assets.

Which choice completes the text so that it conforms to the conventions of Standard English?

- a. They aren't primarily securities

- b. That are not simply securities

- c. Not being directly securities themselves

- d. Which aren't securities in the primary sense

25. Question

Category: SAT Craft & Structure

Modern art, often characterized by its abstract motifs and forms, is a realm where artists endeavour to transcend traditional aesthetic boundaries. Through their creations, they aim to evoke a profound, often _____ response from the observer, challenging conventional perceptions.

Which choice completes the text with the most logical and precise word or phrase?

- a. tepid

- b. visceral

- c. trite

- d. derivative

26. Question

Category: SAT Craft & Structure

Within the vast realm of art history, Impressionism stands as a testament to the radical departure from strict representational art. Originating in the 19th century, this movement was spearheaded by artists determined to capture fleeting moments, moods, and atmospheres. <u>This paradigm shift, rather than just a mere stylistic evolution, marked a profound philosophical divergence, emphasizing the subjective perception of reality.</u> Subsequent art movements, while varied in style and intent, owed much to the trailblazing spirit of the Impressionists.

Which choice best states the function of the underlined sentence in the text as a whole?

- a. It provides a chronological context for the Impressionist movement.

- b. It elaborates on the technical aspects of Impressionist art.

- c. It accentuates the significant philosophical change brought about by Impressionism.

- d. It draws a comparison between Impressionism and later art movements.

27. Question

Category: SAT Craft & Structure

Passage 1

In the dialectics of art history, one confronts the intricate dance of form and substance. The Byzantine epoch, for instance, illustrated this tension vividly in its mosaics and frescoes, where form often subsumed content, leading to an opulent display of intricate patterns often overshadowing the intended narrative. This phenomenon, emblematic of the era's proclivity for aesthetic grandeur, also mirrored the society's predisposition towards valuing surface manifestations, sometimes at the expense of intrinsic meaning.

Passage 2

Art's evolutionary trajectory has been punctuated by epochs wherein form and content engage in an enthralling tango. A salient example can be found in the modernist movement, where artists deliberately obfuscated content to emphasize form. This was not merely an aesthetic choice but a reflection of the zeitgeist—a world grappling with rapid change and seeking solace in the familiar, even if that meant prioritizing aesthetic over narrative. The inherent tension between appearance and essence, it seems, is perennial.

Based on the two passages, with which statement regarding the relationship between form and content in art would the author of Passage 1 most likely disagree with the author of Passage 2?

- a. Artistic epochs are defined by the interplay between form and content.

- b. The prioritization of form over content is a reflection of broader societal tendencies.

- c. All artistic movements prioritize form over content due to societal influences.

- d. Art evolves in response to societal changes, affecting the balance between form and narrative.

Solutions Reading & Writing Test 1 Module 2: Detailed Answer Explanations

1. Question

Category: SAT Expression of Ideas

D: Option D is the correct choice because it makes a generalization about the kind of work created by Leonardo da Vinci and Michelangelo.

The option states that their works are characterized by certain qualities, and that they often collaborated on their works. This generalization is supported by the information in the notes, and it provides a useful overview of the kind of work created by these two renowned artists.

2. Question

Category: SAT Standard English Conventions

C: Option C is the correct choice because the phrase "giving rise to a series of mesmerizing artworks" serves as an essential part of the sentence, providing crucial information about Mia Hernandez's creative process and the outcome of her artistic endeavors.

The phrase describes how she incorporates elements from Salvador Dali's works into her own creations and the effect it has on her art. This information is necessary to complete the sentence and convey the intended meaning.

3. Question

Category: SAT Standard English Conventions

A: Option A is the correct choice because the colon (:) is used to introduce additional information or a specific explanation of the preceding phrase.

In this context, the colon effectively introduces the explanation of the essence of their love, which is described as "a timeless bond of laughter, shared dreams, and unconditional support."

4. Question

Category: SAT Craft & Structure

B: In Text 1, the author focuses on the importance of early childhood education and highlights its numerous benefits, such as better academic performance and improved social and emotional skills.

The passage presents a positive viewpoint of early education, emphasizing its role in laying a strong foundation for future learning. In contrast, Text 2 acknowledges the potential limitations and challenges of early childhood education.

It raises concerns about the pressure and stress that formal education at a young age may put on children, especially if they are not developmentally ready for structured learning.

The passage also discusses the disparities in access to quality early education and highlights the need for addressing these challenges to ensure equal opportunities for all children.

4. Question

Category: SAT Information & Ideas

C: Option C is the correct choice because it is the most logical and appropriate way to complete the passage. The passage mentions that coral bleaching poses a "grave danger" to coral reefs, and it also mentions that this danger has "raised concerns" about the future of coral reefs.

5. Question

Category: SAT Expression of Ideas

D: Choice D is the correct choice because it indicates that in addition to human activities being major contributors to greenhouse gas emissions and climate change, natural factors also play a role in influencing the Earth's climate.

This transition helps to expand upon the causes of climate change and presents a more comprehensive understanding of the issue. It shows a logical connection between the two ideas, emphasizing that both human activities and natural factors contribute to the complexity of climate change.

6. Question

Category: SAT Information & Ideas

A: According to the passage, managers who were in quieter settings tended to make more conservative forecasts. The passage states that "managers who were exposed to higher levels of ambient noise in their work environment tended to make more conservative forecasts, while those in quieter settings exhibited a greater inclination towards optimistic predictions."

This means that the managers in quieter settings were more cautious and conservative in their financial predictions.

7. Question

Category: SAT Information & Ideas

D: Option D is correct because the table shows that the total retail sales of clothing, footwear, and leather goods in the European Union increased from 2011 to 2020, and the population of the European Union also increased over this period.

As a result, the retail sales of clothing, footwear, and leather goods per capita must have increased

8. Question

Category: SAT Information & Ideas

C: Option C is correct because This option is correct because it specifically mentions the importance of self-awareness and self-acceptance.

It also states that the journey of self-discovery is a transformative one, which is a key theme of the poem.

9. Question

Category: SAT Information & Ideas

A: Option A is correct because the bar graph shows that corn has the highest total production of any grain, with 1,151.36 million metric tons. This is followed by wheat, with 783.8 million metric tons, and rice, with 502.98 million metric tons.

10. Question

Category: SAT Craft & Structure

C: The passage is about the collaboration between local farmers and agricultural research institutions to develop innovative farming techniques. The passage begins by stating that local farmers and agricultural research institutions are forming mutually beneficial partnerships in crop experimentation and development. This is because both groups have something to offer the other: farmers have the knowledge and experience of growing crops in a particular region, while research institutions have the knowledge and expertise in agricultural science.

The passage then goes on to describe one such collaborative initiative between a farming cooperative and a renowned agricultural university. The passage concludes by stating that the farmers and scientists continue to work together in gathering and analyzing agricultural data. **Innovative** suggests that the farming techniques are new and groundbreaking. This is consistent with the passage, which states that the farmers and scientists are actively collaborating to co-create new farming techniques.

The word **innovative** means "new and original." This suggests that the farming techniques that are being co-created are new and groundbreaking. The word **innovative** is consistent with the tone and style of the passage. The passage is written in a serious and matter-of-fact tone, and the word **innovative** reflects this tone.

11. Question

Category: SAT Craft & Structure

D: This option is correct because it accurately summarizes the views of both authors. The author of Text 1 highlights the potential benefits of solar energy, while the author of Text 2 acknowledges the limitations and challenges of solar energy.

Both authors agree that solar energy has the potential to be a major source of clean energy, but it is important to be aware of its limitations and challenges.

12. Question

Category: SAT Craft & Structure

C: Option C is correct because the underlined sentence provides a contrast between the cityscape, which is described as "towering skyscrapers and concrete jungles," and George's artistic sensibilities, which are described as an appreciation for the harmony of architectural symmetry and design.

The underlined sentence provides a contrast between the cityscape and George's artistic sensibilities. The contrast is relevant to the passage because it helps to explain why George felt a sense of connection to the urban landscape, even though he was surrounded by towering skyscrapers and concrete jungles.

13. Question

Category: SAT Standard English Conventions

A: Option A is the correct choice because it uses the present perfect tense. The present perfect tense is used to describe actions that have been completed but have some connection to the present. In this sentence, the connection to the present is the fact that the GWC is still at the forefront of global conservation efforts.

Moreover, the subject of the sentence is plural in form "the GWC's scope and impact." Thus, the verb should also be plural in form "have."

14. Question

Category: SAT Information & Ideas

B: Option B is correct because it is based on direct evidence. The children's memories of John's parenting style are more likely to be accurate than their opinions or their feelings about his parenting style.

Additionally, the fact that the children have fond memories of John reading them bedtime stories and writing personalized stories for them suggests that he was an active and involved father.

15. Question

Category: SAT Information & Ideas

C: Option C is correct because it captures the full meaning of the text. The text describes hope as a bird that sings in the soul, and that it is strongest in the face of adversity. This suggests that hope is an intangible force that can help us to find strength and resilience in difficult times.

16. Question

Category: SAT Craft & Structure

B: The passage is about Dr. Alex Johnson, a former marine biologist who believes that humanity will eventually face the necessity of inhabiting environments beyond Earth's boundaries. He acknowledges that he cannot predict the exact timeline for this to happen, but he is confident that it will happen eventually. This conviction drives his passion for advocating further exploration and research missions to the depths of the ocean.

Option B is correct because it suggests that humanity will eventually face the necessity of inhabiting environments beyond Earth's boundaries. This is consistent with Dr. Johnson's belief that this is a certainty, but it also acknowledges that it may not happen immediately.

17. Question

Category: SAT Standard English Conventions

C: Option C is the correct choice because it uses a comma to separate the independent clause from the phrase "known as the flamboyant leafhopper." The comma is used to indicate that the phrase is an appositive, which is a noun phrase that renames or identifies another noun phrase.

The phrase "known as the flamboyant leafhopper" provides additional information about the peculiar creature.

18. Question

Category: SAT Information & Ideas

B: Option B is the correct choice because it logically completes the text and aligns with the context provided in the previous sentences. The passage discusses how black holes are captivating and puzzling entities in the cosmos. The phrase "As researchers delve deeper into the intricacies of black holes, they have uncovered tantalizing evidence" suggests that there is ongoing research and discoveries about black holes.

Therefore, the most fitting completion for the sentence would be an idea that builds on the notion of black holes holding profound truths. Option B states that black holes "may hold the keys to unveiling profound truths about the nature of space, time, and the fabric of reality," which fits coherently with the discussion of astronomers' tireless efforts to unlock the mysteries of the universe and the allure and fascination surrounding black holes.

19. Question

Category: SAT Expression of Ideas

A: Option A is the correct choice because it directly refers to the relevant information present in the student's notes. In the notes, it is mentioned that the Industrial Revolution brought about profound social changes, including the formation of the working class and the rise of labor movements.

The question "How did the Industrial Revolution impact the working class and labor movements?" aligns perfectly with this information, seeking to explore the effects of the Industrial Revolution on these specific social aspects.

21. Question

Category: SAT Standard English Conventions

C: Option C is the correct choice because it uses a comma to separate the independent clause from the phrase "particularly the intricate structures of their cellular proteins." The comma is used to indicate that the phrase is an aside or a parenthetical remark.

The phrase "particularly the intricate structures of their cellular proteins" provides additional information about the impact of the relentless heat and dryness on the physiological processes of desert-dwelling creatures.

22. Question

Category: SAT Information & Ideas

A: The pie chart clearly shows that the U.S. holds the maximum share in the art auction revenue in 2022. This further supports the claim made by the researchers in the passage.

23. Question

Category: SAT Information & Ideas

D: The passage discusses how illuminated manuscripts created by monks have multiple layers of significance, including the spiritual and knowledge-related aspects.

The completion "reflects the harmonious fusion of artistic craftsmanship and spiritual devotion" best captures the idea that the meticulous attention given to illuminating texts was a blend of both artistic skill and the monks' deep reverence for their spiritual and intellectual pursuits.

24. Question

Category: SAT Standard English Conventions

B: Choice B is the best answer. This option effectively introduces the main distinction of derivatives in a clear and concise manner.

Also, it is grammatically correct as a restrictive clause is being introduced.

25. Question

Category: SAT Craft & Structure

B: Choice B, "visceral," is the most fitting, as it implies a deep, emotional, or instinctual response, which aligns with artists' intentions in modern art.

26. Question

Category: SAT Craft & Structure

C: Option C is correct. The underlined sentence underscores the importance of Impressionism not just as an artistic style, but as a significant philosophical shift in understanding and representing reality.

The answer can also be arrived at by the process of elimination; the sentence does not highlight the "technical aspects" or the chronology of the Impressionist movement.

It is in the subsequent sentence that a comparison is suggested between Impressionism and later art movements. Thus, option C is correct.

27. Question

Category: SAT Craft & Structure

C: Both authors, in Passage 1 and Passage 2, allude to the relationship between form and content in art and how it reflects broader societal tendencies (Option B).

They also agree that the balance between form and narrative has been a defining feature of different artistic epochs (Option a. and that art often mirrors societal shifts (Option D).

However, Passage 1 specifically discusses the Byzantine epoch and how form dominated content in that period, while Passage 2 talks about the modernist movement with a similar dynamic.

The specificity of their examples suggests that they don't believe all artistic movements have this characteristic, making Option C the point of potential disagreement.

Practice Test 2 Module 1: Reading & Writing Practice Sets

The questions in this section cover a range of important reading and writing skills. Each

question consists of one or more passages, which may include a table or graphic. Read each passage and question carefully, and then choose the best answer to the question based on the passage(s).

All questions in this section are multiple-choice with four possible answers. Each question has a single best answer.

1. Question

Category: SAT Standard English Conventions

Existentialism, a philosophical stance _____, posits that individuals are free and responsible agents determining their own development through acts of the will.

Which choice completes the text so that it conforms to the conventions of Standard English?

- a. Emerging prominently during the 20th century

- b. It made its mark in the 20th century

- c. Where its significance rose in the 20th century

- d. The 20th century being its era of dominance

2. Question

Category: SAT Craft & Structure

Passage 1

In the lexicon of neoclassical economics, the assumption of 'rational actors' is sacrosanct. These actors, according to staunch neoclassical purists, are invariably guided by self-interest, striving to maximize their utility in a world of scarcity. The result is an equilibrium wherein supply meets demand at an optimal price point. Yet, many contemporaneous thinkers have critiqued this worldview, positing that the human psyche, with its panoply of emotions and biases, seldom behaves in strictly rational ways. Factors such as societal norms, behavioral idiosyncrasies, and even irrational exuberance can skew this pristine economic model.

Passage 2

Behavioral economics has ascended the academic echelons, challenging traditional economic models that have long dominated the discourse. At its heart, behavioral economics acknowledges the quixotic nature of human decision-making. It is a repudiation of the notion that individuals are consistently rational, devoid of biases or emotions. Instead, behavioral theorists argue that our decisions are frequently influenced by a mélange of cognitive biases, heuristics, and societal imperatives. This, in turn, has profound implications for understanding market dynamics and predicting consumer behavior.

Based on the perspectives elucidated in the passages, with respect to which statement would the author of Passage 1 most likely disagree with the author of Passage 2, regarding human decision-making in economic contexts?

- a. Behavioral idiosyncrasies play a pivotal role in human decision-making.

- b. Traditional economic models are infallible and universally applicable.

- c. Human emotions and biases frequently interfere with strictly rational decision-making.

- d. The ascent of behavioral economics challenges the dominance of neoclassical models.

3. Question

Category: SAT Craft & Structure

The global economy, an intricate web of trade, finance, and commerce, often exhibits signs of _____ fluctuations based on geopolitical events, natural disasters, or technological advancements. Predicting these changes is both art and science.

Which choice completes the text with the most logical and precise word or phrase?

- a. static

- b. indolent

- c. sismici

- d. tertiary

4. Question

Category: SAT Craft & Structure

Passage 1

The intricacies of fiscal policy, especially in an era where globalization is profoundly reshaping economic landscapes, are not to be understated. Consider, for instance, the ephemeral nature of capital flows which, when unbridled, can lead to volatile economic climates, often exacerbating recessions. Many economists, rooted in the Keynesian tradition, advocate for stringent regulation of these flows, ensuring that economies remain insulated from unpredictable global shifts. Such an approach, while seemingly antithetical to laissez-faire capitalism, is essential in preserving the integrity of national economies, especially those of developing nations.

Passage 2

Modern economies, as they grapple with the consequences of unfettered globalization, often face a conundrum. On one hand, the allure of unrestricted capital flows promises rapid economic growth and prosperity. On the other, the accompanying volatility can be detrimental. While the Keynesian paradigm suggests cloistering economies from such volatilities through regulation, it's imperative to recognize the benefits of a free market system. Restrictive measures can stifle innovation and deter foreign investments, potentially stagnating an economy. Striking a balance, therefore, is crucial.

Based on the given passages, which statement best describes a point of contention between the authors of Passage 1 and Passage 2 regarding fiscal policy in the face of globalization?

- a. The significance of Keynesian economics in modern fiscal policies.
- b. The inherent risks associated with unregulated capital flows in global economies.
- c. The potential adverse effects of stringent regulations on economic growth and innovation.
- d. The need to prioritize the protection of developing nations in the global economic landscape.

5. Question

Category: SAT Craft & Structure

Historical analyses of ancient civilizations frequently illuminate patterns of trade, warfare, and societal evolution. In contrast, the socio-cultural practices of these societies, such as rites, rituals, and folktales, often remain enshrouded in ambiguity. Yet, these esoteric traditions provide invaluable windows into the psyches of bygone populations, revealing much about their deepest fears, aspirations, and worldviews. Scholars, through rigorous ethnographic studies, attempt to decode these traditions, offering contemporary audiences a glimpse into ancient societal mores.

Which choice best states the function of the underlined sentence in the text as a whole?

- a. It emphasizes the importance of studying ancient economies and warfare.
- b. It delineates the methodologies employed by scholars in their research.
- c. It underscores the intrinsic value of understanding ancient socio-cultural practices.
- d. It elaborates on the reasons behind the ambiguity of ancient rites and rituals.

6. Question

Category: SAT Expression of Ideas

While diving deep into the annals of economic theory, Mark found these points of interest:

- Geoffrey Keynes was a renowned British economist.
- His theories were integral to shaping economic policies in the mid-20th century.
- Many of his works revolved around government intervention in markets.
- His paper 'Economic Webs' (1952) examined the role of governments in free markets.
- Another paper, 'Market Dynamics' (1955), explored the interplay of private enterprises and government regulations.

Mark desires to underscore a thematic link between the two papers. Which option employs the pertinent details from the notes to fulfill this purpose most effectively?

- a. 'Economic Webs' in 1952 and 'Market Dynamics' in 1955 are two of Keynes's celebrated works.

- b. Reflecting Keynes's focus, both 'Economic Webs' and 'Market Dynamics' delve into the interplay between markets and government interventions.

- c. Keynes, whose ideas shaped mid-20th-century economics, wrote 'Economic Webs' and 'Market Dynamics' to illustrate his economic theories.

- d. Keynes discussed free markets in 'Economic Webs' and shifted his focus to private enterprises in 'Market Dynamics'.

7. Question

Category: SAT Information & Ideas

In the intricate tapestry of global finance, the concept of neo-monetary fluidity stands juxtaposed with classical pecuniary paradigms. Historically, liquid assets adhered to predictable channels of flow, delineated largely by geopolitical exigencies and dictated by centralized fiscal authorities. However, the advent of digital currencies and decentralized finance, abbreviated as DeFi, has engendered a paradigmatic shift. This nascent financial model, emancipated from the tethering of traditional banking edifices, has proffered an arena for instantaneous, borderless transactions. Yet, while these innovations evoke a sense of unfettered financial liberation, they also plunge the domain into realms of unforeseen volatility. One cannot overlook the perturbations that these uncharted fiscal waters might usher, challenging the erstwhile stable notions of wealth, solvency, and economic equilibrium.

What can be inferred about the implications of the emergence of digital currencies and decentralized finance on global finance?

- a. Traditional banking structures are completely obsolete due to digital currencies.

- b. Neo-monetary fluidity ensures economic stability by mitigating volatility.

- c. The rise of digital currencies has ushered in new possibilities as well as challenges in the financial landscape.

- d. Centralized fiscal authorities have been entirely replaced by decentralized finance.

8. Question

Category: SAT Standard English Conventions

In ancient Mesopotamia, the cuneiform script, a system of writing using wedge-shaped symbols _____ was revolutionary for its time. This early form of writing paved the way for more advanced systems.

Which choice completes the text so that it conforms to the conventions of Standard English?

- a. employed on clay tablets;

- b. employed on clay tablets,

- c. employed on clay tablets:

- d. employed on clay tablets

9. Question

Category: SAT Information & Ideas

In the sprawling tapestry of global economic paradigms, the ephemeral dance of currency values continually perplexes financial savants. The ethereal fluctuation of these currencies, often obfuscated by transitory market sentiments, bears an uncanny resemblance to the capricious nature of Baroque art. Delving deeper, the art of economic prediction is not so much a science as it is an interpretation of kaleidoscopic patterns, much like discerning the variegated hues in a Byzantine mosaic. Indeed, the financial world, with its myriad intricacies, can be viewed as an expansive gallery where every fiscal decision is analogous to a painter's brushstroke, shaping the overarching narrative and influencing the global economic portrait.

Which one of the following statements, if true, would be the most direct extension of the arguments in the passage?

- a. The value of a currency is determined by the immutable laws of supply and demand.

- b. Baroque art, in its essence, reflects unpredictable and often whimsical patterns akin to market sentiments.

- c. Byzantine mosaics are simple and easily decipherable, unlike the world of finance.

- d. The unpredictability of global economic movements can be attributed solely to geopolitical events.

10. Question

Category: SAT Expression of Ideas

In her studies of literature, Anna came across insights about:

- Dr. Walter Hennessey, a pioneer of neo-modernist poetry.

- His writings have been recognized in France, Argentina, India, and South Korea.

- Hennessey's poems often use nature as an allegory for human emotions.

- His anthology, 'Whispers of Willow' (1997), draws parallels between trees and human despair.

- 'Dawn's Dew' (2000) employs the metaphor of morning dew to depict fleeting joy.

Anna intends to highlight a shared thematic element between the two anthologies. Which choice utilizes the relevant insights from her studies to most effectively accomplish this?

- a. Hennessey's writings, namely 'Whispers of Willow' and 'Dawn's Dew', have earned acclaim across several nations including France and India.

- b. Both 'Whispers of Willow' and 'Dawn's Dew' by Hennessey use elements of nature to symbolically represent profound human emotions.

- c. In 'Whispers of Willow', trees mirror human sorrow, while 'Dawn's Dew' poetically presents the ephemeral nature of happiness.

- d. Hennessey released 'Whispers of Willow' in 1997 and 'Dawn's Dew' three years later in 2000.

11. Question

Category: SAT Information & Ideas

In the panoramic landscape of philosophy, discussions surrounding the immutable nature of existential truths have captivated scholars since antiquity. The 'Metaphysical Construct', a lesser-known doctrine, avers that existential realities are neither transient nor shifting but are rather embedded in the continuum of the cosmos. A secondary school of thought, often described as the 'Temporal Paradigm', advocates that existential verities are fleeting, deeply intertwined with the epoch they emerge from. In essence, while the former perceives existence as a fixed tapestry woven into the vast expanse of the universe, the latter envisions it as ephemeral footnotes within ever-changing chapters of cosmic history.

Which of the following can be most accurately inferred from the passage?

- a. The Temporal Paradigm denies the long-term significance of existential truths.

- b. Existential realities are only appreciated by philosophical scholars.

- c. The Metaphysical Construct and the Temporal Paradigm have drastically different views on the permanence of existential realities.

- d. Philosophical doctrines seldom consider the impact of cosmic occurrences on existential truths.

12. Question

Category: SAT Standard English Conventions

The Keynesian economic theory, formulated during the tumultuous years of the Great Depression, _____ governments to actively participate in regulating economies to manage demand and prevent economic downturns.

Which choice completes the text so that it conforms to the conventions of Standard English?

- a. They profess an advocacy for

- b. This theory clearly endorses

- c. It has a lean towards compelling

- d. A clear emphasis by it is on urging

13. Question

Category: SAT Information & Ideas

The intricate interplay of socio-cultural matrices has perennially shaped human cognition, rendering most of our decisions a mere reflex to the ethereal cultural constructs. In philosophical realms, one might argue that individual agency is predominantly a mirage, a vestige of the overarching societal tapestry that persistently weaves its pattern on the loom of consciousness. Scholars of history can attest to the recurrent paradigms where civilizations, believing in their autonomy, were but marionettes dancing to the tunes of cultural imperatives. This pervasive influence of culture is not to be seen as deterministic, but rather as a subtle nudge, a gentle persuasion that shapes our ethos and, consequently, our actions.

Which one of the following, if true, would weaken the author's claims in the passage?

- a. Many individuals often make decisions that are contrary to their cultural norms.

- b. The loom of consciousness is predominantly influenced by genetic predispositions.

- c. Philosophical realms often exaggerate the influence of culture on human behavior.

- d. Scholars of history have observed consistent cultural influences across all civilizations.

14. Question

Category: SAT Standard English Conventions

In the realm of investment banking, derivatives are complex financial contracts _____, like stocks or bonds, but derive their value from other assets.

Which choice completes the text so that it conforms to the conventions of Standard English?

- a. They aren't primarily securities

- b. That are not simply securities

- c. Not being directly securities themselves

- d. Which aren't securities in the primary sense

15. Question

Category: SAT Expression of Ideas

During a discourse on influential figures in philosophy, Emma jotted down these observations:

- Immanuel Kant was a pivotal figure in modern Western philosophy.

- His writings have been interpreted and discussed extensively across continents.

- Kant was a proponent of the critique of pure reason.

- 'Aesthetics of Reality' (1783) delved into the nature of reality and perception.

- 'Moral Metrics' (1785) investigated the foundation of ethics and moral reasoning.

Emma aims to establish a link in Kant's methodological approach in these works. Which choice employs the information from the notes most effectively to achieve this?

- a. Kant's influential works such as 'Aesthetics of Reality' and 'Moral Metrics' were published in the 1780s.

- b. In 'Aesthetics of Reality' and 'Moral Metrics', Kant critically examines foundational concepts of reality and morality respectively, demonstrating his deep analytical approach.

- c. Kant, a cornerstone of Western philosophy, provided in-depth insights into reality in one work and ethics in another.

- d. Kant wrote 'Aesthetics of Reality' in 1783 and followed with 'Moral Metrics' in 1785, discussing different philosophical themes.

16. Question

Category: SAT Information & Ideas

In the esoteric realms of post-modernist historiography, a paradigmatic shift has been observed in the last half-century. This departure from conventional norms elucidates the increased weightage given to subaltern narratives over dominant discourses. These subaltern voices, which were previously muffled in the cacophony of grand historical retellings, have begun to find their place under the sun. Historians, armed with a more discerning and empathetic lens, are increasingly challenging the monolithic interpretations of history that have long held sway. It is in this landscape that the stories of marginalized communities, often devoid of written records and relegated to oral traditions, are gaining traction. This new wave, far from being a mere academic trend, reflects a societal recognition of the multiplicity of truths and the imperative to embrace diverse historical experiences.

Based on the passage, which of the following best captures the main idea conveyed by the author?

- a. Historians have always recognized the importance of marginalized voices in historical narratives.

- b. The significance of dominant discourses has completely diminished in contemporary historiography.

- c. Post-modernist historiography has opened avenues for diverse historical experiences previously overshadowed by dominant narratives.

- d. Oral traditions are the only reliable sources for understanding the history of marginalized communities.

17. Question

Category: SAT Standard English Conventions

The abstract expressionist movement, predominantly associated with New York in the mid-20th century. _____ provided a means to express themselves through spontaneous, non-representational means. This movement sought to bring the subconscious to the surface, allowing for a more direct interaction between artist and viewer.

Which choice completes the text so that it conforms to the conventions of Standard English?

- a. artists in this domain,
- b. artists in this domain:
- c. artists in this domain;
- d. artists in this domain

18. Question

Category: SAT Craft & Structure

Passage 1

In the dialectics of art history, one confronts the intricate dance of form and substance. The Byzantine epoch, for instance, illustrated this tension vividly in its mosaics and frescoes, where form often subsumed content, leading to an opulent display of intricate patterns often overshadowing the intended narrative. This phenomenon, emblematic of the era's proclivity for aesthetic grandeur, also mirrored the society's predisposition towards valuing surface manifestations, sometimes at the expense of intrinsic meaning.

Passage 2

Art's evolutionary trajectory has been punctuated by epochs wherein form and content engage in an enthralling tango. A salient example can be found in the modernist movement, where artists deliberately obfuscated content to emphasize form. This was not merely an aesthetic choice but a reflection of the zeitgeist—a world grappling with rapid change and seeking solace in the familiar, even if that meant prioritizing aesthetic over narrative. The inherent tension between appearance and essence, it seems, is perennial.

Based on the two passages, with which statement regarding the relationship between form and content in art would the author of Passage 1 most likely disagree with the author of Passage 2?

- a. Artistic epochs are defined by the interplay between form and content.
- b. The prioritization of form over content is a reflection of broader societal tendencies.
- c. All artistic movements prioritize form over content due to societal influences.
- d. Art evolves in response to societal changes, affecting the balance between form and narrative.

19. Question

Category: SAT Information & Ideas

In economic deliberations, the Quintessential Capital Theory (QCT) posits that the foundational underpinnings of capital aren't strictly tethered to tangible assets but also encompass intangible resources like knowledge and innovation. This departure from traditional economic paradigms, which prioritized physical assets, underscores the evolving dynamics of value creation in a post-modern era. Concurrently, the Ambient Economic Hypothesis (AEH) argues that modern economies, being deeply enmeshed in global networks, derive their strength not merely from domestic configurations but also from intricate external alliances and trade relationships. Distilled, while QCT underscores the augmented role of non-material assets, AEH emphasizes the external interconnections vital for contemporary economic prosperity.

Based on the passage, which of the following is a valid inference?

- a. Physical assets are now obsolete in determining economic value.
- b. Modern economies exclusively rely on international trade relationships.
- c. QCT and AEH both challenge certain traditional economic viewpoints.
- d. Knowledge and innovation are the sole determinants of economic strength in the post-modern era.

20. Question

Category: SAT Information & Ideas

In the annals of economic historiography, one discerns a subtle yet profound tension between proponents of free-market capitalism and those espousing regulated interventions. The inexorable momentum of globalization, bolstered by technological advancements, has dramatically widened the chasm between the affluent and the penurious. This glaring economic bifurcation, some scholars argue, is an unpalatable consequence of laissez-faire economics, wherein market forces operate uninhibited. Others, however, posit that periodic downturns, such as recessions, are not the mere offspring of deregulation but arise from multifarious factors, including geopolitical dynamics and fiscal imprudence. Yet, in the crucible of economic debate, the clarion call remains: is unfettered capitalism inherently predisposed to engendering disparities, or are there other shadowy actors at play?

Which one of the following, if true, would strengthen the author's claims in the passage?

- a. Historically, nations with strict economic regulations have witnessed more equitable wealth distribution among its citizens.

- b. The rise of global conglomerates can be attributed solely to the adoption of free-market principles in major economies.

- c. Some of the world's wealthiest individuals have amassed their fortunes primarily through leveraging geopolitical instabilities.

- d. Research has shown that fiscal imprudence is a minor factor when considering the root causes of major economic downturns.

21. Question

Category: SAT Information & Ideas

In the arcane echelons of modern financial epistemology, the oscillation between fiduciary responsibility and aggressive portfolio expansion represents a persistent conundrum. On one spectrum, adherence to prudent fiscal principles safeguards stakeholders' interests, often leading to the preservation of capital. Contrarily, the other spectrum extols the virtues of audacious financial adventurism, beckoning investors to venture into uncharted territories in the pursuit of maximized returns. This duality, subtly underpinned by the age-old battle between fear and greed, further finds its roots embedded in behavioral economics, suggesting a confluence of cognitive biases and emotional predilections influencing investment decisions. Indeed, the quest to harmonize these seemingly dichotomous paradigms continues to elude even the most seasoned financiers, necessitating a perpetually evolving strategic approach.

Which of the following inferences is most closely aligned with the underlying sentiment of the passage?

- a. Traditional fiscal principles are invariably superior to aggressive investment strategies.

- b. Investment decisions are purely mathematical and devoid of emotional influence.

- c. The balancing act between conserving capital and seeking high returns poses a complex challenge in modern finance.

- d. Behavioral economics has no significant role in shaping financial strategies.

22. Question

Category: SAT Expression of Ideas

While perusing the domain of modern management thought, Priya made the following notes:

- Dr. Leah Remington is a leading voice in contemporary management theory.

- Her work has inspired numerous companies to change their operational tactics.

- She emphasizes the value of collaborative leadership.

- Her book 'Synchronous Synergies' (2012) advocates for collaborative team structures.

- Another, 'Echelons of Empowerment' (2014), underscores leadership that empowers at all hierarchical levels.

Priya seeks to highlight the common leadership philosophy in these books. Which option most effectively uses the data from the notes to achieve this objective?

- a. Dr. Remington, through 'Synchronous Synergies' and 'Echelons of Empowerment', addresses management and leadership.

- b. Both 'Synchronous Synergies' and 'Echelons of Empowerment' convey Dr. Remington's endorsement of an inclusive, empowering form of leadership.

- c. Remington's 'Synchronous Synergies' speaks of team structures, while 'Echelons of Empowerment' focuses on hierarchical leadership.

- d. Dr. Remington's profound contributions in 2012 and 2014 revolutionized modern management principles.

23. Question

Category: SAT Standard English Conventions

During the Renaissance era, humanism, a cultural movement _____, emphasized the value and agency of human beings, often in opposition to religious dogma and institutionalized practices.

Which choice completes the text so that it conforms to the conventions of Standard English?

- a. Revolving around philosophical ideals

- b. It was centered around philosophical ideals

- c. Where the core was philosophical ideals

- d. Philosophical ideals were its crux

24. Question

Category: SAT Craft & Structure

Economic models, by their very nature, attempt to simulate the multifaceted dynamics of real-world markets. Though mathematical in structure, these models often incorporate sociological and psychological variables to enhance their accuracy. However, the inherent limitation of such models lies in their inability to predict anomalies arising from unforeseen geopolitical events. Policymakers, hence, often couple these models with qualitative analyses to ensure comprehensive economic forecasting.

Which choice best states the function of the underlined sentence in the text as a whole?

- a. It stresses the mathematical nature of economic models.

- b. It introduces the topic of geopolitical events and their impact.

- c. It critiques the methodology of policymakers in economic forecasting.

- d. It highlights a significant limitation of relying solely on economic models.

25. Question

Category: SAT Information & Ideas

The complexities of income inequality pose obtrusive challenges for both policymakers and global societies. The multidimensional conundrum of income inequality entails more than just a skewed distribution of wealth and resources. The adjunct issues of unequal opportunities and varying living standards barely receive the attention they should. Income inequality has grave and debilitating ramifications. Income disparities cause arrested social mobility and challenge political and economic stability. The crux of the problem is that there is no effective consensus, within and among economies, as to how to mitigate these inequalities, whether to optimize a "trade-off" approach or laissez-faire orientation, which can potentially topple anything orderly. The problem with aggressively redistributive policy is that it can stymy innovation.

Based on the passage, which of the following is a valid inference?

- a. Income inequality is impossible to resolve, thus contemplating economic policies around it would be futile.

- b. Modern economies must find an innovation-led solution for income inequality to be uprooted or at least mitigated.

- c. Divergent and often contentious perspectives on how to resolve income inequality are pervasive and unsettling.

- d. Income inequality cannot be tackled until its by-products are acknowledged and weeded out.

26. Question

Category: SAT Information & Ideas

In the intricate corridors of economic philosophy, the notion that wealth creation is an end in itself has often been juxtaposed against the belief that wealth is but a means to achieving societal harmony. The former, referred to as the 'Affluent Paradigm', posits that nations ought to maximize their economic output without undue emphasis on equitable distribution. Such an emphasis, it claims, would stifle innovation and deter capital accumulation. The latter perspective, termed the 'Equitable Doctrine', asserts that mere accumulation of capital, devoid of its just distribution, results in societal discord and eventually erodes the very fabric of a nation. The tug-of-war between these doctrines has shaped fiscal policies across epochs, influencing the destinies of nations and the prosperity of their denizens.

Which one of the following, if false, would weaken the author's claims in the passage?

- a. Societal harmony is invariably linked with the equitable distribution of wealth.

- b. Innovation is primarily driven by the promise of accruing wealth.

- c. Economic output is the primary determinant of a nation's prosperity.

- d. Fiscal policies have never been influenced by economic philosophies.

27. Question

Category: SAT Craft & Structure

Passage 1

Historical materialism, in its pursuit to comprehend societal evolution, predicates itself on the dialectical relationship between the superstructure and the base. The latter, comprising the forces and relations of production, plays a pivotal role in shaping the ideological and institutional framework—the superstructure. Nonetheless, one must caution against embracing a reductive determinism; the interplay isn't merely unidirectional. Though the base frequently molds the superstructure, the converse also holds veracity, albeit to a lesser degree.

Passage 2

Any rigorous analysis of societal change must be predicated upon the dynamics between the economic foundations and the emergent societal ideologies. These two, though intrinsically entwined, don't always exhibit a straightforward causal relationship. While the economic substrate often acts as a catalyst for societal norms, to argue that ideologies, in turn, never influence economic modalities would be an oversimplified postulation. The flux is cyclical, not linear.

Given the two passages, which of the following statements about the relationship between economic foundations and societal ideologies would the author of Passage 1 most likely disagree with the author of Passage 2?

- a. The economic base often plays a foundational role in shaping societal ideologies.

- b. The relationship between the economic structures and societal norms is bidirectional.

- c. Ideologies never have a significant influence on the economic modalities.

- d. The interplay between economic foundations and societal ideologies is complex and doesn't adhere to simple causality.

Solutions Reading & Writing Test 2 Module 1: Detailed Answer Explanations

1. Question

Category: SAT Standard English Conventions

A: Choice A is the best answer. It smoothly transitions from the philosophy's name to its primary belief, and the only choice that is grammatically and syntactically consistent.

2. Question

Category: SAT Craft & Structure

B: Both Passage 1 and Passage 2 acknowledge the significance of behavioral factors in economic decision-making, rendering Options A and C consistent with both perspectives.

Furthermore, they both recognize that behavioral economics stands in contrast to neoclassical models, as indicated in Option D.

However, Passage 1 does not assert the infallibility of traditional economic models but merely mentions the assumptions of neoclassical economics.

Passage 2 explicitly states that behavioral economics challenges traditional models.

Thus, Option B, suggesting the perfection and universal application of traditional models, is the correct answer.

3. Question

Category: SAT Craft & Structure

C: Choice C, "seismic," aptly conveys the idea of large, impactful shifts in the global economy, aligning with the influences mentioned like geopolitical events.

4. Question

Category: SAT Craft & Structure

C: While both authors discuss the challenges of managing capital flows in a globalized economy, they diverge in their perspectives on the implications of regulations.

The author of Passage 1 leans towards endorsing stringent regulations to protect economies, especially of developing nations, from the caprices of global shifts.

In contrast, the author of Passage 2 acknowledges the benefits of a free market and suggests that overly restrictive measures can hinder economic growth and innovation.

Therefore, Option C, which captures this nuanced disagreement on the potential drawbacks of stringent regulations, is the most accurate.

5. Question

Category: SAT Craft & Structure

C: Option C is correct. The underlined sentence emphasizes the deep insights that can be gleaned from studying the traditions of ancient civilizations, underscoring their significance.

The underlined sentence does not focus on the specific nature of these social practices; instead, its aim is to highlight that the real value of these rituals lies in the broad scope of what they revealed about the people—their fears, aspirations and worldviews.

Option C best encapsulates this idea.

6. Question

Category: SAT Expression of Ideas

B: Choice B is the best fit. It cites two of Keynes' seminal works: 'Economic Webs' and 'Market Dynamics'. These two works signify the consistent theme of the relationship between markets and government intervention across both papers.

7. Question

Category: SAT Information & Ideas

C: The crux of this query centers on understanding the impact of digital currencies and DeFi on the global financial system. Option C reflects the passage's sentiment, suggesting that while digital currencies present new opportunities ("an arena for instantaneous, borderless transactions"), they also introduce challenges ("realms of unforeseen volatility").

This is in line with the passage's nuanced view on the topic. While digital currencies and DeFi present groundbreaking possibilities in the financial world, they are accompanied by new challenges, as captured adeptly by Option C.

8. Question

Category: SAT Standard English Conventions

B: Choice B is the best answer. The comma correctly separates the specific information about the cuneiform script from the statement about its revolutionary nature.

9. Question

Category: SAT Information & Ideas

B: The central premise of the passage revolves around drawing parallels between art (specifically Baroque art and Byzantine mosaics) and the complexity of the financial world, particularly the unpredictability of currency values.

The passage makes a direct connection between the "capricious nature of Baroque art" and the unpredictable shifts in currency values.

This option, in echoing the unpredictable nature of Baroque art as being akin to market sentiments, is a direct continuation of the passage's argument and is neither Broad, Alien, Narrow, nor Extreme.

It retains the passage's nuanced examination of the unpredictable nature of both art and finance.

10. Question

Category: SAT Expression of Ideas

B: Option B best captures the essence of Hennessey's thematic unity in both anthologies: the use of nature as allegories for human emotions.

Option A also talks about the two works' immense popularity; however, the question elicits the exposition of a thematic link, and not the works' literary status.

11. Question

Category: SAT Information & Ideas

C: The question asks for an inference based on the details provided in the passage. The passage delineates that the 'Metaphysical Construct' views existential realities as fixed, while the 'Temporal Paradigm' sees them as ephemeral.

This sharp contrast suggests a drastic difference in their views on the permanence of existential truths. Option C aligns most coherently with the passage's information.

It encapsulates the contrasting views of the 'Metaphysical Construct' and the 'Temporal Paradigm' on existential realities.

12. Question

Category: SAT Standard English Conventions

B: Choice B is the best answer. It concisely and correctly states that the Keynesian economic theory endorses government intervention.

It is also grammatically most accurate and accessible in expression.

13. Question

Category: SAT Information & Ideas

A: The passage primarily highlights the significant influence of socio-cultural factors on human cognition and decision-making. The author even goes on to suggest that individual agency might often be a by-product of these factors.

If it's true that many individuals frequently make decisions that go against their cultural norms, it directly contradicts the author's central claim of cultural constructs influencing decisions.

Thus, Option A is the most potent in undermining the passage's central claim, emphasizing the overwhelming influence of culture on human cognition and decision-making.

14. Question

Category: SAT Standard English Conventions

B: Choice B is the best answer. This option effectively introduces the main distinction of derivatives in a clear and concise manner.

Also, it is grammatically correct as a restrictive clause is being introduced.

15. Question

Category: SAT Expression of Ideas

B: Choice B is the most accurate answer because it emphasizes Kant's analytical method in examining base concepts across both writings: 'Aesthetics of Reality' explores the nature of reality and perception, and 'Moral Metrics' navigate the framework of moral and ethical reasoning.

They illustrate Kant's theoretical and analytical preoccupations that inform his methodological approach.

16. Question

Category: SAT Information & Ideas

C: Option C posits that post-modernist historiography has created opportunities for diverse experiences previously overshadowed.

This is substantiated by the portion of the passage: "a paradigmatic shift increased weightage given to subaltern narratives over dominant discourses."

The narrative of the passage corroborates this, making it the most fitting choice. By understanding the subtleties of the passage and its emphasis on the evolving nature of historiography, it becomes evident that Option C aptly encapsulates the passage's main idea.

17. Question

Category: SAT Standard English Conventions

D: Choice D is the best answer. No punctuation is needed. 'Artist in this domain' is the main subject of the sentence, so using punctuations here would be grammatically incorrect.

18. Question

Category: SAT Craft & Structure

C: Both authors, in Passage 1 and Passage 2, allude to the relationship between form and content in art and how it reflects broader societal tendencies (Option B).

They also agree that the balance between form and narrative has been a defining feature of different artistic epochs (Option a. and that art often mirrors societal shifts (Option D).

However, Passage 1 specifically discusses the Byzantine epoch and how form dominated content in that period, while Passage 2 talks about the modernist movement with a similar dynamic.

The specificity of their examples suggests that they don't believe all artistic movements have this characteristic, making Option C the point of potential disagreement.

19. Question

Category: SAT Information & Ideas

C: The passage deals with intricate economic theories and their deviations from older paradigms. Both the QCT and AEH present ideas that seem to diverge from traditional economic views: QCT brings in the importance of intangibles, while AEH stresses on the role of external interconnections.

The passage says, "This departure from traditional economic paradigms..." and discusses the Ambient Economic Hypothesis in a similar vein, indicating that both theories challenge traditional viewpoints.

On careful analysis, Option C appears to be the most valid inference as it encapsulates the essence of the passage in highlighting the progressive nature of the two discussed theories, QCT and AEH, in challenging certain traditional economic paradigms.

20. Question

Category: SAT Information & Ideas

A: The crux of the passage revolves around the ongoing debate regarding the role of free-market capitalism and its impact, specifically concerning economic disparities.

Option A implies that strict economic regulations, the antithesis of laissez-faire economics, lead to more equitable wealth distribution. This strengthens the author's assertion regarding the "unpalatable consequence of laissez-faire economics" and the resultant "economic bifurcation."

Hence, this option acts in favor of the claim that unregulated markets can lead to disparities. It isn't Broad, Alien, Narrow, or Extreme; it directly correlates with the passage's theme.

21. Question

Category: SAT Information & Ideas

C: Option C highlights the intricate challenge in modern finance of finding a balance between safeguarding capital and chasing higher returns.

This aligns with the narrative of the passage, particularly where it mentions the "oscillation between fiduciary responsibility and aggressive portfolio expansion" and the "duality" present in finance.

Hence, this is the most appropriate choice. To synthesize, the passage delves deep into the intricacies of modern finance, oscillating between caution and risk.

The essence of this balance and its challenges is best captured by Option C.

22. Question

Category: SAT Expression of Ideas

B: Choice B is the most suitable since it encapsulates the shared philosophy of inclusive leadership across both books

23. Question

Category: SAT Standard English Conventions

A: Choice A is the best answer. It provides a succinct introduction to humanism's emphasis on philosophical ideals. It is also the most grammatically and syntactically accurate answer because of its choice of modifier.

24. Question

Category: SAT Craft & Structure

D: Option D is correct. The underlined sentence serves to identify a critical drawback of economic models: their inability to account for unpredictable geopolitical occurrences.

Only option D captures the essence of the underlined sentence. The other options highlight the crux of either the preceding and or the subsequent sentences.

25. Question

Category: SAT Information & Ideas

C: The passage highlights the complexity and not the 'presumed' impossibility of resolving income inequality issues. One aspect of the complexity emphatically alluded to in the passage is the how there is no consensus on a viable solution to this universal problem.

Thus, on careful analysis, Option C appears to be the most valid inference as it encapsulates the aforementioned idea.

26. Question

Category: SAT Information & Ideas

D: This passage delves deep into economic philosophies and their implications on fiscal policies and the well-being of nations. It provides a contrast between two schools of thought: the 'Affluent Paradigm' and the 'Equitable Doctrine'.

The passage explicitly states, "The tug-of-war between these doctrines has shaped fiscal policies across epochs." If it were false that fiscal policies have never been influenced by economic philosophies, it would directly contradict and thus weaken the claim made in the passage.

From a thorough analysis, Option D stands out as the one that, if proven false, would substantially weaken the author's claims in the provided passage.

27. Question

Category: SAT Craft & Structure

C: Both authors, in Passage 1 and Passage 2, acknowledge the complexity of the relationship between economic structures (or bases) and societal ideologies (or superstructures).

They both concur that the economic base often shapes societal ideologies (Option A), that the relationship is bidirectional (Option B), and that this relationship is intricate (Option D).

However, Passage 1 explicitly mentions that the superstructure can influence the base "to a lesser degree," while Passage 2 states that ideologies don't always influence economic structures but doesn't rule out their influence entirely.

The only option suggesting an absolute stance, which the author of Passage 1 would likely disagree with, given the more nuanced stance they've taken, is Option C.

Practice Test 2 Module 2: Reading & Writing Practice Sets

The questions in this section cover a range of important reading and writing skills. Each

question consists of one or more passages, which may include a table or graphic. Read each passage and question carefully, and then choose the best answer to the question based on the passage(s).

All questions in this section are multiple-choice with four possible answers. Each question has a single best answer.

1.Question

Category: Standard English Conventions

Overfishing is a serious threat to our seafood supply. It's not just about the fish we eat; it's also about the entire marine ecosystem. When we overfish, we disrupt the balance of the ocean. This can lead to the extinction of certain _____ can have a domino effect on other marine life. If we don't take action now, we may not have enough seafood to meet the growing demand in the future.

Which choice completes the text so that it conforms to the conventions of Standard English?

- a: species-which
- b: species:which
- c: species; which
- d: species, which

2.Question

Category: Expression of Ideas

While researching a topic, a student has taken the following notes:

- The Treaty of Kiel, signed in 1814, ended hostilities between the United Kingdom and Sweden.

- It allowed Norway to enter a personal union with Sweden, ending Denmark-Norway's union.

- The treaty had an indirect impact on Asia, particularly on the British colonies.

- It allowed the British to focus more on their Asian colonies, which led to the expansion of British imperialism in Asia.

The student wants to explain how the Treaty of Kiel influenced British imperialism in Asia. Which choice most effectively uses relevant information from the notes to accomplish this goal?

- a: The treaty of Kiel ended the union of Denmark-Norway, allowing Norway to enter a personal union with Sweden

- b: The treaty of Kiel, signed in 1814, ended hostilities between the United Kingdom and Sweden, leading to changes in the European geopolitical landscape

- c: By endid hostilities with Sweden in the Treaty of Kiel, the United Kingdom was able to redirect its focus to its Asian colonies, leading to the expansion of British Imperialism in Asia
- d: The treaty of Kiel had a significant impact on Asia, as it led to the expansion of several European colonies

3.Question

Category: Information and Ideas

The Southern Ocean is crucial for global climate due to its unique oceanic and atmospheric properties. It acts as a vast sink, absorbing about 40% of anthropogenic carbon dioxide and 75% of excess heat trapped in the Earth's atmosphere. The Southern Ocean's deep water circulation also distributes these absorbed elements globally, impacting weather patterns and sea levels. However, drastic climate changes could destabilize this ocean's role, posing a significant threat to global climate stability.

Which choice best states the main purpose of the text?

- a. to provide a detailed account of the atmospheric and oceanic properties of the Southern Ocean
- b. To argue that the Southern Ocean is the only ocean that has a signficant impact on global climate
- c.to explain the various weather patterns influenced by the Southern Ocean's deep water circulation
- To emphasize the critical role of the Southern Ocean in global climate regulation and the potential risks posed by climate change

4.Questions

Category: Information and Ideas

Ant colonies exhibit complex social structures, with each ant having a specific role. Workers, the most numerous, gather food and maintain the colony. Soldiers, larger and stronger, protect the colony. The queen, the only fertile female, lays all the eggs. Some scientists believe the queen controls the colony through pheromones. However, a study by Dr. Eleanor Spence suggests otherwise. She observed that when the queen's pheromone was artificially introduced, the ants did not respond as if the queen was present. Dr. Spence hypothesizes that ants communicate through a more complex system of signals.

Which of the following observations, if true, would most directly undermine Dr. Spence's hypothesis?

- a. In another study, ants were observed to respond differently to the pheromones of their own queen compared to those of a different colony's queen
- b. In a separate experiment , ants were sen to change thei behavior significantly after exposure to an artificial mix of signals identical to the queen's
- c. In a different colony, it was observed that the removal of the queen did not disrupt the colony's functioning signficantly
- d.In colonies where artificial pheromenos were introduced, ants were seen to exhibit increased levels of aggression

5.Question

Category: Craft and Structure

_____ in seed dispersal, which is vital for the survival of many plant species. They consume fruits and inadvertently carry the seeds within their digestive system. These seeds are then excreted in different locations, often far from the parent plant. This process helps in the propagation of plant species and maintains biodiversity.

Which choice completes the text so that it conforms to the conventions of Standard English?

- a.Birds play a crucial role

- b.Birds played a crucial role
- c.Birds plays a crucial role
- d. Birds playing a crucial role

6.Question

Category: Craft and Structure

William Faulkner's The Sound and the Fury is a paragon of modernist literature, with its groundbreaking narrative techniques and unconventional structure. The novel is divided into four distinct sections, each narrated by a different member of the Compson family. This fragmentation, combined with Faulkner's dense, stream-of-consciousness prose, renders the novel a complex, often _____ labyrinth that challenges even the most astute readers. Despite the initial difficulty, those who manage to navigate through its complexities are rewarded with a profound exploration of human nature and the inexorable passage of time.

Which choice completes the text with the most logical and precise word or phrase?

- a.irrelevant
- b.impenetrable
- c. immaculate
- d.inexpensive

7.Question

Category: Craft and Structure

In the 1930s, anthropologist Margaret Mead conducted extensive ethnographic research on adolescent behavior in Samoa and New Guinea; this _____ work involved learning local languages, observing cultural practices, and interviewing many youths and families.

Which choice completes the text with the most precise and relevant word or phrase?

- a. cursory
- b. meticulous
- c.intermittent
- d. theoretical

8.Question

Category: Information and Ideas

During the War of 1812, the United States faced significant challenges against the British naval power. Despite their lack of maritime strength, the Americans held their ground using innovative defensive strategies. One of these was the construction of coastal fortifications, which proved crucial in repelling naval invasions. The Battle of Fort McHenry, where the American forces successfully resisted a British attack, stands as a testament to the effectiveness of these fortifications, and inspired the writing of 'The Star-Spangled Banner.'

Which choice best states the main purpose of the text?

- a.To argue that the war of 1812 was primarily a naval conflict between the United States and Britain
- b. To highlight the significance of coastal fortifications and their role in the America defense during the War of 1812
- c.To provide a comprehensive history of the war of 1812, focusing on the key battles and outcomes
- d. To argue that the battle of Fort McHenry was the most pivotal event of the war of 1812

9.Question

Category: Information and Ideas

Researcher	Year	Animal Species	Test Result
Smith	2015	Rats	50% Accuracy
Johnson	2019	Monkeys	80% Accuracy
Williams	2017	Mice	60% Accuracy
Jones	2020	Rabbits	70% Accuracy

The use of animals in quality control tests has been a topic of great debate among scientists. Some argue that animals provide a highly accurate model for human health risks, while others contend that the results can vary greatly depending on the animal species used. This has led to a significant variation in test results across different studies, creating uncertainty in the field.

Which choice best describes data from the table that support the contention that the results can vary greatly depending on the animal species used?

- a. The study by Smith used rats and produced the highest accuracy in results, whereas the study by Johnson used monkeys and produced the lowest accuracy

- b.The test results produced by Johnson and by Smith were substantially different from each other, even though both studies were conducted in a three-year period

- c.The accuracy of the results produced by Williams was similar to that of the results produced by Jones, suggesting that the species of animal has a little impact on the test results

- d.The study by Smith showed a lower accuracy than the study by Williams, even though both of them used rodents for their test

10. Question

Category: Standard English Conventions

Neil Gaiman is a renowned British author known for his work in various genres. He has written numerous novels, comic books, and screenplays. His works often blend elements of fantasy, horror, and mythology. Gaiman's unique storytelling style has earned him a dedicated fanbase and numerous awards. Despite his success, he _____ the boundaries of his craft, constantly seeking new ways to engage his readers.

Which choice completes the text so that it conforms to the conventions of Standard English?

- a.continued to push
- b.continue to push
- c.continuing to push
- d.continues to push

11.Question

Category: Information and Ideas

Johann Gottlieb Fichte was a German philosopher who became a founding figure of the philosophical movement known as German idealism, which developed from the theoretical and ethical writings of Immanuel Kant. Fichte's philosophy, known as Wissenschaftslehre or science of knowledge, was a reaction to Kant's critical philosophy. He sought to develop a concept of the self that was not grounded in empirical observations, but rather in the self's activity of positing itself. Fichte's radical emphasis on the primacy of the ego resonated with many thinkers, influencing the development of German Romanticism. However, critics have pointed out that this emphasis on the self could potentially lead to an unchecked individualism and a disregard for the community. This critique has led to a reconsideration of Fichte's philosophy in the light of _____.

Which choice most logically completes the text?

- a.The contemporary discourse on the balance between individual rights and social responsibilities

- b.The ongoing debate about influence of German idealism on modern scientific thought

- c.the recent re-evaluation of Kant's philosophy in academic circles
- d. the modern exploration of the concept of self in the fields of psychology and neuroscience

12.Question

Category: Information and Ideas

The following lines are from Robert Browning's poem "Meeting at Night": The grey sea and the long black land; And the yellow half-moon large and low; And the startled little waves that leap In fiery ringlets from their sleep, As I gain the cove with pushing prow, And quench its speed i' the slushy sand. Then a mile of warm sea-scented beach; Three fields to cross till a farm appears; A tap at the pane, the quick sharp scratch And blue spurt of a lighted match, And a voice less loud, thro' its joys and fears, Than the two hearts beating each to each!

Which choice best describes the overall structure of the text?

- a.It conveys a mysterious mood through descriptive imagery
- b.it chronicles a journey from expectant to disappointed
- c. It contrasts dark, somber settings with moments of energy
- d. It depicts a lover sneaking across a dim, quiet landscape

13.Question

Category: Expression of Ideas

While researching a topic, a student has taken the following notes:

- African sculpture has significantly influenced the development of modern art globally.

- Pablo Picasso, a renowned modern artist, was profoundly inspired by African sculpture.

- African masks and figurines were referenced in Picasso's revolutionary painting, Les Demoiselles d'Avignon.

- The abstraction and stylization found in African sculpture directly challenged and expanded Western ideas of representation and form.

- The 'primitive' aesthetic of African sculpture has been both admired and criticized for its influence on Western modernism.

The student wants to illustrate how African sculpture has redefined Western ideas of representation and form. Which choice most effectively uses relevant information from the notes to accomplish this goal?

- a.African sculpture has influenced the development of modern art globally, particularly through the works of Pablo Picasso

- b.Pablo Picasso's painting, Les Demoiselles d'Avignon, references African masks and figurines

- c. The "primative" aestethic of African sculpture has been both admired and criticized

- d. Through its observation and stiylization, African sculpture challenged and expanded Western ideas of representation and form, influencing artists like Picasso

14.Question

Category: Standard English Conventions

In Ancient Roman literature, comedy played a significant role. It was not only a source of entertainment, but also a means of social commentary. Through humor, authors could subtly criticize societal norms and political issues. Comedy was a tool for _____, and it was often used to mock the powerful and the corrupt. This form of literature was popular among the masses, and it had a profound impact on the culture and society of Ancient Rome.

Which choice completes the text so that it conforms to the conventions of Standard English?

- a.satire or parody
- b.satire and parody
- c.satire, parody
- d.satire, parody

15 Question

Category: Information and Ideas

Animal	Year	Method	Impact on Urban Planning (Units)
Deer	2015	Population Density	30-50
Raccoons	2018	Habitat Distribution	15-35
Birds	2012	Biodiversity Index	60-80
Squirrels	2019	Population Density	25-45

Urban planning has long been influenced by the population of animals in the area. Different species have different impacts on planning decisions, such as the placement of roads, parks, and residential areas. Studies have shown that the presence of certain animals can significantly affect these decisions. However, the methods used to quantify the impact of these animals may vary, leading to different results.

Which choice best describes data from the table that support the idea that the method used can significantly affect the quantified impact of animals on urban planning?

- a. The studies on Deer and Squirrels used the Population Density method and produced similar impacts, while the studies on Raccoons and Birds used different methods and produced distinctly different impacts.

- b. The study by Raccoons in 2018 used Habitat Distribution and produced the smallest impact, while the study on Birds in 2012 used Biodiversity Index and produced the largest impact.

- c. The study on Deer in 2015 produced a higher impact than Squirrels in 2019, even though both used the same method of Population Density.

- d. The impact produced by the Birds study in 2012 exceeded the impact produced by the Raccoons study in 2018, even though both used different methods.

16.Question

Category: Information and Ideas

Albert Einstein is often regarded as the father of modern physics. He is best known for developing the theory of relativity, which revolutionized the science of physics. However, what is often overlooked is his philosophical ideas. Einstein believed that the laws of physics are merely descriptions of how matter behaves under certain conditions. He asserted that these laws do not provide a complete understanding of the universe but rather serve as a useful tool for predicting phenomena. Furthermore, Einstein contended that the concept of space and time are not absolute but relative to the observer. Despite his remarkable contributions to science, Einstein remained humble. He believed that his theories were not the final word on the nature of reality, but merely stepping stones towards a more comprehensive understanding of the universe. This humility, coupled with his relentless pursuit of knowledge, underscores a critical aspect of Einstein's philosophical outlook: _____.

Which choice most logically completes the text?

- a.his unwavering belief in the supremacy of the human mind over the mysteries of the universe.

- b. his assertion that relativity is the only valid framework for understanding the nature of reality.

- c. his rejection of the notion that the laws of physics can provide a comprehensive understanding of the universe.

- d. his conviction that scientific knowledge is always evolving and no single theory can claim to have all the answers.

17.Question

Category: Standard English Conventions

Amerigo Vespucci, an Italian explorer, embarked on several expeditions to the New World in the late 15th and early 16th centuries. His journeys, unlike those of Christopher Columbus, were primarily focused on exploring the South American coast. Vespucci's accounts of his travels were widely circulated in _____ a result, a German cartographer named Martin Waldseemüller suggested the name 'America' for the New World in honor of Vespucci. This suggestion was accepted, and thus, the continents were named.

Which choice completes the text so that it conforms to the conventions of Standard English?

- a. Europe, as
- b. Europe; as
- c. Europe: as
- d.Europe, and as

18.Question

Category: Craft and Structure

Text 1

Art historian, Clara Simmons, suggests that Rembrandt's paintings are notable for their innovative use of light and shadow. She argues that Rembrandt was ahead of his time in using contrast to create depth and to focus the viewer's attention on key elements of his paintings.

Text 2

Contrarily, art critic Benjamin Fielding argues that Rembrandt's true innovation was not his use of light and shadow, but rather, his ability to capture emotion and portray the human condition. Fielding contends that while Rembrandt's use of contrast was certainly skillful, it was his exceptional observation of human emotion that truly set him apart.

Based on the texts, how would Benjamin Fielding (Text 2) most likely respond to the "innovative use of light and shadow" discussed by Clara Simmons (Text 1)?

- a. By pointing out that Rembrandt's use of contrast was merely a technique to enhance the portrayal of emotional depth in his subjects
- b. By explaining that Rembrandt's use of light and shadow was a common technique among his contemporaries and not particularly innovative
- c. By emphasizing that the real innovation in Rembrandt's work was his ability to capture emotion, overshadowing his use of light and shadow
- d. By suggesting that the light and shadow in Rembrandt's paintings were secondary techniques applied to supplement his primary focus on the human condition

19.Question

Category: Craft and Structure

Text 1

The Treaty of Kanagawa, signed in 1854, was a pivotal moment in Japan's history. It marked the end of Japan's 200-year-old policy of national seclusion, by opening the ports of Shimoda and Hakodate to American vessels. It was negotiated by Matthew Perry, a commodore in the U.S. navy, who threatened Japan with military action if they did not agree to open their ports.

Text 2

Historian John Marshall argues that while the Treaty of Kanagawa is often viewed as a forced agreement, it was also seen by some Japanese leaders as an opportunity. They believed that opening up to foreign trade would enable Japan to acquire the technology and knowledge to stand up against Western powers in the future.

Based on the texts, how would John Marshall (Text 2) most likely respond to the "forced agreement" perspective discussed in Text 1?

- a. By suggesting it was a strategic choice, as it allowed Japan to gain access to Western technology and knowledge.

- b. By asserting that the Treaty was a clear violation of Japan's sovereignty and should have been resisted at all costs.

- c. By offering a nuanced view, arguing that while Japan was coerced, some leaders saw the Treaty as an opportunity to strengthen Japan.

- d.By arguing that the Treaty was a result of Japan's weaker military power and had little to do with their willingness to open up.

20.Question

Category: Information and Ideas

In ancient Greek philosophy, lyric poetry held a distinct position. Famed philosophers like Socrates and Plato often referred to it in their dialogues. Plato, in particular, despite his notorious criticism of poetry's emotional appeal, acknowledged the didactic potential of lyric poetry. He conceded that it could be used to instill moral values and virtues in the society. This perspective, however, was not without contradictions. For instance, in 'The Republic', Plato proposed the censorship of poetry, arguing that it could negatively influence society's moral fabric. Yet, in 'Phaedrus', he alluded to the transformative power of poetic inspiration, suggesting that it could lead to truth. These incongruities in Plato's views reveal an underlying tension in the ancient Greeks' understanding of lyric poetry. They grappled with the question of whether poetry, despite its emotive power, could be a reliable conduit of _____.

Which choice most logically completes the text?

- a.historical narratives that provide insights into the cultural practices of ancient Greek society.

- b.scientific knowledge to the wider public, aiding in the dissemination of technological advancements.

- c. philosophical truth, effectively communicating complex ideas and promoting intellectual discourse.

- d.political propaganda, influencing public opinion and swaying the decision-making process.

21.Question

Category: Craft and Structure

Ocean currents, the continuous movement of water in the Earth's ocean, play a significant role in shaping the marine ecosystem. This movement of water, loaded with nutrients, helps the flourishing of marine life. However, the impact of these currents is a double-edged sword. While they provide sustenance and facilitate migration, they also cause drastic changes in the habitat, making it challenging for certain species to _____. Despite these challenges, marine species display exceptional adaptability, evolving to survive and thrive in the ever-changing marine environment.

Which choice completes the text with the most logical and precise word or phrase?

- a. acclimate
- b. proliferate
- c. navigate
- d.habituate

22.Question

Category: Craft and Structure

The following text is adapted from Daniel Defoe's 'Robinson Crusoe.' In this passage, Crusoe reflects on his life after being stranded on a deserted island. I have often looked back with a sigh at that lonesome island when I have been at sea. I considered it my kingdom, where I was an absolute and rightful ruler. I had all the human necessities at my disposal, and the island was not so bad after all. In fact, it often seemed to me like a paradise, where I was safe from the dangers of the world and lived in peace.

Which choice best states the main purpose of the text?

- a. To illustrate Crusoe's deep longing to return to the civilized world and his dislike for the island.

- b. To convey Crusoe's complex feelings towards the island, seeing it both as a lonely place and a safe haven.

- c. To indicate Crusoe's regret for being stranded on the island and his desperate need for human company.

- d. To emphasize Crusoe's dissatisfaction with his life on the island and his desire for a luxurious life.

23.Question

Category: Information and Ideas

William Blake was an influential figure in the Romantic art movement of the 18th and 19th centuries. His work, often characterized by imaginative and symbolic elements, broke away from the classical norms. Blake had a profound impact on Romanticism, emphasizing the importance of individual imagination as a critical aspect of the human experience. His poetic and pictorial works, such as Songs of Innocence and of Experience, were marked by a revolutionary spirit, challenging the established religious and social orders.

Which of the following, if true, would best support the assertion that Blake's work had a revolutionary impact on the Romantic art movement?

- a.Blake's work was often critiqued by contemporary artists for its departure from traditional artistic conventions.

- b. Many of Blake's works were not widely recognized until after his death, reflecting a lack of understanding from his contemporaries.
- c.Blake was known for his eccentric lifestyle, which often reflected in the unconventional themes of his work.

- d.Several prominent artists of the Romantic movement, including Samuel Taylor Coleridge and William Wordsworth, publicly acknowledged Blake's influence on their work.

24.Question

Category: Expression of Ideas

Edward Weston, one of the most influential American photographers of the 20th century, was known for his meticulously composed, sharply focused images of natural forms, landscapes, and nudes. His work significantly transformed the aesthetic standards of American photography, moving away from the soft-focus pictorialism that was prevalent during his time. _____ he emphasized the potential of the camera to create images of stark precision and tonal range, which was a radical departure from the prevailing norms.

Which choice completes the text with the most logical transition?

- a. Surprisingly,
- b. Similarly,
- c.However,
- d.Moreover,

25.Question

Category: Craft and Structure

Text 1

Organ-on-a-chip (OOC) technology has shown promise in modelling human physiology in vitro. Scientists believe it can reduce reliance on animal models, which often lack predictive validity for human responses. However, some researchers question its scalability and universal applicability, citing the complexity of human biology and the need for multi-organ systems for accurate modelling.

Text 2

Biomedical engineer, Dr. Jane Foster and her team propose a hybrid approach. They suggest combining OOC technology with computational modelling to address the issue of scalability and complexity. This approach would allow for the integration of multi-organ systems in the chip models, overcoming the limitations of standalone OOC technology.

Based on the texts, how would Dr. Jane Foster and her team (Text 2) most likely respond to the "concerns about scalability and universal applicability" of OOC technology discussed in Text 1?

- a. By asserting that concerns about scalability and universal applicability of OOC technology are unfounded as animal models are more problematic.

- b. By suggesting that the limitations of OOC technology are not significant enough to deter its use in modelling human physiology.

- c. By arguing that the concerns about scalability and universal applicability of OOC technology are due to a lack of understanding of the technology.

- d.By advocating for a hybrid approach that combines OOC technology with computational modelling to overcome the scalability and complexity issues.

26.Question

Category: Craft and Structure

The impact of Roman literature on Western civilization is profound. The Romans, through their literature, have shaped the way we think, write, and communicate. Their works, such as the Aeneid, have been studied and revered for centuries. _____ complex ideas and emotions through their writing has had a lasting impact on literature and culture worldwide.

Which choice completes the text so that it conforms to the conventions of Standard English?

A: The Romans' abilities to convey

B: The Romans' ability conveying

C: The Romans' ability to convey

D: The Romans' ability for conveying

27. Question

Category: Information and Ideas

In T.S. Eliot's modernist poem "The Love Song of J. Alfred Prufrock," the speaker expresses feelings of isolation and anxiety in the face of an uncertain, fragmented modern world. Referring to "the chambers of the sea," Eliot writes about Prufrock's meditations, implying that he feels detached and lonely.

Which quotation from the poem most effectively illustrates the claim?

- a. "I should have been a pair of ragged claws / Scuttling across the floors of silent seas."

- b. "I grow old... I grow old... / I shall wear the bottoms of my trousers rolled."

- c. "In the room the women come and go / Talking of Michelangelo."

- d. "We have lingered in the chambers of the sea / By sea-girls wreathed with seaweed red and brown."

Solutions Reading & Writing Test 2 Module 2: Detailed Answer Explanations

1. Question

Category: SAT Standard English Conventions

Correct Answer: D

Explanation: Choice D is correct because the comma is used to introduce a nonrestrictive clause, which adds extra information to the sentence but is not essential to its meaning. The other choices do not use the correct punctuation to introduce this type of clause.

2. Question

Category: Expression of Ideas

Correct Answer: C

Explanation: Choice C is correct because it explains how the Treaty of Kiel influenced British imperialism in Asia by allowing the UK to focus more on its Asian colonies.

3. Question

Category: Information and Ideas

Correct Answer: D

Explanation: Choice D is the best answer because it accords with the main purpose of the text, which is to highlight the significant role of the Southern Ocean in regulating global climate and the potential threats climate change could impose on this role. The text discusses how the Southern Ocean absorbs a significant portion of carbon dioxide and excess heat, influences weather patterns and sea levels through its deep water circulation, and how drastic climate changes could destabilize these functions.

4.Questions

Category: Information and Ideas

Correct Answer: B

Explanation: Option B is correct because it presents a finding that, if true, would weaken Dr. Spence's hypothesis that ants communicate through a more complex system of signals. If ants were seen to change their behavior significantly after exposure to an artificial mix of signals identical to the queen's, it would strongly suggest that the queen's signals (and not a more complex system) play a crucial role in ant communication.

5.Question

Category: Craft and Structure

Correct Answer: C

Explanation: Choice C is correct because the subject 'Birds' is plural and therefore, the verb 'play' should be in its base form to maintain subject-verb agreement.

6.Question

Category: Craft and Structure

Correct Answer: B

Explanation: Choice B is correct because 'impenetrable' best describes the complex, challenging nature of the novel described in the passage.

7.Question

Category: Craft and Structure

Correct Answer: B

Explanation: "Meticulous" is the most precise choice to complete the blank, indicating the careful approach Mead took in her extensive research.

8.Question

Category: Information and Ideas

Correct Answer: B

Explanation: Choice B is the best answer because it accurately reflects the main purpose of the text. The text discusses the challenges faced by the United States during the War of 1812 and highlights the role of coastal fortifications in the American defense. The Battle of Fort McHenry is mentioned as an example of the effectiveness of these fortifications.

9.Question

Category: Information and Ideas

Correct Answer: B

Explanation: Choice B is the best answer because it accurately describes data from the table that support the contention that results can vary greatly depending on the animal species used. The table shows that the study by Johnson, which used monkeys, reported an accuracy of 80%, while the study by Jones, which used rabbits, reported an accuracy of 70%. This difference in results, despite the studies being conducted within a similar timeframe, supports the contention.

10. Question

Category: Standard English Conventions

Correct Answer: D

Explanation: Choice D is correct because the subject 'he' is singular, so the verb should be in the third person singular present tense, which is 'continues'.

11. Question

Category: Information and Ideas

Correct Answer: A

Explanation: Choice A is correct because the passage refers to a critique of Fichte's philosophy that it could lead to an unchecked individualism and a disregard for the community. This critique logically leads to a reconsideration of Fichte's philosophy in the light of contemporary discourse on the balance between individual rights and social responsibilities.

12. Question

Category: Information and Ideas

Correct Answer: D

Explanation: Choice D is correct because the passage depicts a lover sneaking across a dim, quiet landscape. Explanation: The text follows the quiet, secret movements of the speaker crossing the landscape to meet their lover. Overall, the imagery and ideas come together to depict a secretive meeting, with the speaker urgently rowing across a bleak seascape under the faint moonlight to passionately meet their lover waiting in the cove. The text builds an atmosphere of mystery, intimacy and intensity as the journey culminates in the darkened, quiet cove.

13. Question

Category: Expression of Ideas

Correct Answer: D

Explanation: Choice D is correct. The sentence effectively uses notes to illustrate how African sculpture, through its unique abstraction and stylization, has redefined Western ideas of representation and form. It also mentions the influence on Pablo Picasso, linking the concept directly to modern art.

14. Question

Category: Standard English Conventions

Correct Answer: B

Explanation: Choice B is correct because the conjunction 'and' correctly links the two related concepts of 'satire' and 'parody', which are both tools of comedy in Ancient Roman literature.

15 Question

Category: Information and Ideas

Correct Answer: A

Explanation: Choice A is the best answer. It describes data from the table that supports the idea that the method used can significantly affect the quantified impact of animals on urban planning. The studies on Deer and Squirrels used the same method (Population Density) and produced similar impacts, while the studies on Raccoons and Birds used different methods (Habitat Distribution and Biodiversity Index, respectively) and produced distinctly different impacts.

16.Question

Category: Information and Ideas

Correct Answer: D

Explanation: Choice D is the correct answer because it logically completes the statement. The passage discusses Einstein's belief that the laws of physics are merely descriptions and do not provide a complete understanding of the universe. His humility and belief that his theories were merely stepping stones towards a more comprehensive understanding of the universe suggest that he believed that scientific knowledge is always evolving and no single theory can claim to have all the answers. This is precisely what choice D states.

17.Question

Category: Standard English Conventions

Correct Answer: D

Explanation: Choice D is correct because it uses the correct punctuation and conjunction to link two related ideas in a sentence.

18.Question

Category: Craft and Structure

Correct Answer: C

Explanation: Choice C is the best answer because it aligns with Benjamin Fielding's viewpoint in Text 2. While acknowledging Rembrandt's skillful use of contrast (light and shadow), Fielding emphasizes that the artist's true innovation was his ability to capture emotion and portray the human condition. Therefore, he would likely respond to Clara Simmons' assertion (Text 1) by emphasizing Rembrandt's emotional depth rather than his use of light and shadow.

19.Question

Category: Craft and Structure

Correct Answer: C

Explanation: Choice C is correct because according to Text 2, John Marshall posits a more complex perspective on the Treaty of Kanagawa. While acknowledging the coercive nature of the Treaty, as described in Text 1, Marshall also highlights how some Japanese leaders saw an opportunity in it, believing that foreign trade could help Japan acquire the necessary technology and knowledge to resist Western powers.

20.Question

Category: Information and Ideas

Correct Answer: C

Explanation: Choice C is the correct answer because it aligns with the passage's discussion of the ambivalent role of lyric poetry in ancient Greek philosophy. The text suggests that while figures like Plato recognized the potential of lyric poetry as a tool for moral instruction, they also grappled with its reliability for conveying philosophical truth, given its emotional appeal. Therefore, the statement that poetry could be a 'reliable conduit of philosophical truth, effectively communicating complex ideas and promoting intellectual discourse' most logically completes the text.

21.Question

Category: Craft and Structure

Correct Answer: A

Explanation: Choice 'A' is correct because the word 'acclimate' means to become accustomed to a new climate or conditions, which is what marine species must do in response to the changes brought about by ocean currents.

22.Question

Category: Craft and Structure

Correct Answer: B

Explanation: Choice B is correct because it most accurately describes the main purpose of the text. Crusoe expresses a complex range of emotions towards the island. He 'often looked back with a sigh' indicating some loneliness or regret, but also considers the island his 'kingdom' and a 'paradise' where he was safe from the world's dangers. Thus, the main purpose is to convey these mixed feelings.

23.Question

Category: Information and Ideas

Correct Answer: D

Explanation: Choice D is correct because it provides evidence that William Blake's work was acknowledged by other significant figures in the Romantic movement as being influential. This supports the assertion that Blake's work had a revolutionary impact on the Romantic art movement.

24.Question

Category: Expression of Ideas

Correct Answer: D

Explanation: Choice D is the best answer. 'Moreover' logically signals that the detail in this sentence—that Weston emphasized the potential of the camera to create images of stark precision and tonal range—adds to the information in the previous sentence. Specifically, the previous sentence indicates one way in which Weston transformed the aesthetic standards of American photography, and the claim that follows indicates a second, additional way.

25.Question

Category: Craft and Structure

Correct Answer: D

Explanation: Choice D is the best answer because according to Text 2, Dr. Jane Foster and her team would likely respond to the concerns about scalability and universal applicability of OOC technology by suggesting a hybrid approach. This approach combines OOC technology with computational modelling, which they believe would allow for the integration of multi-organ systems in the chip models, thereby addressing the limitations of standalone OOC technology.

26.Question

Category: Craft and Structure

Correct Answer: C

Explanation: Choice C is correct because it uses the correct form of the verb 'to convey'. The phrase 'The Romans' ability to convey' correctly uses the infinitive form of the verb after 'ability', which is the standard English convention.

27.Question

Category: Information and Ideas

Correct Answer: D

Explanation: Choice D is correct because "lingered in the chambers of the sea" directly relates to the claim about Prufrock's meditations and feelings of isolation. The sea symbolizes the unconscious mind.

Practice Test 3 Module 1: Reading & Writing Practice Sets

The questions in this section cover a range of important reading and writing skills. Each

question consists of one or more passages, which may include a table or graphic. Read each passage and question carefully, and then choose the best answer to the question based on the passage(s).

All questions in this section are multiple-choice with four possible answers. Each question has a single best answer.

1.Question

Category: Craft and Structure

In 1886, Mexican-American archaeologist Zelia Maria Magdalena Nuttall published a research paper on sculptures discovered at the ancient indigenous city of Teotihuacan in present-day Mexico, other researchers readily _____ her work as ground breaking; this recognition stemmed from her convincing demonstration that the sculptures were much older than had previously been thought.

Which of the following options best completes the text with the most logical and precise word or phrase?

- a. acknowledged
- b. ensured
- c. denied
- d. underestimated

2.Question

Category: Craft and Structure

Like other tribal nations, the Muscogee (Creek) Nation is self-governing; its National Council generates laws regulating aspects of community life such as land use and healthcare, while the principal chief and cabinet officials _____ those laws by devising policies and administering services in accordance with them.

Which of the following options best completes the text with the most logical and precise word or phrase?

- a. implement
- b. presume
- c. improvise
- d. mimic

3.Question

Category: Craft and Structure

Some economic historians _____ that late nineteenth- and early twentieth-century households In the United States, there was a perception that households with larger numbers of members spent less on food per capita than those with smaller numbers of members. However, an analysis of the available data by economist Trevon Logan demonstrated that this supposition was not supported by the evidence.

Which choice completes the text with the most logical and precise word or phrase?

- a. surmised
- b. contrived
- c. questioned
- d. regretted

4.Question

Category: Craft and Structure

The work of Kiowa painter T.C. Cannon derives its power in part from the tension among his _____ influences: The European tradition of portraiture, with its emphasis on realistic depictions of faces, is contrasted with the American pop art movement, which employs vibrant colors. Flat style, an intertribal painting style that eschews the effects of depth achieved through shading and perspective, is also discussed.

Which of the following options best completes the text with the most logical and precise word or phrase?

- a. complementary
- b. unknown
- c. disparate
- d. interchangeable

5.Question

Category: Craft and Structure

The recently published research conducted by Suleiman A. Al-Sweedan and Moath Alhaj is based on their observation that, despite the numerous studies that have been conducted on the effect of high altitude on blood chemistry, there is still much to be learned, there is a _____ studies of the effect on blood chemistry of living in locations below sea level, such as the California towns of Salton City and Seeley.

Which of the following options best completes the text with the most logical and precise word or phrase?

- a. quarrel about
- b. paucity of
- c. profusion of
- d. verisimilitude in

6.Question

Category: Craft and Structure

The concept of living in an impractical space has been explored by conceptual artists Madeline Gins and Shusaku Arakawa, who designed an apartment building in Japan to be more fanciful than functional. The design features a kitchen counter that is chest-high on one side and knee-high on the other, as well as a ceiling with a door to nowhere. The effect of this design is disorienting but invigorating. After four years in the apartment, filmmaker Nobu Yamaoka reported significant health benefits.

Which choice best states the main idea of the text?

- a. While residing in a domicile embellished with imaginative architectural elements, such as those conceived by Gins and Arakawa, may offer a sense of revitalization, such an environment is ultimately unsustainable.

- b. The design of disorienting spaces, such as those observed in the Gins and Arakawa building, represents the most effective approach to creating a physically stimulating environment.

- c. As a filmmaker, Yamaoka has consistently demonstrated support for the conceptual artwork of artists such as Gins and Arakawa.

- d. Although impractical, the design of the apartment building by Gins and Arakawa may enhance the well-being of the building's residents.

7.Question

Category: Information and Ideas

Given that stars and planets initially form from the same gas and dust in space, some astronomers have proposed that host stars (such as the Sun) and their planets (such as those in our solar system) are composed of the same materials. This implies that the planets contain equal or smaller quantities of the materials that make-up the host star. This idea is also supported by evidence that rocky planets in our solar system are composed of some of the same materials as the Sun.

Which finding, if true, would most directly weaken the astronomers' claim?

- a. The majority of stars are composed of hydrogen and helium, but upon cooling, they are found to contain minute quantities of iron and silicate.

- b. A nearby host star is observed to contain the same proportion of hydrogen and helium as that of the Sun.

- c. New evidence suggests that the iron content of some rocky planets is significantly higher than that of their host stars.

- d. The method for determining the composition of rocky planets has been found to be less effective when applied to the analysis of other planetary types.

8.Question
Category: Information and Ideas

In the early nineteenth century, some Euro-American farmers in the northeastern United States employed agricultural techniques that had been developed by the Haudenosaunee (Iroquois) people centuries earlier. However, it appears that few of those farmers had actually observed Haudenosaunee farms firsthand. It is unlikely that multiple farmers from the same era independently developed techniques that the Haudenosaunee people had already invented, these facts most strongly suggest that _____

Which choice most logically completes the text?

- a. The farmers in question acquired their techniques from other individuals who were more directly influenced by Haudenosaunee practices.

- b. The crops typically cultivated by Euro-American farmers in the northeastern United States were not well suited to Haudenosaunee farming techniques.

- c. The agricultural techniques employed by the Haudenosaunee were utilized extensively in regions beyond the northeastern United States.

- d. It was not until the late nineteenth century that Euro-American farmers began to recognize the benefits of Haudenosaunee farming techniques.

9.Question
Category: Information and Ideas

The dating of artifacts recovered from the Kuulo Kataa settlement in modern Ghana to the thirteenth century CE may lend credence to claims that the settlement was founded before or around that time. However, there is other evidence, including the artifact dates and the fourteenth century CE founding date, which strongly supports a fourteenth century CE founding date for Kuulo Kataa. If both the artifact dates and the fourteenth century CE founding date are correct, that would imply that _____

Which choice most logically completes the text?

- a. It is observed that artifacts from the fourteenth century CE are more commonly recovered than are artifacts from the thirteenth century CE.

- b. The artifacts were originally sourced from elsewhere and subsequently reached Kuulo Kataa through trade or migration.

- c. The origins of Kuulo Kataa have been revealed to be from a different region than previously assumed.

- d. It is possible that the excavations at Kuulo Kataa may have inadvertently damaged some artifacts dating to the fourteenth century CE.

10.Question

Category: Standard English Conventions

A member of the Cherokee Nation, Mary Golda Ross is renowned for her contributions to NASA's Planetary Flight Handbook, which _____ detailed mathematical guidance for missions to Mars and Venus.

Which choice completes the text so that it conforms to the conventions of Standard English?

- a. provided
- b.having provided
- c.to provide
- d.providing

11.Question

Category: Standard English Conventions

Typically, underlines, scribbles, and notes left in the margins by a former owner lower a book's _____ when the former owner is a famous poet like Walt Whitman, such markings, known as

marginalia, can be a gold mine to literary scholars.

Which choice completes the text so that it conforms to the conventions of Standard English?

- a. value,but
- b. value
- c. value,
- d. value but

12.Question

Category: Craft and Structure

Research conducted by planetary scientist Katarina Miljkovic suggests that the Moon's surface may not accurately _____ early impact events. When the Moon was still forming, its surface was softer, and asteroid or meteoroid impacts would have left less of an impression; thus, evidence of early impacts may no longer be present.

Which of the following options best completes the text with the most logical and precise word or phrase?

- a. reflect
- b. receive
- c. evaluate
- d. mimic

13.Question

Category: Craft and Structure

Handedness, or the preferential use of either the right or left hand, is a trait that is typically easy to observe in humans. Because this trait is present but less _____ in many other animals, animal-behavior researchers often employ tasks specially designed to reveal individual animals' preferences for a certain hand or paw.

Which choice completes the text with the most logical and precise word or phrase?

- a. recognizable
- b. intriguing
- c.significant
- d.useful

14.Question

Category: Standard English Conventions

Like other amphibians, the wood frog (Rana sylvatica) is unable to generate its own heat, so during periods of subfreezing temperatures, it _____ by producing large amounts of glucose, a sugar that helps prevent damaging ice from forming inside its cells. Which choice completes the text so that it conforms to the conventions of Standard English?

- a. had survived
- b. survived
- c. would survive
- d. survives

15.Question
Category: Craft and Structure

The Cambrian explosion gets its name from the sudden appearance and rapid diversification of animal remains in the fossil record about 541 million years ago, during the Cambrian period. Some scientists argue that this _____ change in the fossil record might be because of a shift in many organisms to body types that were more likely to be preserved.

Which choice completes the text with the most logical and precise word or phrase?

- a. catastrophic
- b. elusive
- c. abrupt
- d. imminent

16.Question

Category: Craft and Structure

In 2014, a team led by Vicente Lull conducted an archaeological excavation in Spain. Their findings included the remains of a woman from the Early Bronze Age society of El Algar, accompanied by a number of valuable objects that indicated a high position of power. This finding may persuade researchers who have argued that Bronze Age societies were ruled by men to _____ that women may have also held leadership roles

Which of the following options best completes the text with the most logical and precise word or phrase?

- a. waive
- b. concede
- c. refute
- d. require

17.Question

Category: Craft and Structure

A US tax policy expert posits that state taxes are _____ but one factor among many to be considered when contemplating an interstate move. Even significant differences in state taxation have a negligible effect on the majority of individuals' decisions, while differences in employment opportunities, housing availability, and climate exert a considerable influence.

Which choice completes the text with the most logical and precise word or phrase?

- a. consistent with
- b. representative of
- c. overshadowed by
- d. irrelevant to

18.Question

Category: Craft and Structure

The author's claim about the relationship between Neanderthals and Homo sapiens is _____, as it fails to account for several recent archaeological discoveries. To be considered convincing, his argument would need to address the recent finds of additional hominid fossils, such as the latest Denisovan specimens and Homo longi.

Which choice completes the text with the most logical and precise word or phrase?

- a. disorienting
- b.tenuous
- c.nuanced

- d.unoriginal

19.Question

Category: Information and Ideas

In West Africa, jalis have traditionally served as repositories of information about family histories and records of significant events. They have often fulfilled the roles of teachers and advisers. While new technologies have introduced changes to the role of the jali, they continue to be valued for their ability to know and protect their peoples' stories.

Which choice best states the main idea of the text?

- a. Even though there have been some changes in their role, jalis continue to preserve their communities' histories.
- b. Although jalis have many roles, many of them like teaching best.
- c. Jalis have been entertaining the people within their communities for centuries.
- d. Technology can now do some of the things jalis used to be responsible for.

20.Question
Category: Craft and Structure

Among social animals that care for their young, including chickens, macaque monkeys, and humans, newborns appear to exhibit an innate attraction to faces and face-like stimuli. To test whether this trait also occurs in Testudo tortoises, which live alone and do not engage in parental care, Elisabetta Versace and her colleagues used an image of three black dots arranged in the shape of eyes and a nose or mouth. They found that tortoise hatchlings showed a significant preference for the image, suggesting that _____

Which of the following options is the most logical conclusion to the text?

- a. It can be reasonably assumed that face-like stimuli are likely to be perceived as harmless by newborns of social species that practice parental care. However, it can be postulated that such stimuli are perceived as threatening by newborns of solitary species that lack parental care.

- b. It is important to note that an innate attraction to face-like stimuli does not necessarily imply an adaptation related to social interaction or parental care.

- c. It can be posited that the inclination towards face-like stimuli observed in social species that engage in parental care is a learned rather than an innate phenomenon.
- d. Newly hatched Testudo tortoises exhibit a stronger preference for face-like stimuli than adult Testudo tortoises do.

21.Question
Category: Standard English Conventions

The Association of Southeast Asian Nations (ASEAN) was established in 1967 with the objective of promoting political and economic stability within the Asia-Pacific region. Initially comprising five members—Thailand, the Philippines, Singapore, Malaysia, and Indonesia—ASEAN expanded its membership by the end of the 1990s s, the organization _____ its initial membership.

Which choice completes the text so that it conforms to the conventions of Standard English?

- a. has doubled
- b. had doubled
- c. doubles
- d. will double

22.Question

Category: Standard English Conventions

To survive when water is scarce, embryos inside African turquoise killifish eggs _____ a dormant state known as diapause. In this state, embryonic development is suspended for a period of up to two years, which is longer than the lifespan of an adult killifish.

Which of the following options best completes the text in accordance with the conventions of Standard English?

- a.enter
- b. to enter
- c. having entered
- d. entering

23.Question

Category: Standard English Conventions

Food and the sensation of taste are central to Monique Truong's novels. In The Book of Salt, for example, the exiled character of Bình connects to his native Saigon through the food he prepares, while in Bitter in the Mouth, the character of Linda _____ a form of synesthesia whereby the words she hears evoke tastes.

Which choice completes the text so that it conforms to the conventions of Standard English?

- a. experienced
- b.had experienced
- c. experiences
- d. will be experiencing

24.Question
Category: Standard English Conventions

In Racetrack Playa, a flat, dry lakebed in Death Valley National Park, there are 162 rocks, some of which weigh less than a pound, while others weigh almost 700 pounds. These rocks move periodically from place to place, seemingly of their own volition, despite the absence of any discernible cause.

Racetrack-like trails in the _____ mysterious migration.

Which choice completes the text so that it conforms to the conventions of Standard English?

- a. playas sediment mark the rock's
- b. playa's sediment mark the rocks
- c. playa's sediment mark the rocks'
- d. playas' sediment mark the rocks'

25.Question
Category: Standard English Conventions

In numerous landscape paintings from the 1970s and 1980s, Lebanese American artist Etel Adnan sought to encapsulate the essence of California's fog-shrouded Mount Tamalpais region through abstraction, employing splotches of color to symbolize the area's distinctive features. Interestingly, the triangle representing the mountain itself _____ among the few defined figures in her paintings.

Which choice completes the text so that it conforms to the conventions of Standard English?

- a. are
- b.have been
- c. were
- d.is

26.Question

Category: Standard English Conventions

Seneca sculptor Marie Watt's blanket art comes in a range of shapes and sizes. In 2004, Watt sewed strips of blankets together to craft a 10-by-13-inch _____ in 2014, she arranged folded blankets into two large stacks and then cast them in bronze, creating two curving 18-foot-tall blue-bronze pillars.

Which choice completes the text so that it conforms to the conventions of Standard English?

- a. sampler later,
- b.sampler;
- c.sampler,
- d.sampler, later,

27.Question

Category: Craft and Structure

In 2019, researchers Patricia Jurado Gonzalez and Nawal Nasrallah prepared a stew from a 4,000-year-old recipe discovered on a Mesopotamian clay tablet. Upon tasting the dish, known as pašrūtum ("unwinding"), they found that it possessed a mild flavor and induced a sense of tranquility. _____ the researchers, knowing that dishes were sometimes named after their intended effects, theorized that the dish's name, "unwinding," referred to its function: to help ancient diners relax.

Which choice completes the text with the most logical transition?

- a.Therefore,
- b.Alternately,
- c. Nevertheless,
- d. Likewise,

Solutions Reading & Writing Test 3 Module 1: Detailed Answer Explanations

1.Question

Category: Craft and Structure

Choice A is the most logical answer

Because it most logically completes the text's discussion of Nuttall's 1886 research paper. In this context, "acknowledged" means recognized as having a certain status. The text indicates that other researchers recognized Nuttall's work as groundbreaking because of its convincing demonstration related to the age of the ancient sculptures. In other words, the researchers recognized the groundbreaking status of Nuttall's work.

2.Question

Category: Craft and Structure

Choice A is the most logical answer to the question

It most closely corresponds to the text's overall discussion on self-government among the Muscogee (Creek) Nation. In this context, the verb "implement" means to carry out or put into effect. The text states that the National Council generates laws, while the principal chief and cabinet officials are responsible for devising policies and administering services in accordance with those laws, as stated. In light of the aforementioned context, it can be reasonably inferred that the principal chief and cabinet officials are responsible for implementing the laws. This is evidenced by their creation of policies and administration of services that align with the aforementioned laws.

3.Question

Category: Craft and Structure

Choice A is the most logical answer

because it most logically completes the text's discussion of late nineteenth- and early twentieth-century household food purchases. In this context, "surmised" means formed an idea or assumption with little evidence. The text explains that certain economic historians "assumed" that large and small households spent different amounts on food per person, but that another economist found this supposition to be false based on evidence from available data. This context suggests that the economic historians made an erroneous assumption without sufficient consideration of evidence.

4.Question

Category: Craft and Structure

Choice C is the correct answer.

This is because it most closely aligns with the text's discussion of the artistic styles that have influenced Cannon's work. In this context, the term "disparate" is used to describe two or more distinct or dissimilar styles. The text indicates that a tension exists among the styles that have influenced Cannon's work, and goes on to describe how those styles differ. For instance, classic European portraiture favors realism, American pop art uses vivid colors, and intertribal flat style rejects the use of shading and perspective to achieve depth. This context suggests that the styles that have influenced Cannon's work are disparate.

5.Question

Category: Craft and Structure

Choice B is the best answer.

This is because it most accurately reflects the discussion of studies of altitude's effect on blood chemistry. In this context, the term "paucity of" means lack of. In describing the inspiration behind AlSweedan and Alhaj's research, the text employs the word "though" to suggest a contrasting relationship between two types of studies: those examining the effect on blood chemistry of living at a high altitude and those examining the effect on blood chemistry of living in locations below sea level. This contrasting relationship, along with the text's use of the word "many," provides context suggesting that there are few, if any, examples of the second type of study, whereas there are numerous examples of the first type.

6.Question

Category: Craft and Structure

The answer most accurately representing the main idea of the text is **Choice D**.

The text states that conceptual artists Gins and Arakawa have designed an apartment building that is disorienting due to several unconventional elements, including uneven kitchen counters and a door to nowhere. The text goes on to suggest that there may be benefits to this kind of design, citing filmmaker Yamaoka's four-year residency in the apartment building and his reported health benefits. Consequently, although the design may be impractical, it may enhance the well-being of the residents of the apartment building.

7.Question

Category: Information and Ideas

Choice C is the most appropriate response.

It presents a finding that, if true, would challenge the astronomers' assertion regarding the composition of host stars and their planets. The text explains that because stars and planets originate from the same gas and dust, astronomers believe planets should be composed of the same materials as their host stars, but in equal or smaller quantities. The discovery that the quantity of iron in some rocky planets is considerably greater than that of their host stars would challenge the astronomers' assertion, as it would indicate that some planets contain the same material as their host stars, albeit in higher concentrations.

8.Question

Category: Information and Ideas

Choice A is the most logical conclusion

to be drawn from the text's discussion of Euro-American farmers' utilization of Haudenosaunee agricultural techniques. As the text indicates, some Euro-American farmers were employing these techniques in the early nineteenth century, despite the fact that a significant proportion of the farmers had not observed Haudenosaunee farms. One potential explanation for these facts is that the farmers developed techniques on their own that had been invented centuries earlier by the Haudenosaunee people. However, the text explicitly rules out this explanation. If the techniques in question were not observed by Euro-American farmers directly and not invented independently, the most logical explanation would be that they were learned from others who were more directly influenced by Haudenosaunee practices than the farmers themselves. Once learned, these techniques could then be applied to farming practices in a way that was consistent with Haudenosaunee agricultural practices.

9.Question

Category: Information and Ideas

Choice B is the correct answer.

This is because it most logically completes the text's discussion of artifacts and Kuulo Kataa's founding date. If it were true that both Kuulo Kataa was founded in the fourteenth century CE and that artifacts found in excavations of the settlement are from the thirteenth century CE, it would be reasonable to conclude that the artifacts were not created in the Kuulo Kataa settlement. This would suggest that the artifacts originated elsewhere and were subsequently transported to the settlement through trade or migration.

10.Question

Category: Standard English Conventions

The most appropriate response is to select Choice A.

The convention that is being tested is the use of finite and nonfinite verb forms within a sentence. Relative clauses, such as the one that begins with "which," require a finite verb, a verb that can function as the main verb of a clause. This response correctly supplies the clause with the finite past tense verb "provided."

11.Question

Category: Standard English Conventions

The most appropriate response is to select Choice A.

The convention that is being tested is the coordination of clauses within a sentence. This response correctly employs a comma and the coordinating conjunction "but" to join a main clause ("Typically, value") and a subordinate clause ("when, Whitman") that precedes a main clause ("Such, scholars").

12.Question

Category: Craft and Structure

Choice A is the most logical answer

Because it most logically completes the text's discussion of the Moon's surface. In this context, "reflect" means show or make apparent. The text states that because the surface of the Moon was softer when the Moon was still forming than it is now, early asteroid and meteoroid impacts would have left less of an impression and, as a result, evidence of them may no longer exist. This context lends support to the hypothesis that the surface of the Moon may not accurately reflect the evidence of early impact events.

13. Question

Category: Craft and Structure

Choice A is the most logical answer

Because it most logically completes the text's discussion about handedness in animals. As used in this context, "recognizable" means apparent or identifiable. The text indicates that handedness is "easy to observe in humans," but that animal-behavior researchers use special tasks to determine handedness in other animals. This context and the use of "less" before the blank indicate that compared with handedness in humans, handedness in other animals is less recognizable.

14. Question

Category: Standard English Conventions

The most appropriate response to the question is that of Choice D.

The convention being tested is the use of verbs to express tense. In this instance, the present tense verb "survives" correctly indicates that the wood frog regularly survives subfreezing temperatures by producing large amounts of glucose.

15. Question

Category: Craft and Structure

Choice C is the most logical and precise answer

Because it most closely aligns with the text's discussion of the fossil record from the Cambrian period. In this context, "abrupt" means sudden. The text explains that the fossil record reflects the unexpected appearance and rapid diversification, or increase in variety, of animal remains during the Cambrian period. This context establishes that these remains' entry into the fossil record was sudden.

16. Question

Category: Craft and Structure

Choice B is the correct answer.

This is because it most logically completes the text's discussion of the significance of the 2014 archaeological finding at El Algar. In this context, "concede" means to admit something is true after first resisting that admission. The text indicates that some researchers believe "Bronze Age societies were ruled by men." However, the discovery of a Bronze Age burial at El Algar, which included "valuable objects signaling a high position of power," raises the possibility that "women may have also held leadership roles." Consequently, the text challenges the prevailing view that only men were leaders in these societies, prompting those who hold this view to reconsider their opinions.

17.Question

Category: Craft and Structure

The rationale behind the selection of Choice C

is that it most logically completes the text's discussion of the factors that influence individuals' decisions to relocate to a different state. In this context, the phrase "overshadowed by" is used to indicate that a particular factor is surpassed by or causes another factor to seem less important than other factors affecting a move. The text indicates that, according to a US tax policy expert, when people consider an interstate move, state taxes have a minimal impact on their decisions, while employment opportunities, housing availability, and climate have a profound effect. This context suggests that people prioritize these other factors over state taxes.

18.Question

Category: Craft and Structure

Choice B is the correct answer.

This is because it most logically completes the text's discussion of the author's claim about the relationship between Neanderthals and Homo sapiens. As used in this context, "tenuous" means lacking substance or strength. The text states that the author's claim is not convincing because it does not consider certain pieces of evidence—relevant recent discoveries. The context conveys the idea that the author's claim is weak.

19.Question

Category: Information and Ideas

Choice A is the optimal response

The text posits that jalis have traditionally been tasked with maintaining records of their communities' histories and significant events. It further asserts that while technological advancements have prompted some modifications to jalis' roles, they continue to be valued for their contributions to the preservation of their communities' histories.

20.Question

Category: Craft and Structure

Choice B is the most appropriate response

Because it presents the conclusion that most logically completes the text's discussion of the study by Versace and colleagues. The text indicates that newborn animals of some species are attracted to faces and to stimuli that resemble faces. These species share two characteristics: they are social and they practice parental care, meaning that parents care for their young. The text then describes the experiment conducted by Versace and colleagues, which demonstrated that although Testudo tortoises are not social and do not practice parental care, hatchlings of this species were attracted to a stimulus that resembles a face. Given that Versace and colleagues have demonstrated that a species that is not social and does not practice parental care nevertheless possesses the innate characteristic of being attracted to face-like stimuli, it follows that this characteristic should not be assumed to be an adaptation related to social interaction or parental care.

21.Question

Category: Standard English Conventions

The most appropriate response to the question is that provided in Choice B.

The convention being tested is the use of verbs to express tense. In this case, the past perfect verb "had doubled" is an accurate indication that the doubling of the organization's initial membership occurred during a specific period prior to the present (between the organization's founding in 1967 and the end of the 1990s).

22.Question

Category: Standard English Conventions

The most appropriate response to the question is that provided in Choice A.

The convention being tested is that of finite and nonfinite verb forms within a sentence. A main clause requires a finite verb to perform the action of the subject (in this case, "embryos"), and this choice supplies the clause with the finite present tense verb "enter" to indicate how the embryos achieve diapause.

23.Question

Category: Standard English Conventions

The most appropriate response to the question is that of choice C.

The convention being tested is the use of verbs to express tense. In this instance, the present tense verb "experiences" is consistent with the other present tense verbs (e.g., "connects" and "prepares") used to describe the events in Truong's novels. Furthermore, it is conventional to use the present tense when discussing a literary work.

24.Question

Category: Standard English Conventions

The most appropriate response to this question is choice C.

The convention being tested is the use of plural and possessive nouns. The singular possessive noun "playa" and the plural possessive noun "rocks" correctly indicate that the sediment is that of one playa (the Racetrack Playa) and that there are multiple rocks that have mysteriously migrated across the sediment.

25.Question

Category: Standard English Conventions

The correct answer is Choice D.

The convention being tested is subject-verb agreement. In this case, the singular verb "is" agrees in number with the singular subject "the triangle."

26.Question

Category: Standard English Conventions

The most appropriate response to the question is that of Choice B.

The convention being tested is that of the coordination of main clauses within a sentence. This response employs the semicolon in a conventional manner to join the first main clause ("In 2004... sampler") and the second main clause ("In 2014... pillars").

27.Question

Category: Craft and Structure

Choice A is the best answer.

"Therefore" logically signals that the action described in this sentence—the researchers theorizing that the dish was named for its effect on diners—is a result or consequence of the previous observation that the dish had a calming effect.

Practice Test 3 Module 2: Reading & Writing Practice Sets

The questions in this section cover a range of important reading and writing skills. Each

question consists of one or more passages, which may include a table or graphic. Read each passage and question carefully, and then choose the best answer to the question based on the passage(s).

All questions in this section are multiple-choice with four possible answers. Each question has a single best answer.

1.Question

Category: Craft and Structure

Seminole/Muscogee director Sterlin Harjo _____ television's tendency to situate Native characters in the distant past: this rejection is evident in his series Reservation Dogs, which revolves around teenagers who dress in contemporary styles and whose dialogue is laced with current slang.

Which choice completes the text with the most logical and precise word or phrase?

- a. repudiates
- b. proclaims
- c. foretells
- d. recants

2.Question

Category: Craft and Structure

Given that the conditions in binary star systems should make planetary formation nearly impossible, it's not surprising that the existence of planets in such systems has lacked _____ explanation. Roman Rafikov and Kedron Silsbee shed some light on the subject when they used modeling to determine a complex set of factors that could support the evolution of planets.

Which choice completes the text with the most logical and precise word or phrase?

- a. discernible
- b. a straightforward
- c. an inconclusive
- d. an unbiased

3.Question

Category: Craft and Structure

In 2007, computer scientist Luis von Ahn was working on converting printed books to digital format. He found that some words were so distorted that digital scanners couldn't recognize them, but most humans could read them easily. On the basis of this finding, von Ahn invented a simple security test to keep automated "bots" out of web pages. The first version of the reCAPTCHA test asked users to type a known word and one of the many words scanners couldn't recognize. Correct answers proved the users were human. Data was added to the book digitization project.

Which choice best states the main purpose of the text?

- a. To discuss von Ahn's invention of reCAPTCHA
- b. To explain how digital scanners work
- c. To call attention to von Ahn's book-digitizing project
- d. To indicate how popular reCAPTCHA is

4.Question

Category: Information and Ideas

The following is from Edith Wharton's 1905 novel The House of Mirth. Walking through a park is Lily Bart and a companion. Lily had no real intimacy with nature. But she had a passion for the appropriate, and could be acutely sensitive to a scene that was the appropriate background for her own feelings.

The landscape below seemed an enlargement of her present mood, and she found something of herself in its serenity, its vastness, its long open spaces. On the nearer slopes the sugar maples swayed like bonfires of light. Lower down was a mass of gray orchards, and here and there the lingering green of an oak grove.

Which choice best describes the function of the underlined sentence in the text as a whole?

- a. It creates a detailed image of the physical setting of the scene.
- b. It establishes that a character is experiencing an internal conflict.
- c. It makes an assertion that the next sentence then expands on.
- d. It illustrates an idea that is introduced in the previous sentence.

5.Question

Category: Information and Ideas

A study by finance professor Madhu Veeraraghavan and colleagues suggests that exposure to sunshine during the workday may be a source of overly optimistic behavior. Using data from 1994 to 2010 for a set of U.S. companies, the team compared more than 29,000 annual earnings forecasts with the actual earnings those companies later reported. The team found that the more a manager's earnings forecast exceeded what the company actually earned that year, the greater his or her exposure to sunshine at work in the two weeks before submitting the forecast.

Which choice best states the function of the underlined sentence in the overall structure of the text?

- a.To summarize the results of the team's analysis
- b. To present a specific example that illustrates the study's findings
- c. To explain part of the methodology used in the team's study
- d. To call out a challenge the team faced in conducting its analysis

6.Question

Category: Information and Ideas

The following is from Edith Nesbit's 1906 novel The Railway Children.

Mother did not spend all her time paying dull [visits] to dull ladies and sitting dull at home waiting for dull ladies to pay [visits] to her. She was almost always there, ready to play with the children, read to them, and help them with their homework. She also used to write stories for them while they were at school and read them to them after tea, and she always made up funny verses for their birthdays and other big occasions.

According to the text, what is true about Mother?

- a. She wishes that more ladies would visit her.
- b. Birthdays are her favorite special occasion.
- c. She creates stories and poems for her children.
- d. Reading to her children is her favorite activity.

7.Question

Category: SAT Standard English Conventions

In the realm of investment banking, derivatives are complex financial contracts _____, like stocks or bonds, but derive their value from other assets.

Which choice completes the text so that it conforms to the conventions of Standard English?

- a. They aren't primarily securities

- b. That are not simply securities

- c. Not being directly securities themselves

- d. Which aren't securities in the primary sense

8.Question

Category: SAT Craft & Structure

Modern art, often characterized by its abstract motifs and forms, is a realm in which artists strive to transcend traditional aesthetic boundaries. Through their creations, they aim to evoke a profound, often _____ response from the viewer, challenging conventional perceptions.

Which choice completes the text with the most logical and precise word or phrase?

- a. tepid

- b. visceral

- c. trite

- d. derivative

9.Question

Category: SAT Craft & Structure

Impressionism stands as a testament to the radical departure from strictly representational art in the vast realm of art history. This movement began in the 19th century. It was led by artists determined to capture fleeting moments, moods, and atmospheres. This paradigm shift was not merely a stylistic evolution, but a profound philosophical divergence that emphasized the subjective perception of reality. Subsequent art movements, while diverse in style and intent, owed much to the pioneering spirit of the Impressionists.

Which choice best states the function of the underlined sentence in the text as a whole?

- a. It provides a chronological context for the Impressionist movement.

- b. It elaborates on the technical aspects of Impressionist art.

- c. It accentuates the significant philosophical change brought about by Impressionism.

- d. It draws a comparison between Impressionism and later art movements.

10.Question

Category: Craft and Structure

The following text is from Maggie Pogue Johnson's 1910 poem "Poet of Our Race." In this poem, the speaker is addressing Paul Laurence Dunbar, a Black author.

Thou, with stroke of mighty pen,
Hast told of joy and mirth,
And read the hearts and souls of men
As cradled from their birth.
The language of the flowers,
Thou hast read them all,
And e'en the little brook
Responded to thy call.

Which choice best states the main purpose of the text?

- a. To praise a certain writer for being especially perceptive regarding people and nature
- b.To establish that a certain writer has read extensively about a variety of topics
- c.To call attention to a certain writer's careful and elaborately detailed writing process
- d.To recount fond memories of an afternoon spent in nature with a certain writer

11.Question

Category: Information and Ideas

Martín Chambi was born in 1891 to a Quechua-speaking family in the Peruvian Andes. Today, he is considered one of the most important figures in Latin American photography. In a paper written for an art history class, one student asserts that Chambi's photographs have considerable ethnographic value - in his work, Chambi was able to capture the most diverse elements of Peruvian society and to portray his subjects with both dignity and authenticity.

Which finding, if true, would most directly support the student's claim?

- a. Chambi took many commissioned portraits of wealthy Peruvians, but he also produced hundreds of images carefully documenting the peoples, sites, and customs of Indigenous communities of the Andes.
- b. Chambi's photographs demonstrate a high level of technical skill, as seen in his strategic use of illumination to create dramatic light and shadow contrasts.
- c. During his lifetime, Chambi was known and celebrated both within and outside his native Peru, as his work was published in places like Argentina, Spain, and Mexico.
- d. Some of the peoples and places Chambi photographed had long been popular subjects for Peruvian photographers.

12.Question

Category: SAT Craft & Structure

Passage 1

In the dialectic of art history, one is confronted with the intricate dance between form and substance. The Byzantine period, for example, vividly illustrated this tension in its mosaics and frescoes, where form often subsumed content, resulting in an opulent display of intricate patterns that often overshadowed the intended narrative. This phenomenon, emblematic of the era's penchant for aesthetic grandeur, also reflected society's tendency to value superficial manifestations, sometimes at the expense of intrinsic meaning.

Passage 2

The evolutionary trajectory of art has been punctuated by periods in which form and content engage in a compelling tango. A prominent example is the modernist movement, in which artists deliberately obscured content to emphasize form. This was not just an aesthetic choice, but a reflection of the zeitgeist - a world struggling with rapid change and seeking comfort in the familiar, even if it meant prioritizing aesthetics over narrative. The inherent tension between appearance and essence, it seems, is perennial.

Based on the two passages, with which statement regarding the relationship between form and content in art would the author of Passage 1 most likely disagree with the author of Passage 2?

- a. Artistic epochs are defined by the interplay between form and content.

- b. The prioritization of form over content is a reflection of broader societal tendencies.

- c. All artistic movements prioritize form over content due to societal influences.

- d. Art evolves in response to societal changes, affecting the balance between form and narrative.

13.Question

Category: Information and Ideas

In the mountains of Brazil, Barbacenia tomentosa and Barbacenia macrantha - two plants in the Velloziaceae family - colonize soilless, nutrient-poor patches of quartzite rock. Plant ecologists Anna Abrahão and Patricia de Britto Costa used microscopic analysis to determine that the roots of B. tomentosa and B. macrantha that grow directly into the quartzite contain tufts of fine hairs near the root apex; further analysis revealed that these hairs secrete both malic and citric acids. The researchers hypothesize that the plants depend on the dissolution of the underlying rock with these acids. This process not only creates channels for further growth, but also releases phosphates, which provide the vital nutrient phosphorus.

Which finding, if true, would most directly support the researchers' hypothesis?

- a. Other species in the Velloziaceae family are found in terrains with more soil but have root structures similar to those of B. tomentosa and B. macrantha.

- b. Though B. tomentosa and B. macrantha both secrete citric and malic acids, each species produces the acids in different proportions.

- c.The roots of B. tomentosa and B. macrantha carve new entry points into rocks even when cracks in the surface are readily available.

- d. B. tomentosa and B. macrantha thrive even when transferred to the surfaces of rocks that do not contain phosphates.

14.Question

Category: SAT Expression of Ideas

As David explored avant-garde movements in the art world, he catalogued these observations:

Elise Moran is a visionary of post-abstract expressionism.

Her work is exhibited in major galleries in Brazil, Italy, Spain, and China.

Moran's compositions are often a fusion of geometric and organic forms.

Juxtaposing structured squares with fluid forms, 'Fractured Facades' (2013) symbolizes conflict.

Convergence' (2015) blends circles and undulating lines to represent harmony.

David aims to emphasize a consistent stylistic approach throughout these works. Which option draws most effectively from his observations to achieve this goal?

- a. 'Fractured Facades' and 'Convergence' are exemplary artworks by Moran, exhibited in renowned galleries globally.

- b. Both 'Fractured Facades' and 'Convergence' exemplify Moran's signature style, merging geometric and organic forms to convey profound themes.

- c. In 'Fractured Facades', squares meet fluid shapes, while 'Convergence' brings circles into contact with wavy patterns.

- d. Moran has significantly influenced post-abstract expressionism with works like 'Fractured Facades' in 2013 and 'Convergence' in 2015.

15.Question

Category: Craft and Structure

Disruptions in the supply chain for microchips used in personal electronics have cast doubt on an economist's assertion that retailers can expect robust growth in sales of such devices in coming months. The delays are unlikely to completely _____ her forecast, but will almost certainly extend its time frame.

Which choice completes the text with the most logical and precise word or phrase?

- a. dispute
- b. withdraw
- c. underscore
- d. invalidate

16.Question

Category: Craft and Structure

Some scientists have suggested that the mammals of the Mesozoic era weren't a very _____ group, but the research of paleontologist Zhe-Xi Luo suggests that the early mammals that lived in the shadow of the dinosaurs weren't all ground-dwelling insectivores. Fossils of several plant-eating mammals have been found in China. They include species such as Vilevolodon diplomylos, which Luo says could glide like a flying squirrel.

Which choice completes the text with the most logical and accurate word or phrase?

- a. predatory
- b. obscure
- c. diverse
- d. localized

17.Question

Category: Craft and Structure

The following text is adapted from Gwendolyn Bennett's 1926 poem "Street Lamps in Early Spring.

Night wears a garment

All velvety soft, all violet-blue

And over her face she draws a veil

As fine as floating dew

And here and there

In the black of her hair

The subtle hands of the night

Move slowly with their jeweled light.

Which choice best describes the overall structure of the passage?

- a. It presents alternating descriptions of night in a rural area and in a city.
- b. It sketches a picture of nightfall, then a picture of sunrise.
- c. It makes an extended comparison of the night to a human being.
- d. Describes how night changes from one season to the next.

18.Question

Category: SAT Standard English Conventions

In ancient Mesopotamia, cuneiform, a system of writing using wedge-shaped symbols _____, was revolutionary for its time. This early form of writing paved the way for the more advanced systems of writing.

Which choice completes the text so that it conforms to the conventions of Standard English?

- a. employed on clay tablets;
- b. employed on clay tablets,

- c. employed on clay tablets:

- d. employed on clay tablets

19.Question

Category: SAT Information & Ideas

The concept of neo-monetary fluidity is juxtaposed with classical monetary paradigms in the intricate tapestry of global finance. Historically, liquid assets adhered to predictable channels of flow, largely defined by geopolitical imperatives and dictated by centralized fiscal authorities. However, the advent of digital currencies and decentralized finance, or DeFi for short, has led to a paradigm shift. Emancipated from traditional banking edifices, this nascent financial model has provided an arena for instantaneous, borderless transactions. But while these innovations evoke a sense of unfettered financial liberation, they also plunge the domain into realms of unpredictable volatility. It is impossible to ignore the disruptions that these uncharted fiscal waters may bring. They challenge previously stable notions of wealth, solvency, and economic equilibrium.

What can be said about how digital currencies and decentralized finance affect global finance?

- a. Traditional banking structures are completely obsolete due to digital currencies.

- b. Neo-monetary fluidity ensures economic stability by mitigating volatility.

- c. The rise of digital currencies has ushered in new possibilities as well as challenges in the financial landscape.

- d. Centralized fiscal authorities have been entirely replaced by decentralized finance.

20.Question

Category: SAT Standard English Conventions

Existentialism, a philosophical stance _____, posits that individuals are free and responsible agents determining their own development through acts of the will.

Which choice completes the text so that it conforms to the conventions of Standard English?

- a. Emerging prominently during the 20th century

- b. It made its mark in the 20th century

- c. Where its significance rose in the 20th century

- d. The 20th century being its era of dominance

21.Question

Category: SAT Expression of Ideas

While researching a topic, a student makes the following

the following notes:

- The Atlantic Monthly magazine was published in 1857.
- The magazine focused on politics, art, and literature.
- In 2019, historian Cathryn Halverson will publish book *Faraway Women and the Atlantic Monthly*.
- Her subject is women writers whose autobiographies appeared in the magazine in the

in the early 1900s.

- One of the authors discussed is Juanita Harrison.

The student would like to present Cathryn Halverson's Cathryn Halverson's book to an audience already familiar with *Atlantic Monthly*.

Which choice most effectively uses relevant information from the notes to accomplish this

to accomplish this goal?

- a. Cathryn Halverson's Faraway Women and the "*Atlantic Monthly*" discusses female authors whose autobiographies whose autobiographies appeared in the magazine in the early in the early 1900s.
- b. A magazine called "*Atlantic Monthly*," referred to in Cathryn Halverson's book title, was first published in 1857.
- c. *Faraway Women and the Atlantic Monthly* features contributors to the Atlantic Monthly, which was first published in 1857 as a magazine focusing on politics, art, and literature.
- d. One author discussed by Cathryn Halverson is Juanita Harrison, whose autobiography was published in the appeared in the Atlantic Monthly in the early 1900s.

22. Question

Category: SAT Expression of Ideas

"*The Young Girl*" is a 1920 short story by Katherine Mansfield. In the story, the narrator introduces an unnamed unnamed seventeen year old girl and her younger brother to dinner. In describing the teenager, Mansfield often contrasts the character's pleasant unpleasant attitude, as when Mansfield writes of the When Mansfield writes about the teenager,

———

Which quote from "*The Young Girl*" most effectively illustrates the claim?

- a. "I heard her murmur, 'I can't bear flowers on a table.' They had evidently been giving her intense pain, for she positively closed her eyes as I moved them away."

- b. "While we waited she took out a little, gold powder-box with a mirror in the lid, shook the poor little puff as though she loathed it, and dabbed her lovely nose."

- c. "I saw, after that, she couldn't stand this place a moment longer, and, indeed, she jumped up and turned away while I went through the vulgar act of paying for the tea."

217

- d. "She didn't even take her gloves off. She lowered her eyes and drummed on the table. When a faint violin sounded she winced and bit her lip again. Silence."

23.Question

Category: SAT Information & Ideas

In the vast tapestry of global economic paradigms, the ephemeral dance of currency values continues to perplex financial experts. The ethereal fluctuation of these currencies, often obscured by transient market sentiments, bears an uncanny resemblance to the capricious nature of Baroque art. A more detailed examination of economic prediction reveals that, rather than a precise science, it is more accurately described as an interpretation of complex patterns, comparable to the discernment of variegated hues in a Byzantine mosaic. Indeed, given its intricate nature, the financial world can be likened to a vast gallery, with each fiscal decision being analogous to a painter's brushstroke, shaping the overarching narrative and influencing the global economic portrait.

Which one of the following statements, if true, would be the most direct extension of the arguments in the passage?

- a. The value of a currency is determined by the immutable laws of supply and demand.

- b. Baroque art, in its essence, reflects unpredictable and often whimsical patterns akin to market sentiments.

- c. Byzantine mosaics are simple and easily decipherable, unlike the world of finance.

- d. The unpredictability of global economic movements can be attributed solely to geopolitical events.

24.Question

Category: Craft and Structure

Anthropologist Kristian J. Carlson and colleagues conducted an analysis of the fossilized clavicle and shoulder bones of a 3.6-million-year-old early hominin known as "*Little Foot*." Their findings indicated that these bones were _____ the clavicle and shoulder bones of modern apes that are frequent climbers, such as gorillas and chimpanzees. This suggests that Little Foot had adapted to life in the trees.

Which of the following best completes the text with the most logical and precise word or phrase?

- a. surpassed by
- b.comparable to
- c.independent of
- d.obtained from

25.Question

Category: SAT Information & Ideas

Since antiquity, philosophers have been engaged in discussions surrounding the immutable nature of existential truths within the broader landscape of philosophical discourse. One such doctrine, the "Metaphysical Construct," posits that existential realities are not transient nor shifting but are instead embedded within the cosmic continuum. Another school of thought, the "Temporal Paradigm," often described as the "Temporal Paradigm," argues that existential verities are fleeting, deeply intertwined with the epoch they emerge from. In essence, the Metaphysical Construct views existence as a fixed tapestry woven into the vast expanse of the universe. In contrast, the Temporal Paradigm perceives existence as ephemeral footnotes within ever-changing chapters of cosmic history.

Which of the following can be most accurately inferred from the passage?

- a. The Temporal Paradigm denies the long-term significance of existential truths.

- b. Existential realities are only appreciated by philosophical scholars.

- c. The Metaphysical Construct and the Temporal Paradigm have drastically different views on the permanence of existential realities.

- d. Philosophical doctrines seldom consider the impact of cosmic occurrences on existential truths.

26.Question

Category: Craft&Structure

Rydra Wong, the protagonist of Samuel R. Delany's 1966 novel Babel-17, is a poet, an occupation which, in Delany's work, is not _____: nearly a dozen of the characters that populate his novels are poets or writers. Which choice completes the text with the most logical and precise word or phrase?

- a.infallible
- b.atypical
- c.lucrative
- d.tedious

27.Question

Category: SAT Expression of Ideas

In her studies of literature, Anna encountered insights about Dr. Walter Hennessey, a pioneer of neo-modernist poetry. Hennessey's writings have been recognized in France, Argentina, India, and South Korea. Hennessey's poems often utilize nature as an allegory for human emotions. His anthology, "Whispers of Willow" (1997), draws parallels between trees and human despair.

In "Dawn's Dew" (2000), the metaphor of morning dew is employed to depict fleeting joy. Anna's intention is to highlight a shared thematic element between the two anthologies.

Which choice effectively accomplishes this goal by utilizing the relevant insights from her studies?

- a. Hennessey's writings, namely 'Whispers of Willow' and 'Dawn's Dew', have earned acclaim across several nations including France and India.

- b. Both 'Whispers of Willow' and 'Dawn's Dew' by Hennessey use elements of nature to symbolically represent profound human emotions.

- c. In 'Whispers of Willow', trees mirror human sorrow, while 'Dawn's Dew' poetically presents the ephemeral nature of happiness.

- d. Hennessey released 'Whispers of Willow' in 1997 and 'Dawn's Dew' three years later in 20

Solutions Reading & Writing Test 3 Module 2: Detailed Answer Explanations

1.Question

Category: Craft and Structure

Choice A is the best answer

Because it most logically completes the text's discussion of Sterlin Harjo's approach to representing Native characters on television. In this context, "repudiates" means to reject or refuse to have anything to do with. The text suggests that television shows tend to portray Native characters as having lived long ago, but that Harjo's series Reservation Dogs focuses on Native teenagers in the present, representing a "rejection" of the typical approach to Native character representation. In this context, then, Harjo's rejection of the general tendency of television with regard to Native characters is evident.

2.Question

Category: Craft and Structure

Choice B is the best answer

because it most logically completes the text's description of efforts to explain the existence of planets in binary star systems. In this context, the description of an explanation as a "straightforward" one would mean that the explanation is direct and uncomplicated. The text claims that since it should be "nearly impossible" for planets to form in binary star systems, it is "not surprising" that there is no simple explanation for the existence of planets in such systems; the fact that one possible approach includes "complex" factors provides further contextual support for this idea.

3.Question

Category: Craft and Structure

Choice A is the best answer

because it most accurately states the main purpose of the text. The text focuses on discussing how von Ahn's digitization work led to the invention of a digital security test known as reCAPTCHA, after a brief introduction to computer scientist Luis von Ahn.

4.Question

Category: Information and Ideas

Choice D is the best answer

because it best describes how the underlined sentence functions in the passage as a whole. The first sentence of the passage establishes that Lily can be "very sensitive" to scenes that serve as "appropriate backdrops" for her feelings-that is, she's very aware of when a setting seems to reflect her mood. This awareness is then demonstrated in the next sentence, which is underlined: Lily sees the landscape she's in as a large-scale reflection of her current mood. She identifies with elements such as its tranquility. Thus, the function of the underlined sentence is to illustrate an idea introduced in the previous sentence.

5.Question

Category: Information and Ideas

Choice C is the best answer

because it best describes how the underlined sentence works in the passage as a whole. The first sentence states the implication of Veeraraghavan's team's study: exposure to sunlight during working hours can lead to overly optimistic behavior. It then describes what data Veeraraghavan's team looked at and how Veeraraghavan's team made use of it (comparing predicted profits with actual profits), and finally it presents what Veeraraghavan's team found when looking at this data. Thus, the underlined sentence primarily serves to explain some of the methodology used in the team's study.

6.Question

Category: Information and Ideas

Choice C is the best answer

because it describes something that is true about Mother as presented in the passage. The passage indicates that, among other activities, Mother writes stories for her children while they are at school and makes up "funny poems" for certain occasions.

7.Question

Category: SAT Standard English Conventions

B: Choice B is the best answer.

This option effectively introduces the main distinction of derivatives in a clear and concise manner.

Also, it is grammatically correct as a restrictive clause is being introduced.

8.Question

Category: SAT Craft & Structure

B: Choice B, "visceral,"

is the most fitting, as it implies a deep, emotional, or instinctual response, which aligns with artists' intentions in modern art.

9.Question

Category: SAT Craft & Structure

C: Option C is correct.

The underlined sentence emphasizes the importance of Impressionism, not only as a style of art, but also as a major philosophical shift in the understanding and representation of reality.

The sentence does not emphasize the "technical aspects" or the chronology of the Impressionist movement; the answer can also be arrived at by process of elimination.

The following sentence suggests a comparison between Impressionism and later art movements. Therefore, choice C is correct.

10.Question

Category: Craft and Structure

Choice A is the best answer

because it most accurately states the main purpose of the text. In the first part of the text, the speaker speaks of Paul Laurence Dunbar's ability to understand human beings (he has "read the hearts and souls of the people" and has written of their "joy and mirth"). The speaker describes Dunbar's deep understanding of nature (he has read "the language of flowers" and studied "the little stream") in the second part of the text. Thus, the text mainly praises Dunbar for being particularly perceptive about people and nature.

11.Question

Category: Information and Ideas

Choice A is the best answer

Because it presents a finding that, if true, would support the claim about Chambi's photographs. The passage describes a student who claims that Chambi's photographs "have considerable ethnographic value"-that is, they are valuable as records of cultures-and that they "capture diverse elements of Peruvian society" in a respectful way. If it's true that Chambi carefully photographed people from different communities in Peru, as well as photographed the customs and places of different communities, that would support the claim that the photographs have ethnographic value as depicting diverse elements of Peruvian society.

12.Question

Category: SAT Craft & Structure

C: Both authors, in passages 1 and 2, allude to the relationship between form and content in art and how it reflects broader social trends (Option B).

They also agree that the balance between form and narrative has been a defining characteristic of different artistic periods (choice A) and that art often reflects societal changes (choice D).

However, passage 1 specifically discusses the Byzantine period and how form dominated content in that period, while passage 2 discusses the modernist movement with a similar dynamic.

The specificity of their examples suggests that they don't believe that all artistic movements have this characteristic, making Option C the point of potential disagreement.

13.Question

Category: Information and Ideas

Choice C is the best answer

because it presents a finding that, if true, would support the researchers' hypothesis about the plants' dependence on dissolving rock. The passage states that the roots of the two plant species grow directly into quartzite rock, where hairs on the roots secrete acids that dissolve the rock. The researchers hypothesize that the plants depend on this process because the dissolving rock opens up space for the roots to grow and releases phosphates, which provide the plants with phosphorus, a vital nutrient. If the plants do this process of dissolving rock even when the rock already has spaces for roots to grow into, this would support the researchers' hypothesis because it suggests that the plants are getting some benefit - such as access to phosphorus - from the action of dissolving rock. If the plants don't benefit from dissolving rock, they would be expected to grow in the cracks that already exist, because that would mean the plants don't have to expend energy making and secreting acids; but if the plants create new entry points by dissolving rock, even where cracks already exist, that would support the hypothesis that they depend on dissolving rock for some benefit.

14.Question

Category: SAT Expression of Ideas

B: Choice B is the ideal option

because it emphasizes Moran's unique stylistic approach of blending geometric and organic elements, a feature evident in both works.

15.Question

Category: Craft and Structure

Choice D is the best answer

Because it most logically completes the text's discussion of the economist's claim about sales of personal electronic devices. In this context, "invalidate" most closely means to nullify or make invalid. The text indicates that the economist's claim that sales of personal electronics will show strong growth in the coming months has been "invalidated" by disruptions in the supply of microchips for personal electronics. The text goes on to explain the effect of the delays on the economist's forecast, stating that the delays are "very likely to extend the time frame over which the projected sales growth will occur. This context suggests that the delays are unlikely to invalidate the economist's forecast altogether. The delays are likely to alter the time frame of the forecast, not nullify or invalidate it.

16.Question

Category: Craft and Structure

Choice C is the best answer

because it most logically completes the text's discussion of the types of mammals that lived during the Mesozoic era. In this context, "diverse" means to have a significant amount of variety. The text notes that some scientists have suggested that Mesozoic mammals can't be characterized in any particular way, and then contrasts the view of those scientists with Luo's research, which shows that Mesozoic mammals "were not all ground-dwelling insectivores" and were instead "diverse. The implication here is that some scientists have a view that Mesozoic mammals were all the same, or not a very diverse group.

17.Question

Category: Craft and Structure

Choice C is the best answer

because it most accurately describes the overall structure of the passage. Throughout the text, the speaker characterizes night as if it were a person. She wears a garment ("a garment" that is "velvety soft" and "violet-blue") and a veil "over her face," and she moves her hands "slowly with their gem-studded light" through her dark hair. The text is thus structured as an extended comparison of the night with a human being.

18.Question

Category: SAT Standard English Conventions

Choice B is the best answer.

The comma correctly separates the specific information about the cuneiform script from the statement about its revolutionary nature.

19.Question

Category: SAT Information & Ideas

Choice C is the best answer.

The crux of this question is understanding the impact of digital currencies and DeFi on the global financial system. Option C reflects the sentiment of the passage, suggesting that while digital currencies present new opportunities ("an arena for instant, borderless transactions"), they also present challenges ("realms of unpredictable volatility").

20.Question

Category: SAT Standard English Conventions

Choice A is the best answer.

It smoothly transitions from the philosophy's name to its primary belief, and the only choice that is grammatically and syntactically consistent.

21.Question

Category: SAT Expression of Ideas

Choice A is the best answer.

The sentence effectively introduces Cathryn

Halverson's book to an audience already familiar with Atlantic Monthly,

by stating the title of Halverson's book and describing its contents without providing

Providing background information about Atlantic Monthly

22.Question

Category: SAT Expression of Ideas

Choice B is the best answer.

The most effective way of illustrating the claim in the text that Mansfield contrasts the character's pleasant appearance with her unpleasant attitude is to select Choice B as the best answer. In the quotation, Mansfield describes the teenage girl as having a "lovely nose" (a compliment about her appearance) but also states that she treats her makeup puff "as though she loathed it" (a judgment suggesting her unpleasant attitude).

23.Question

Category: SAT Information & Ideas

Choice B is the best answer.

The core argument put forth in this passage concerns the comparison between art, in particular Baroque art and Byzantine mosaics, and the complexity of the financial world, with a specific focus on currency value fluctuations.

This passage directly connects the "capricious nature" of Baroque art to the unpredictability of currency values.

This option, which echoes the notion that the unpredictable nature of Baroque art is comparable to market sentiments, serves to reinforce the central argument presented in the text. Consequently, it may be described as neither broad, alien, narrow, nor extreme.

Furthermore, it maintains the text's nuanced examination of the unpredictable nature of both art and finance.

24.Question

Category: Craft and Structure

Choice B is the correct answer

This is because it most closely aligns with the text's discussion of the fossilized bones of the hominin known as Little Foot. In this context, the phrase "comparable to" would be best understood as meaning "similar to." The text implies that the fossilized clavicle and shoulder bones of Little Foot are similar to those of other animals known to climb frequently, such as chimpanzees and gorillas. This suggests that Little Foot was capable of adapting to moving around in trees. Therefore, the similarities between the fossilized bones of Little Foot and those of chimpanzees and gorillas are likely to be significant.

25.Question

Category: SAT Information & Ideas

Choice C is the correct answer

The question requires an inference based on the details presented in the passage. The passage delineates that the "Metaphysical Construct" views existential realities as fixed, while the "Temporal Paradigm" sees them as ephemeral. This stark contrast suggests a significant divergence in their perspectives on the permanence of existential truths. Option C is most closely aligned with the information presented in the passage.

It encapsulates the contrasting views of the "Metaphysical Construct" and the "Temporal Paradigm" on existential realities.

26.Question

Category: Craft&Structure

Choice B is the most logical answer

because it most logically completes the text's discussion of Samuel R. Delany's character Rydra Wong. As used in this context, "atypical" would mean unrepresentative or not common. The text indicates that Wong is one of "nearly a dozen" characters in Delany's novels who are poets or writers. This context indicates that the occupation of poet is not an atypical one for a character in one of Delany's works.

27.Question

Category: SAT Expression of Ideas

Choice B is the most logical answer

Option B most effectively encapsulates the underlying thematic unity present in both anthologies, namely the utilization of nature as a metaphor for human emotions.

THIS PAGE IS INTENTIONALLY LEFT BLANK

Digital SAT Score Calculator

In the journey towards SAT preparation and success, understanding your potential score is pivotal. To aid in this crucial aspect of test preparation, we are introducing an innovative tool: the Digital SAT Score Calculator. Accessible via a convenient QR code, this tool is designed to demystify the scoring process, providing students with an immediate and accurate estimation of their SAT scores based on practice test results.

The Digital SAT Score Calculator is not just a tool; it's a bridge to greater insight and preparedness. By inputting your raw scores—simply the number of questions you answered correctly—into the calculator, you can obtain a scaled score for both the Math and Evidence-Based Reading and Writing sections. This calculator employs the same principles and statistical equating processes used by the official SAT scoring system to ensure accuracy and reliability.

How to Use the Calculator

Simply scan the provided QR code with your mobile device to access the **Digital SAT Score Calculator**. Enter your raw scores for the respective sections, and the calculator will do the rest, presenting you with an estimated scaled score. It's recommended to use the calculator after each practice test to track your progress and adjust your study plan as needed.

SAT SCORE

Chapter 4: Test-Taking Psychology

Introduction

Embarking on the SAT journey is as much a mental endeavor as it is an academic one. Understanding the psychology behind test-taking can significantly enhance a student's ability to perform under pressure, turning potential stress into a catalyst for success. This chapter delves into the psychological aspects of preparing for and taking the SAT, offering insights and strategies to navigate the mental challenges that accompany this pivotal exam. By mastering the art of test-taking psychology, students can approach the SAT with confidence, resilience, and a positive mindset.

The Psychology of Preparation

1. **Growth Mindset:** Embrace the belief that your abilities can be developed through dedication and hard work. This perspective fosters a love for learning and resilience essential for great accomplishment.

2. **Goal Setting:** Define clear, achievable goals for your SAT preparation. Setting specific targets can help maintain motivation and focus throughout your study journey.

3. **Stress Management Techniques:** Incorporate relaxation techniques such as deep breathing, meditation, or yoga into your preparation routine to reduce anxiety and improve concentration.

The Mental Game of Test Day

1. **Anxiety Reduction:** Learn to recognize and manage test-day anxiety. Techniques such as positive visualization, affirmations, and tactical breathing can help calm nerves and focus the mind.

2. **Focus and Concentration:** Develop strategies to enhance your concentration during the test. This can include mindfulness exercises that train you to bring your focus back to the task at hand when your mind wanders.

3. **Endurance and Stamina:** Building mental endurance is crucial for the SAT, which demands sustained concentration. Practice under simulated test conditions to improve your mental stamina over time.

Post-Test Reflection

1. **Self-Assessment:** After the test, engage in a reflective practice to assess your performance. Identify what strategies worked well and what areas need improvement for future tests.

2. **Coping with Disappointment:** If results are not as expected, it's important to learn how to deal with disappointment constructively. Reflect on the experience as a learning opportunity and plan for the next steps.

3. **Celebrating Success:** Acknowledge and celebrate your efforts and achievements, regardless of the outcome. Recognizing your hard work and dedication is vital for maintaining a positive attitude and motivation.

Anxiety Reduction: Navigating Test-Day Nerves

The phenomenon of test anxiety is widespread and can manifest in various forms, ranging from mild nervousness to debilitating stress. Understanding how to effectively manage this anxiety is crucial for maximizing performance on the SAT. This section explores comprehensive strategies to mitigate test-day nerves, enabling students to approach the exam with clarity and confidence.

Recognize the Symptoms

First, it's essential to recognize the physical and psychological signs of anxiety: rapid heartbeat, shallow breathing, excessive sweating, and negative thought patterns. Awareness of these symptoms is the first step toward managing them.

Preparation is Key

Anxiety often stems from fear of the unknown or feeling unprepared. Rigorous, consistent study, familiarity with the test format, and practicing under timed conditions can reduce uncertainties and bolster confidence.

Develop a Pre-Test Routine

Establish a calming pre-test routine that can help signal to your body and mind that it's time to focus. This might include light stretching, deep breathing exercises, or listening to calming music. A consistent routine can be a powerful antidote to anxiety.

Breathing Techniques

Deep breathing activates the body's relaxation response. Techniques such as the 4-7-8 method (inhale for 4 seconds, hold for 7, exhale for 8) can slow the heart rate and promote calmness. Practice these techniques regularly and especially on test day to alleviate anxiety.

Positive Visualization

Imagine yourself succeeding on the test. Visualization is a potent tool for combating negativity. Regularly practicing positive visualization can reframe your mindset toward optimism and success.

Mindfulness and Meditation

Mindfulness exercises and meditation can enhance your ability to stay present and focused, reducing the impact of distracting anxious thoughts. Even short daily practices leading up to the test day can have significant benefits.

Affirmations

Positive affirmations can shift your mindset from self-doubt to self-empowerment. Phrases like "I am prepared and capable" or "I can handle this challenge" can be mentally or verbally repeated to build confidence.

Tactical Breaks During the Test

If anxiety peaks during the test, allow yourself a brief moment to close your eyes, breathe deeply, and refocus. These tactical breaks can reset your mental state and prevent panic from taking hold.

Physical Activity

Regular physical activity can reduce stress levels, improve mood, and enhance cognitive function. Incorporating exercise into your SAT preparation can have a positive impact on both your physical well-being and test performance.

Seek Support

Remember, you're not alone. Discussing anxieties with teachers, parents, or peers can provide comfort and valuable strategies for managing stress. Sometimes, just verbalizing your fears can diminish their power.

Conclusion

Anxiety reduction for the SAT is not about eliminating nerves altogether but about managing them effectively. By employing these strategies, students can transform their test-day nerves from a hindrance into a focused energy that propels them towards achieving their best possible scores. Remember, anxiety is a natural response, and learning to navigate it is a valuable skill that extends far beyond the SAT.

Building Confidence for Success in the Digital SAT

Confidence is a pivotal factor in the success of students taking the Digital SAT. It is not merely a byproduct of preparation but a critical component of effective test-taking. This section delves into practical strategies to build and maintain confidence, enabling students to approach the SAT not just with preparedness but with a robust sense of self-assurance.

Foundational Knowledge

Confidence begins with a solid foundation in the required material. Ensure comprehensive coverage of all topics on the SAT, with an emphasis on understanding rather than memorization. Utilize varied resources—books, online courses, and practice tests—to deepen your mastery of subjects. When you know your material inside and out, confidence naturally follows.

Deepening Stress Management Techniques for the Digital SAT

Effectively managing stress is crucial for performing optimally on the Digital SAT. Stress, if left unchecked, can impair cognitive functions such as memory recall, concentration, and problem-solving, which are essential for a test-taking environment. This section expands on various advanced techniques for managing stress, enabling students to approach the SAT with a calm, focused mindset.

Advanced Deep Breathing Techniques

Deep breathing is a foundational stress management tool that can be performed anywhere, anytime, making it particularly useful before and during the SAT.

- **Box Breathing:** Also known as square breathing, this technique involves inhaling for four counts, holding the breath for four counts, exhaling for four counts, and then holding again for four counts. This method is used by athletes and in military training to increase concentration and performance under pressure.

- **Alternate Nostril Breathing:** This yoga technique involves closing one nostril and breathing through the other. By alternating nostrils after each breath, it helps to balance the body's systems and calm the mind, reducing stress and increasing focus.

Cognitive Behavioral Techniques

Cognitive-behavioral strategies involve addressing the mental aspects of stress, particularly how negative thinking patterns can contribute to anxiety.

- **Thought Record:** Keep a journal of stressful thoughts and challenge them systematically. Write down the evidence for and against these thoughts and try to come up with a more balanced perspective.

- **Mindfulness Meditation:** Develop a regular practice of mindfulness meditation where you observe your thoughts and feelings without judgment. This practice enhances your ability to remain present and calm, reducing the impact of stressors.

Physical Strategies

Engaging your body can help manage the physiological responses to stress.

- **High-Intensity Interval Training (HIIT):** Engage in HIIT workouts, which are shown to rapidly reduce stress levels through short bursts of intense exercise followed by brief recovery periods. This type of exercise can improve mood and reduce anxiety through the release of endorphins.
- **Yoga Sequences for Stress Relief:** Certain yoga poses, particularly those that open the chest like backbends and those that promote grounding like standing poses, can be particularly effective at reducing stress.

Nutritional Approaches

What you eat can significantly affect how you handle stress.

- **Balanced Diet:** Maintain a diet that stabilizes your blood sugar levels. Avoid high-sugar snacks and focus on complex carbohydrates, proteins, and healthy fats which provide sustained energy and mood stabilization.
- **Adaptogens:** Consider incorporating adaptogens such as ashwagandha or rhodiola. These herbs are known for their ability to help the body handle stress more effectively. However, consult with a healthcare provider before starting any new supplement regimen.

Environmental Adjustments

The environment in which you study and take the test can influence your stress levels.

- **Optimal Study Space:** Create a calm, organized study environment. This could include elements like plants, natural light, or soothing colors. A well-organized space can reduce anxiety and boost focus.
- **Sound and Music:** Utilize the calming effects of sound. Ambient noise or classical music can enhance concentration and alleviate stress during study sessions.

Regular Practice under Simulated Conditions

Regularly taking practice tests under conditions that simulate the actual test day can desensitize you to the test environment, reducing anxiety and increasing confidence.

- **Mock Tests:** Schedule regular mock tests where you mimic the testing conditions of the SAT, including timing, breaks, and even the room layout if possible.

By integrating these deeper, more structured stress management techniques into your SAT preparation, you can significantly improve not only your ability to handle stress but also enhance your overall test performance. These strategies go beyond simple relaxation; they prepare you to face the SAT with resilience and a proactive, empowered mindset.

Chapter 5: Effective Revision Techniques

In the rigorous journey towards mastering the Digital SAT, effective revision stands as a cornerstone of successful test preparation. This chapter delves into sophisticated strategies that harness pedagogical research and cognitive psychology to optimize your review sessions. These methods are not only rooted in academic theory but are also proven in practice, providing a structured approach to enhancing retention and understanding.

Strategic Overview of Revision Techniques

Effective revision is an art that balances breadth and depth while employing diverse techniques to solidify knowledge and improve recall. Mastery of the Digital SAT demands a revision strategy that is both methodical and adaptable, tailored to the unique challenges presented by the test's format and content.

Techniques for Maximizing Retention

1. **Distributed Practice:**

   - Spread your revision sessions over time rather than condensing them into a few lengthy sessions. This approach, based on the spacing effect, helps improve long-term retention and recall, as it allows time for material to consolidate in your memory.

2. **Retrieval Practice:**

   - Engage actively with the material through testing yourself on the concepts rather than passively reading or reviewing notes. Utilizing flashcards, practice tests, and self-assessment quizzes triggers cognitive processes that enhance learning and memory consolidation.

3. **Interleaved Practice:**

   - Mix different topics and types of SAT questions within a single study session. This technique helps build connections between ideas and improves problem-solving skills by teaching you how to apply knowledge flexibly in varied contexts.

Advanced Techniques for Deepening Understanding

4. **Elaborative Interrogation:**

   - Foster a deeper understanding by asking yourself 'why' a concept is true or how it connects to what you already know. This form of self-explanation clarifies understanding and cements information in your memory.

5. **Concept Mapping:**

   - Create visual representations of the material, such as diagrams or mind maps. This technique helps organize and integrate knowledge visually, making it easier to recall and apply during the test.

6. **Dual Coding:**

   - Combine verbal and visual information in your study practices. For example, annotate graphs and diagrams with explanatory notes, or create summaries of reading passages that include both text and relevant visuals.

Practical Application of Revision Techniques

7. **Feedback-Informed Practice:**

   - Use feedback from practice tests to identify areas of weakness. Focus your revision efforts on these topics, adapting your strategies based on performance analytics to ensure continuous improvement.

8. **Simulated Testing Conditions:**

   - Mimic the conditions of the actual Digital SAT during practice sessions. This not only familiarizes you with the test format and timing but also reduces anxiety and enhances performance under exam conditions.

Effective revision is not merely about reviewing content but about engaging with material in a manner that is scientifically proven to enhance learning and retention.

The techniques outlined in this chapter are designed to equip students with the tools necessary for not just passing the Digital SAT, but excelling at it.

By integrating these advanced strategies into your study routine, you can approach the Digital SAT with confidence, armed with a thorough understanding and superior ability to recall and apply knowledge effectively under pressure.

Identifying Weaknesses

One of the first steps in effective revision is accurately identifying areas of weakness. This requires a thorough and analytical approach to reviewing performance data from past assessments. Students should compile results from all available practice tests, quizzes, and homework to look for trends and patterns. It is crucial to analyze not just what questions were missed, but why they were missed. Was it a lack of understanding of the material, a misreading of the question, or a simple calculation error? Distinguishing between knowledge gaps and careless mistakes is essential for targeting revision effectively.

Utilizing Diagnostic Tools

Leveraging diagnostic tools, often provided by SAT prep software, can help pinpoint specific content areas and skills that need improvement. These tools analyze your responses and can offer detailed insights into your performance across various test sections. For example, they might reveal a consistent struggle with algebraic functions or reading comprehension questions involving inference. Armed with this information, students can create a focused study plan that prioritizes these weaker areas.

How Diagnostic Tools Work

When you complete a section of a practice test, the diagnostic tool evaluates each answer, not just for correctness but for underlying patterns. For instance, it might notice that you struggle with quadratic equations or grammatical parallelism. This isn't just about identifying right or wrong answers; it's about understanding the 'why' behind your mistakes. This could be a fundamental misunderstanding of a concept or a recurring error in approach.

Customized Reports and Feedback

These tools often generate customized reports that break down your performance by section, question type, and difficulty level. They provide actionable feedback, suggesting targeted exercises and recommending specific study materials. For example, if you're struggling with critical reading sections, the tool might suggest additional readings or practice exercises that focus on inference and evidence-based questions.

Seeking External Feedback

Sometimes, self-assessment isn't enough. Seeking feedback from teachers, tutors, or study groups can provide a new perspective on where you might be struggling. Often, these individuals can offer additional insights or alternative explanations that clarify difficult concepts and enhance understanding.

While self-assessment is crucial, external feedback introduces a new dimension of insight that can be critical for overcoming blind spots in your preparation. This feedback can come from various sources, including tutors, teachers, online forums, or study groups.

Engaging with Educators and Tutors

Teachers and tutors who specialize in SAT preparation can offer a wealth of knowledge and experience. They can provide explanations and insights that are tailored to your specific needs. A tutor might use your diagnostic results to help refine your study plan, focusing on areas that offer the most significant opportunity for score improvement. They can also provide strategies for approaching the test that you might not have considered.

Utilizing Peer Review and Study Groups

Study groups offer mutual benefits through peer learning. Discussing problems, explaining your reasoning to others, and hearing different approaches to the same question can deepen your understanding and expose you to new techniques. Peers can also provide moral support and help maintain motivation during the often intense preparation period.

Feedback in Practice

To effectively incorporate feedback, actively engage with your sources. Ask specific questions to deepen your understanding, and be open to critique. For instance, after a practice test session, you could discuss each wrong answer with a tutor to understand your mistakes thoroughly, or you could have a study partner quiz you on key concepts.

Conclusion

Utilizing diagnostic tools and seeking external feedback are practices that, when effectively integrated into your SAT preparation, can dramatically enhance both the efficiency and effectiveness of your study sessions. These strategies ensure that you are not just practicing but improving, with each session tailored to address your specific needs and challenges. As you prepare for the SAT, remember that these tools and resources are not just about finding where you went wrong—they are about paving a clear path to where you need to be.

Chapter 6: Beyond the SAT

Introduction

As students approach the culmination of their SAT preparation, it's crucial to recognize that the SAT is not an end in itself but a gateway to broader academic and professional opportunities. This test is a significant step in the college admissions process, serving as a benchmark that colleges use to assess academic preparedness across a diverse applicant pool. However, the impact of the SAT extends beyond college admissions, influencing future academic choices and career paths. "**Beyond the SAT**" aims to provide students with insights and strategies to effectively transition from SAT preparation to making informed decisions about higher education and lifelong learning.

The preparation for and completion of the SAT equips students with a set of skills that are invaluable in both academic and real-world settings. Critical thinking, analytical reasoning, and disciplined study habits developed during this time are assets that will serve students well beyond the test itself. This chapter explores how to leverage these skills and your SAT scores to enhance your college applications, select educational paths that align with your long-term goals, and embrace a mindset of continual growth and learning.

Navigating College Admissions with SAT Scores

The strategic utilization of SAT scores in college applications is more than just submitting your highest scores; it involves a nuanced understanding of how different institutions value these scores within the context of their holistic review processes. To maximize the impact of your SAT results, it's essential to consider how they fit into the broader narrative you are presenting to admissions committees.

Understanding Score Preferences and Requirements

Different colleges have varying preferences and requirements when it comes to SAT scores. Some institutions might place a heavier emphasis on standardized test scores, while others might consider them as just one factor among many. Research each target school's admissions statistics to understand the SAT score range for admitted students. This data can help you identify where your scores stand in comparison and how they might influence your chances of admission.

Where your scores exceed a school's average, highlight this achievement as part of your academic strength. Conversely, if your scores are on the lower end, it's crucial to bolster other aspects of your application, such as your personal statement, extracurricular activities, and letters of recommendation. In contexts where your SAT scores align closely with a program's specific requirements—such as engineering or other quant-heavy fields—emphasizing your math scores can demonstrate preparedness and aptitude for the major.

If there is a significant disparity in your performance across different sections of the SAT, use your application essays or additional interviews to address these discrepancies. For instance, a lower score in verbal sections can be offset by demonstrating strong communication skills through essays or a personal blog. This approach shows admissions officers that you are more than just your SAT score, providing a fuller picture of your capabilities and potential.

Using Scores to Guide Application Strategy

Strategically leveraging your Digital SAT scores in the college application process is a crucial component of optimizing your admissions potential. Your SAT score can significantly impact your application by highlighting your academic strengths and aligning with the admissions criteria of your chosen colleges. Understanding how to use these scores effectively can set you apart from other applicants and improve your chances of admission into your desired institutions.

Assessing Your Score in Context

Before you can use your SAT scores effectively, you must understand their context within your broader application profile:

1. **Benchmark Against College Requirements**: Each college has its own range of SAT scores typically accepted from previous applicants. Research these ranges through college websites or college admission tools to understand where your scores fall within this spectrum. If your scores are in the upper quartile, they can be a strong point in your application. If they are lower, you will need to compensate with stronger essays, extracurriculars, or recommendations.

2. **Understand the Program Requirements**: Some programs, especially those in fields like engineering, business, or pre-med, might place a higher emphasis on quantitative scores. If you're applying for such programs, emphasize your math score if it's a strength or, conversely, highlight your verbal skills if they align better with programs in the humanities or social sciences.

Strategic Use of SAT Scores

With a clear understanding of how your SAT scores fit into the context of your chosen schools and programs, you can begin to strategize:

1. **Highlighting Strengths in Applications**: Use your personal statement or additional essays to discuss how your SAT scores reflect your academic preparedness and intellectual curiosity. For instance, a strong score in the Writing and Language sections can be leveraged if you are applying to programs that value communication skills.

2. **Choosing Where to Apply**: Consider applying to a range of schools where your SAT scores fall into different categories (reach, match, and safety schools). This diversifies your chances of admission and ensures that you have options when acceptances are announced.

3. **Early Decision/Early Action**: If your SAT scores are well above the average at a particular school, applying early decision or early action can sometimes give you an advantage, signaling strong interest and a good fit for the institution.

Tailoring Applications Based on Scores

Your SAT scores can inform the tone and content of your applications:

1. **Balancing the Application**: If your SAT scores are not as strong as other components of your application, it becomes crucial to ensure that your essays, letters of recommendation, and interview (if applicable) are compelling. Conversely, excellent scores can bolster an application that might be slightly weaker in extracurricular achievements.

2. **Addressing Disparities**: If there's a significant difference between your scores in different sections, consider addressing this in your applications. For instance, if your math score is low but your chosen major does not heavily rely on quantitative skills, point out your strengths in other relevant areas.

Conclusion

Effectively using your Digital SAT scores in college applications involves more than just submitting them along with your forms. It requires a strategic approach that considers how these scores align with each school's criteria, your program of interest, and your overall application strategy. By thoughtfully integrating your **SAT scores** into your applications, you can enhance your profile, making a compelling case for your admission.

Appendices

Quick Reference: Formulas and Rules

Math Formulas:

This section includes a compiled list of essential mathematical formulas and rules that are frequently tested on the SAT, such as quadratic formulas, properties of geometric shapes, and rules of exponents. Keeping this list handy during practice sessions can help reinforce your familiarity with their application.

Mathematics is a pivotal section of the SAT, demanding not only understanding of concepts but also the ability to apply formulas and rules efficiently under timed conditions. This section provides an in-depth look at the essential math formulas you need to master for the SAT. Familiarity with these formulas can significantly enhance your ability to solve problems quickly and accurately, which is crucial for achieving a high score.

Key Math Formulas and Their Applications

1. **Quadratic Formula**: $x=\frac{-b \pm\sqrt{b^2-4ac}}{2a}$

    - **Application**: This formula is used to find the roots of any quadratic equation $ax^2+bx+c=$

    It's especially useful when factoring is not straightforward or possible.

2. **Area and Perimeter Formulas**:

    - **Rectangle**: Area = length × width, Perimeter = 2(length + width)

    - **Circle**: Area = πr^2, Circumference = $2\pi r$

    - **Triangle**: Area = 0.5 × base × height

    - **Application**: These are vital for solving geometry problems involving space and dimensions, which often appear in both multiple-choice and grid-in questions.

3. **Pythagorean Theorem**: $a^2+b^2=c^2$

    - **Application**: Essential for solving right triangle problems and is often used in conjunction with trigonometric ratios to solve more complex geometry problems.

4. **Slope Formula**: Slope = $\frac{y_2-y_1}{x_2-x_1}$

    - **Application**: Crucial for problems involving linear equations and graphing lines, helping you understand the rate of change and direction of a line.

5. **Trigonometric Ratios**:

    - Sine, Cosine, Tangent (SOH-CAH-TOA)

- **Application**: These ratios are indispensable for problems involving triangles, particularly in non-right triangles and when working with angles and distances.

6. **Distance Formula**: Distance = $\sqrt{(x_2 - x_1)^2 + (y_2 - y_1)^2}$

    - **Application**: Used to calculate the distance between two points in the coordinate plane, valuable for questions on geometry and algebra that involve points and distances.

7. **Exponent Rules**:

    - $a^n \cdot a^m = a^{n+m}$

    - $a^n / a^m = a^{n-m}$

    - $(a^n)^m = a^{nm}$

    - **Application**: Frequently used in simplification problems, solving equations with variables in exponents, and manipulating algebraic expressions.

How to Effectively Memorize and Use These Formulas

- **Active Practice**: Regularly practicing problems that incorporate these formulas is the best way to internalize them. This active engagement helps transition knowledge from short-term to long-term memory.

- **Flashcards**: Create flashcards for each formula with a problem example on one side and the formula on the other. Regular review, especially in spaced intervals, can reinforce memory retention.

- **Real-World Applications**: Connecting each formula to a real-world context can aid in understanding and remembering its use. For example, consider how the Pythagorean theorem is used in construction or how trigonometric ratios are applied in engineering.

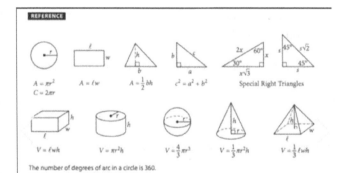

Math reference

In the Mathematics section, the necessity for memorization of common formulas is eliminated. Instead, a reference pop-out is made available during the test, which includes reminders such as how to calculate the circumference or area of a circle, the hypotenuse of a right triangle, and the volume of cylinders and cones.

Grammar and Writing Rules for the SAT

The Writing and Language section of the SAT evaluates your command of English grammar and your ability to write clearly and effectively. To excel, you'll need to demonstrate mastery over a range of grammar rules and writing principles. This quick reference provides a snapshot of key rules that you'll want to have at your fingertips for review at any time.

Punctuation Rules

- **Commas (,):** Used to separate items in a list, after introductory words or phrases, and to set off non-essential clauses.

- **Periods (.):** Mark the end of a declarative sentence.

- **Semicolons (;):** Link closely related independent clauses and can replace commas in a list if the items themselves contain commas.

- **Colons (:):** Introduce lists, quotes, or explanations.

- **Apostrophes ('):** Indicate possession or contractions.

- **Quotation Marks (""):** Enclose direct speech, titles of short works, or used to highlight a word or phrase.

Sentence Structure

- **Parallel Structure:** Ensure parallelism by matching grammatical forms within a sentence. If you start with an '-ing' verb, all subsequent actions should also be '-ing' verbs, unless a shift in the sequence or emphasis is logically justified.

- **Subordination and Coordination:** Use subordinate clauses to present information that is less important and coordinate clauses for equal emphasis.

Agreement Rules

- **Subject-Verb Agreement:** Subjects and verbs must agree in number (singular or plural). Be mindful of tricky subjects that might seem plural but are singular, like "everyone" or "each."

- **Pronoun-Antecedent Agreement:** Pronouns must agree in number and gender with the antecedents they refer to.

Modifier Placement

- **Modifiers:** Place descriptive words and phrases as close as possible to the words they modify to avoid confusion.

Usage and Style

- **Word Choice:** Select the most precise words for clarity and conciseness.

- **Concision:** Eliminate unnecessary words or redundant expressions.

- **Tone:** Maintain a consistent style and tone appropriate to the passage's context.

Avoiding Common Errors

- **Run-on Sentences:** Avoid run-ons by separating independent clauses with periods, semicolons, or conjunctions.

- **Sentence Fragments:** Ensure every sentence has a subject and a predicate and expresses a complete thought.

- **Misplaced and Dangling Modifiers:** Ensure modifiers are placed next to the word they describe.

By integrating these grammatical rules and writing principles into your SAT preparation, you can approach the Writing and Language section with confidence. Regularly consulting this reference will reinforce your understanding and help you quickly identify and correct errors, making it an indispensable tool for SAT success. Remember, these rules not only serve you for the SAT but also form the foundation for effective writing in college and beyond.

Effective Weekly Study Plan for SAT Preparation

A structured weekly study plan is essential for thorough SAT preparation. This plan will help you organize your study time efficiently, ensuring that you cover all necessary content areas with enough revision and practice tests to solidify your understanding. The following is a suggested weekly framework, which can be adjusted to suit your personal schedule and areas of focus.

Week 1-4: Foundational Knowledge Building

Monday: Mathematics - Focus on Algebra

- 2 hours of algebra practice, including linear equations, systems of equations, and inequalities.

- Review algebraic functions and practice problem sets from SAT prep resources.

Tuesday: Evidence-Based Reading

- 2 hours of reading comprehension practice with a focus on literature and historical documents.

- Practice active reading strategies and note-taking.

Wednesday: Writing and Language - Grammar

- 2 hours of grammar practice focusing on sentence structure, punctuation, and common usage errors.

- Complete grammar exercises in SAT prep books or online platforms.

Thursday: Mathematics - Advanced Topics

- 2 hours covering geometry, trigonometry, and the Pythagorean theorem.

- Solve geometry problems from practice tests or textbooks.

Friday: Evidence-Based Reading - Social Science and Sciences

- 2 hours reading social science and science passages.

- Develop strategies for graph and data interpretation.

Saturday: Full Practice Test

- Take a full-length practice test under timed conditions.

- Score the test and note areas of difficulty for further review.

Sunday: Rest and Reflect

- Take the day off to rest.

- Reflect on the week's progress and adjust the upcoming week's study plan accordingly.

Week 5-8: Intermediate Skill Development

Monday: Mathematics - Focus on Problem Solving

- 2 hours of problem-solving practice with a mix of algebra, geometry, and other math topics.

- Incorporate SAT math problem-solving and data analysis questions.

Tuesday: Writing and Language - Writing Style

- 2 hours examining writing style, including consistency, tone, and organization.

- Edit and revise sample paragraphs to improve clarity and cohesion.

Wednesday: Mathematics - Advanced Problems

- 2 hours on higher-order polynomial functions, exponential growth, and decay.

- Work on complex problem sets and review strategies for tackling difficult questions.

Thursday: Evidence-Based Reading - Synthesis and Application

- 2 hours synthesizing information across multiple texts and applying ideas.

- Practice making inferences and identifying authors' arguments and purposes.

Friday: Writing and Language - Advanced Grammar

- 2 hours deepening knowledge of advanced grammar and effective language use.

- Engage in revising longer passages for grammatical precision and variety.

Saturday: Full Practice Test

- Take another full-length practice test with a focus on improving speed and accuracy.

- Analyze results to identify persisting challenges.

Sunday: Rest and Reflect

- Continue with a day of rest to recharge.

- Reflect on the week's learning and adjust strategies as needed.

Week 9-12: Intensive Review and Practice

Monday through Friday: Focused Review

- Spend 2 hours each day on the subject area identified as needing the most review based on practice test results.

- Alternate between math, reading, and writing to cover all topics comprehensively.

Saturday: Full Practice Test

- Continue the routine of full-length practice tests.

- Pay particular attention to time management and endurance.

Sunday: Analyze and Adapt

- Review test results from the previous day thoroughly.

- Spend 1-2 hours adapting the study plan for the week based on these insights.

Final Week: Pre-Test Preparation

Monday through Wednesday: Light Review

- Limit study sessions to 1 hour per day, focusing on light review and practice of familiar problems.

- Avoid new material to reduce last-minute stress.

Thursday: Mental Preparation

- Engage in a light activity, such as reading or solving a few practice problems.

- Begin mental and relaxation exercises to build confidence and reduce anxiety.

Friday: Rest and Visualization

- Avoid any strenuous study or new material.

- Visualize the test day, walk through the test process, and prepare test materials.

Saturday: Test Day

Sunday: Post-Test Reflection

- After the test, take time to reflect on the experience.

- Jot down any immediate thoughts or areas for future improvement.

This weekly study plan is designed to build your knowledge, develop test-taking skills, and ensure you are prepared for the SAT. Remember to customize the plan based on your individual needs and maintain balance to avoid burnout. With dedication and strategic planning, you will be well-equipped to perform at your best on test day.

BONUS FLASHCARDS DIGITAL SAT

Vocabulary questions have consistently been included on the SAT in various forms. We have compiled a list of the most frequently tested words and made them available in the flashcard tool below to assist students in memorizing them.

Flashcards are a well-established study tool utilized by individuals preparing for the SAT and other standardized tests that require a comprehensive understanding of vocabulary. A systematic approach is the recommended study strategy when employing flashcards. This approach involves first acquainting oneself with a word and its definition, then progressing to learning its synonyms, antonyms, and usage in sentences. This method ensures that students are not merely memorizing isolated words; rather, it ensures an understanding of the nuances, connotations, and applications of these words.

Regularly reviewing new words using the flashcard tool can significantly enhance a student's ability to recall and use these words accurately under the pressure of the exam.

SCAN SAT FLASHCARDS

We Value Your Fedback

Thank You for Choosing Our Book!

As you reach the conclusion of this guide, we hope you have found the strategies, insights, and exercises within these pages both enriching and instrumental in your preparation for the Digital SAT. Our goal has been to provide you with comprehensive tools and knowledge to not only achieve success on the SAT but also to enhance your overall academic skills.

<u>Share Your Experience</u>

If this book has aided in your SAT preparation and you feel better equipped for your upcoming test, we would be grateful if you took a moment to share your experience. Your feedback is invaluable as it helps us to improve and continue providing high-quality resources to students like you.

Leave your feedback

Please consider leaving a review wherever you purchased this book or on any online platform where this book is featured. Your insights and satisfaction help future students make informed decisions about their SAT preparation choices. Additionally, your reviews can provide us with direct feedback on what worked well and what might need more enhancement.

Beyond the SAT, we encourage you to keep pushing your limits and pursuing your educational goals. Stay connected with us through our website and social media channels for more resources, updates, and support as you continue your academic journey.

Thank you once again for trusting us with your SAT preparation. We are honored to have been a part of your educational path, and we wish you all the best in your test and future endeavors. May your hard work and dedication lead you to the success you deserve

Your success is our success. Let's achieve greatness together

Made in United States
Cleveland, OH
14 November 2024

10665781R00136